The Anti-Keynesian Tradition

The Anti-Keynesian Tradition

Edited by

Robert Leeson

macmillan

First published 2008 by
PALGRAVE MACMILLAN

Palgrave Macmillan in the UK is an imprint of Macmillan Publishers Limited,
registered in England, company number 785998, of Houndmills, Basingstoke,
Hampshire RG21 6XS.

Palgrave Macmillan in the US is a division of St Martin's Press LLC,
175 Fifth Avenue, New York, NY 10010.

Palgrave Macmillan is the global academic imprint of the above companies
and has companies and representatives throughout the world.

Palgrave® and Macmillan® are registered trademarks in the United States,
the United Kingdom, Europe and other countries.

ISBN-13: 978-1-4039-4959-2 hardback
ISBN-10: 1-4039-4959-X   hardback

This book is printed on paper suitable for recycling and made from fully
managed and sustained forest sources. Logging, pulping and manufacturing
processes are expected to conform to the environmental regulations of the
country of origin.

A catalogue record for this book is available from the British Library.

Library of Congress Cataloging-in-Publication Data
The anti-Keynesian tradition / edited by Robert Leeson.
      p.   cm. — (Archival insights into the evolution of economics)
   Includes index.
   ISBN 978-1-4039-4959-2 (alk. paper)
   1. Chicago school of economics.   2. Friedman, Milton, 1912-2006.
   3. Keynesian economics.   I. Leeson, Robert.
   HB98.3.A58 2008
   330.15′53—dc22   2008020799

10   9   8   7   6   5   4   3   2   1
17   16   15   14   13   12   11   10   09   08

Printed and bound in Great Britain by
CPI Antony Rowe, Chippenham and Eastbourne

Contents

List of Tables

Tables

List of Contributors

Ross B. Emmett is at James Madison College, Michigan State University, USA.

J. Daniel Hammond is Hultquist Family Professor, Department of Economics, Wake Forest University, USA.

Enrico Sergio Levrero is Associate Professor, University of Roma Tre, Italy.

Thomas Gale Moore is Senior Fellow, Hoover Institution, Stanford University, USA.

Fiorenzo Mornati is Assistant Professor, School of Law, University of Turin, Italy.

Michael J. Oliver is Professor of Economics, École Supérieure de Commerce de Rennes.

Warren J. Samuels is Professor Emeritus of Economics, Department of Economics, Michigan State University, USA.

Warren Young is an Associate Professor, Bar-Ilan University, Israel.

1
Introduction

Robert Leeson

The first volume of this trilogy examined the Keynesian Tradition; this second volume examines aspects of the Anti-Keynesian Tradition. These chapters illustrate the argument that economists neglect at their peril the subterranean world in which our subject is constructed. Archival evidence provides numerous unique insights and can also resolve disputes that may otherwise meander along, endlessly. Equally, archival evidence can expose as hollow some of the creation myths and unflattering caricatures that pervade accounts of intellectual and policy revolutions.

Warren Samuels (Chapter 2) provides an analysis of the purposes to which archival research can be put, also drawing attention to the possibilities of an archival-based analysis of the First and Second Chicago Schools, if indeed interwar Chicago qualifies for such a designation. Such systematic comparisons of Chicago Old and New are long overdue; they will doubtless provide numerous insights into the process by which Frank Knight *et al.* had only marginal immediate policy impacts, but major 'second round' impacts (with 'long and variable lags') through their students, Milton Friedman, George Stigler and Allen Wallis. Archival research also illuminates aspects of the Third Chicago School: the rational expectations revolution of Robert Lucas *et al.* and the ongoing (but often unacknowledged) influence of Henry Simon's 1936 *JPE* essay 'Rules versus Authorities in Monetary Policy'.

Ross Emmett (Chapter 3) provides an account of Frank Knight's three-decade-long attempt to write a textbook (1910s–1940s). In the end, Knight settled for a Chicago 'local use' teaching supplement (although his mimeograph was finally published in 1951, apparently without his consent). The lack of a systematic effort to 'spread the gospel' did not characterize either the Second Chicago School or the Keynesian Paul Samuelson, another of Knight's students.

Enrico Sergio Levrero (Chapter 4) examines Friedman between his two stays at Chicago: his statements and writings during his period in wartime Treasury's Division of Tax Research. 'Washington Friedman' (1941–1943) was different from the Friedman that emerged after his return to Chicago (September 1946), and somewhat horrified 'Autobiographical Friedman' (1998); yet there are distinct continuities. Friedman was embarrassed to have developed the system of taxation-at-source (with all the associated anti-libertarian implications); yet on 16 April 1946 (before his return to Chicago) Friedman referred to the supply of cash and bank deposits as 'the basic causes of inflation'.

Thomas Gale Moore (Chapter 5) was a Chicago graduate student at a pivotal moment: the publication of Friedman's *Studies in the Quantity Theory of Money* (1956) and *A Theory of the Consumption Function* (1957), Stigler's return to Chicago and the 'Coase conversion evening' all occurred around this time. Moore explains how this Chicago environment transformed him from 'flaming socialist to flaming libertarian', and attributes this metamorphosis, in part, to the influence of Friedman's mimeographed microeconomics textbook.

J. Daniel Hammond (Chapter 6) explores the process by which Friedman came to write his famous and highly influential 'The Methodology of Positive Economics' (1953). The first draft was written in early 1948, as Samuelson was finishing his (subsequently best-selling) introductory textbook. Hammond argues that Samuelson was pushing economics in a formalist direction, whilst Friedman (1946, 283) disparaged the agenda that, he believed, would trap economists in 'formal models of imaginary worlds'.

Warren Young and Robert Leeson (Chapter 7) describe the process by which Friedman obtained – from A. W. H. Phillips – the adaptive inflationary expectations formula that would later be used to undermine the Keynesian Phillips Curve. This chapter also argues that the role Phillips allocated to inflationary expectations in the theoretical Phillips Curve was far more damaging to macroeconomic stability than the role that Friedman subsequently allocated in his famous American Economic Association Presidential address. For Phillips, inflationary expectations were destabilising; for Friedman, they were stabilizing (as expectations are corrected, and the economy moved back to expectational equilibrium at the natural rate of unemployment). The archival evidence reinforces the textual evidence: the standard story by which Monetarism overthrew its naïve (static expectation) Keynesian adversary is mythical. Indeed, Phillips was aware of the limitations of the optimal control agenda and developed a Lucas-type critique before Lucas.

Michael Oliver (Chapter 8) provides an insight into a Chicago article of price flexibility faith: the consequences of fixed exchange rates. One of the hardy perennials of British politics is the conflation of national strength with an overvalued exchange rate. Despite this national priority, both during and after this Sisyphean challenge, Sterling fell from US$4.03 to US$1.57 (1949–1976), falling again to US$1.05 in February 1985.

The costs of this loss-of-face obsession were widespread: the threat of revolution (the General Strike, 1926), imperial humiliation (Suez, 1956) and financial hemorrhage (Black Wednesday, 16 September 1992). In the first episode (the return to the Gold Standard at pre-war parity), the cost of a rigidly defended inappropriate price was borne by the coal miners (whose wages were seen – by the mine owners – as the only available equilibrating instrument). Scuttling from imperial misadventure in Suez (to protect Sterling) intensified ancient French suspicions about British reliability: Britain was thus only belatedly admitted to the European Economic Community – just as the post-war boom gave way to stagflation. In 1992, the major cost was borne by the British Treasury and the housing sector (hit by high Sterling-rescue interest rates); the value to George Soros of this British obsession was over $1 billion.

Governments that overvalue the exchange rate have their economic competence appropriately valued by the electorate – typically resulting in periods of prolonged opposition. British Labour Governments were especially apprehensive of the electoral taint of being 'the party of devaluation': one (by then a 'National' Government) left the Gold Standard (1931); two (1949 and 1967) presided over devaluation (a fourth, 1976, would later go cap in hand to the International Monetary Fund). The Conservative Party was also committed to exchange rate fixity (free market rhetoric not withstanding). In July 1967 Edward Heath referred to the case for flexible exchange rates as 'bollocks'; in September 1970 he declined to be persuaded by Friedman in person. This chapter uses archival evidence to illuminate the pre-November 1967 devaluation and the pre-June 1972 float periods. During this episode, the fixers were overcome by Friedman's heretical price flexibility solution.

Warren Young (Chapter 9) examines the genesis and evolution of another Anti-Keynesian research program: the process by which Robert Lucas's work, and the Lucas Critique in particular, developed into the Kydland–Prescott real business cycle school. In their *JPE* article 'Rules Rather than Discretion: The Inconsistency of Optimal Plans', Finn Kydland and Ed Prescott (1977, 487) concluded that 'policymakers should follow rules rather than have discretion'. Friedman (1967, 1) described

Simons as 'a shaper of my ideas'; and Kydland and Prescott are also implicitly members of Simons' 'rules party'. Indeed, 30 years later, Prescott acknowledged the importance of Simon's article after reading it for the first time:

> Simons sees it as rules versus authorities. I see things very differently. An independent central bank, which is an authority or mechanism, is proving effective in sustaining a good monetary policy rule, namely price targeting... There are some ideas here. Maybe decentralized systems perform better because they better deal with the time inconsistency problem than do centralized systems. This requires a theoretical framework where the concept of decentralized is well defined. Better theory in the language sense of 'theory' is needed.
>
> (Prescott to Young, 19 February 2007)

It would seem that even after 70 years, Simons' seminal published work is still relevant for theorists, despite having sunk into an archival-type subterranean world.

Fiorenzo Mornati (Chapter 10) uses Vilfredo Pareto's correspondence to explore the evolution of some of the ideas that became part of Chicago microeconomics. Pareto was a pivotal player in the second-generation Neoclassical School: a 'liberal' (in the European sense), indeed a 'liberalist militant', who sought to provide solid theoretical foundations for 'rational political economy', minimal government action, free trade and 'preference'-based microeconomics. Diminishing marginal utility and measurable (cardinal) utility provided a foundation for income and wealth redistribution according to the 'greatest good to the greatest number' criteria. The ordinal utility revolution denied the legitimacy of such measurable interpersonal comparisons: its 'victory' in the 1930 provided the foundations of modern neoclassical microeconomics (the Coase conversion evening strengthened still further the Chicagoans' faith in market outcomes).

There are similarities between the Paretian ordinalist revolution and the rational expectations revolution. Both revolutions sought to deny the validity of the intellectual justification for government intervention. Moreover, the consumer's equilibrium connecting (subjective, preference-based) indifference curves to (objective) budget constraints has a parallel in the rational expectations equilibrium (which equates an objective mathematical expectation with a subjective evaluation or expectation). Lucas (1976) focused on the microeconomic foundations of macroeconomics and argued that preferences were part of the 'deep parameters' that should be modelled. Lucas, Prescott and Kydland sought to break the nexus between the macroeconometric models of the time and (discretionary) policy inferences, while Pareto sought to remove the connection between cardinal utility and utilitarian social welfare inferences. For Pareto, preferences were deep parameters and ordinal utility represented preference-ordering. Kydland and Prescott (1977, 479, 475) connected Phillips Curves to indifference curves, concluding that with rational expectations the marriage of optimal control theory to aggregate demand management was 'absurd'. Pareto claimed to have discovered a universal law of income and wealth distribution, an inter-temporal, pan-cultural constraint on policy interventions. Thus the New Classical Policy Ineffectiveness Proposition resembles the Policy Restrictiveness of Pareto Optimality and Pareto's Law of Income Distribution.

2
Resources in the Archival Supplements to *Research in the History of Economic Thought and Methodology*

Warren J. Samuels

The origins of the archival supplements

The first volume of the annual *Research in the History of Economic Thought and Methodology* was published in 1983. A principal motivation was to provide opportunity for people to publish articles that were normally too long for conventional journals. The editorial design of the annual provided for two sections. The first section would publish original materials that had been approved by peer review, as in a conventional journal. The second section would consist of essays reviewing new books in the two fields covered by the annual. The authors of these review essays would have ample space to deal with their subjects. Some of these essays were to be sent out for peer review; all were at least reviewed and edited by me, and later by my co-editors, Jeff Biddle and Ross Emmett. Another motivation was to commission review essays on new publications that were long enough to be seriously substantive.

The first volume, however, did not follow that design. Entitled *The Craft of the Historian of Economic Thought*, it comprised essays on the work of leading historians of economic thought. A sequel to that collection, *Historians of Economics and Economic Thought: The Construction of Disciplinary Memory*, co-edited with Steven G. Medema, was published independent of the series of annuals in 2001 by Routledge.

By the 1980s I had collected a considerable volume of archival materials. Some materials had been given to me, notably by Edwin E. Witte, my major professor at the University of Wisconsin. He retired in June 1957, coincidentally the same month I received my doctorate. Clearing out his office, he found materials that he did not want destroyed, and kindly offered them to me. Some other materials, such as lecture notes and, more recently, conference reports (see below), I developed on my own. A few other materials came to me by purchase, many others by request, and still others quite fortuitously (see below). Several groups of materials were both provided and edited by other scholars (also see below). Alas, I have forgotten the provenance of some items acquired decades ago. My mistake was in failing to keep a record.

I had had the idea of someday doing something with these materials. I had already published in the *Journal of Economic Issues* the correspondence between Clarence E. Ayres and Frank H. Knight, between James M. Buchanan and myself, and between Robert Lee Hale and Thomas Nixon Carver. In the mid-1980s the idea occurred to me that an archival supplement to the annual could make such materials available to other historians of economic thought and other interested scholars. Herbert Johnson, of JAI Press, my original publisher, agreed to my proposal of publishing one archival supplement a year. Archival Supplement 1 (hereafter AS 1) was published in 1989. It contained only one document, lectures by John Dewey on moral and political philosophy, edited by my philosopher colleague Donald F. Koch and myself. After having published the first seven archival supplements, Herb Johnson agreed to publishing two a year, which we did commencing with AS 8 and 9 published in 1999. The arrangement has been continued by Elsevier, which acquired JAI Press during 1999–2000; my editor at Elsevier, Jeroen Loos, has been as supportive as Herb Johnson. A few archival items have found their way into regular annual volumes.

The identification and numbering of archival volumes underwent a change when Elsevier took over the series. The first nine archival supplements were numbered AS 1 through AS 9 and were published from 1989 through 1999. No volume was published in 1990 and 1993; two were published in 1999. Thereafter the archival supplements became the B and C volumes each year.

The rationale of using archival collections and publishing archival materials

Archival materials typically have not hitherto been published. They may be lecture notes used by the lecturer or taken by students in class. They may be private correspondence. They may be early drafts of papers subsequently published – permitting readers to see the author's evolution of ideas and language – or papers not yet papers. They may have been published but are so fugitive as to be lost to current scholars (I have published one of these, Jacob Warshaw's memoir on Thorstein Veblen). Archival materials may help with one's own research or simply provide interesting and informative reading.

The following points, however, are worth keeping in mind.

1. The usefulness of archival materials depends on the purpose of one's research. What will be useful for one purpose or project may not be useful for another. Utility is a function of interest. The publisher of archival materials for the most part cannot predict their use. Most, if not all, documents have introductions; some have more or less extended commentaries serving at least two functions: (a) placing the document in historical perspective and (b) calling attention to potentially interesting or useful matters therein.

2. It is sometimes difficult, even impossible, to say in advance how particular materials will be useful on the basis only of knowledge of the archival materials themselves.

3. Class notes – the lecturer's or a student's – may or may not parallel the lecturer's publications; they may or may not provide more subtle or more extreme, less hedged, positions. Class notes may provide the lecturer's condensed version of ideas given (possibly) in writing in more detail, indicating or suggesting what in the writing is more important or more salient – saliency, however, is not necessarily important.

4. Much depends on the quality of the archival materials themselves.

5. Archival materials can contribute to the biography of their author: what he or she was thinking about at various points in time, hence the development of his or her thinking. Archival materials may help fill in the interstices of the subjects' ideas, including what was considered and used, or considered and not used. Archival materials may facilitate the discovery of major developments, or enable the comparison of lesser and more sophisticated versions of ideas.

6. Archival materials can contribute to a richer and deeper history of economic thought.

7. Archival materials may address issues either not dealt with in formal writing or done so in a different way. Archival materials can raise issues not hitherto seen or appreciated.

8. Archival materials can provide source materials as grist for the interpretive mill.

9. Archival materials can provide evidence of what hitherto had transpired.

10. Archival materials, either alone or in conjunction with non-archival materials – even, perhaps especially, when contradictory – can provide details or lines of development that comport well with the overall content and structure of a story or that suggest a different story. If only one part of the user's overall topic is enriched by archival materials, some evidential imbalance may result; still, it is better to have uneven evidence than not to have it.

The first point must be emphasized. One cannot say in advance, or can do so only rarely, from knowledge of the archival source alone, what use that material will be for researchers. The material may be useful differently for different projects and/or different researchers. Archival materials may fill an already known lacuna, may indicate and fill a lacuna, may lead research along known parallel lines, may raise new questions, may lead research along new lines, and may suggest entirely new research.

Research is undertaken for many reasons – because it is interesting, possibly important, and so on. Research is a process to be enjoyed. That is true of archival research and much other research. New archival materials have the potential advantage of being unknown, of carrying one off into a more or less unknown domain.

One can only imagine being Edwin Cannan and reading student notes taken in Adam Smith's course on jurisprudence (law and government) a century and a third or so earlier! What a difference those notes have made to Smith scholarship and our understanding of Smith!

Antecedent to the use of archival materials is their discovery and their preparation in such a way as to make them available to and useful for scholars. If their use can be a matter of joy, so too is the process of their discovery and availability, as well as the anticipation of their use by others. I will turn in a moment to the materials I have made available in the archival volumes and, in general, to the process by which the raw materials are turned into archival documents. I also note for the record that all original documents are deposited through donation to the archival collections of the appropriate colleges and universities, immediately upon publication of each document.

But first I call attention to serendipitous coincidence – an aspect of use noted above.

A coincidental example of serendipity

During the same period in which I was preparing this chapter for Robert Leeson's collection, I was asked to write a review of his two-volume work

Chicago and Friedman (Leeson, 2003) for EH.NET. The collection ~~~ with publications concerned with whether or not, prior to Milton Friedman's publication in 1956 of his restatement of the quantity theory, there had been (as he claimed) an oral tradition of the quantity theory at Chicago; and if there was, of what did it consist? Friedman attributed to that oral tradition a model in which the quantity theory was 'in the first instance' a theory of the demand for money; indeed, a stable demand for money. Friedman claimed that the tradition was spawned by Henry Simons and Lloyd Mints directly, and by Frank Knight and Jacob Viner at one remove. Thirteen years later, Don Patinkin questioned the validity of Friedman's interpretation of the quantity theory and his 'Chicago' version. Patinkin identified 'The Other Chicago' version thusly:

> The quantity theory is, first and foremost, not a theory of the demand for money, but a theory which relates the quantity of money (M) to the aggregate demand for goods and services (MV), and thence to the price level (P) and/or level of output (T); all this in accordance with Fisher's $MV = PT$.
>
> (Leeson, 2003, Vol. 1, pp. 89, 91)

After a further 22 years Patinkin held that the disagreement was not about 'whether or not there was such an oral tradition, but what the nature of that tradition was' (Vol. 1, p. 381). Friedman also has modified his position.

Leeson's conclusions place a great deal of interpretive weight on Friedman's having taken Lloyd Mints's graduate course in money and banking (Economics 330) during his first year as a graduate student at Chicago in 1932–1933. Leeson has been fortunate in having been given access by Friedman to his notes from Mints's Economics 330. Leeson notes that 'Friedman's lecture notes are currently in his possession and have not been processed into his archives at the Hoover Institution' (Vol. 2, p. 515, n. 1). The next important round may well center on the notes. The course was organized around Keynes's *Treatise*, one feature of which was 'an increased emphasis on money demand in a revised quantity theory framework' (Vol. 2, p. 486).

Additional interpretive weight is placed by Leeson on a private seminar held by graduate students; quite a group, for they included Friedman, Albert G. Hart, Stigler, Allen Wallis, Kenneth Boulding, and others, as well as a stream of visiting economists.

Leeson concludes,

> It therefore seems likely that Friedman took the ideas he was exposed
> to in Economics 330 and used them as an organising framework
> with which to understand the 'macroeconomic' dislocation of the
> 1930s. If intense student discussion is admissible as an 'oral tradi-
> tion' then Friedman's assertion has some validity. A version of the
> quantity theory which was 'in the first instance a theory of the
> demand for money' was apparently 'a central and vigorous part of
> the oral tradition' at Chicago at least among graduate students in
> 1932–3 (and possibly until the *General Theory* made Keynes a suspect
> figure).
>
> (Vol. 2, p. 488)

One difficulty with Friedman's initial position has to do with the concept
of an 'oral tradition.' Friedman was part of the 1932–1933 (and beyond)
discussion; the 'oral' part of the concept is unobjectionable. But the
'tradition' part is highly suspect.

The first difficulty is that Friedman knew – and perhaps could only
have known – of the discussions in 1932–1933 and not earlier. A second
difficulty is that many different readings were given in the *Treatise* (not
unlike the later *General Theory*), each reading stressing different combinations of variations within a general quantity theory framework. This
meant, on the one hand, that a variety of oral 'traditions' likely coexisted
throughout the discipline and, on the other hand, that some or many of
them included significant attention to the demand for money. Leeson
stresses that 'Friedman's initial assertion about Chicago uniqueness in
this context must now appear unreliable. . . . It is therefore improbable
that the Treatise – with its emphasis on money demand – informed
"macroeconomic" discussions in Chicago only. Indeed, Friedman in the
preface to these volumes has retreated from his initial assertion about
Chicago uniqueness' (Vol. 2, pp. 488, 489). In his preface to Leeson's
collection, Friedman begins his defense saying that he early 'was baf-
fled . . . at what all the fuss was about. . . . very little was at stake.' He then
takes, correctly but irrelevantly, the position that if he has been 'confused
about the origin of the ideas . . . it would not affect by an iota the validity
or usefulness of those ideas.' He concludes that he remains 'persuaded
that I was the beneficiary of a Chicago oral tradition, but this evidence
convinces me that I gave Chicago more credit for uniqueness than was
justified. . . . The issue,' he repeats, 'is entirely about the origin of ideas,
not about the validity of content' (Vol. 1, p. x). Friedman seems to have

taken too much for granted; Chicago was no more homogeneous than was the discipline as a whole on the quantity theory.

My review went on to examine, first, certain historiographical considerations and, second, the question of how different versions of the quantity theory could exist.

Mints, however, was not the only instructor in Economics 330. In volume 23-C (2005) of *Research in the History of Economic Thought and Methodology*, I published F. Taylor Ostrander's notes from Charles O. Hardy's course in Economics 330 given in 1933–1934, the next academic year following Friedman's enrollment in Mints's course (Friedman was at Columbia, not at Chicago, during 1933–1934). I have also published in AS 23-B (2005) Ostrander's notes from Economics 332, Monetary Theory, taught by Melchior Palyi.

The volume was already in production when I began work on both my review of Leeson's two volumes and this chapter for his collection. The notes suggest that the demand for money was part of Hardy's and Palyi's courses but by no means as central as the notion of an oral tradition centering on the demand for money would have it be.

At the time Hardy taught the course taken by Ostrander during 1933–1934, monetary economics was represented by Melchior Palyi and Lloyd Mints as well as Simon, Viner, and Knight, in addition to Hardy. Hardy was clearly a leading student of monetary policy. Though apparently not regarded as a leading monetary theorist, he evidently knew his theory, as he easily grounded policy in theory and was respected for his contributions to policy analysis. Palyi was a well-known economist both in the profession and to readers of business-oriented newspapers in both the United States and Europe. Each of the Chicago economists specializing, at least in part, in monetary economics went his own way, concentrating on some combination of what interested them and what they considered important. Peering over all their shoulders was the well-known anti-quantity theory orientation of the long-time chair of the Department of Economics, Laughlin.

There is more but altogether what is shown (1) indicates more or less conventional attention to the quantity theory as the core of monetary theory and (2) does not indicate a distinctive Chicago approach centering on the demand for money. Even the earlier negative position of Laughlin has fallen prey to the selective memory of any oral tradition. Laughlin, who opposed the quantity theory, was chair of the Department of Economics for many years and was a conspicuous person in the profession. Any complete rendition of Chicago 'tradition' presumably would have to include his anti-quantity theory position. Perhaps he was an embarrassment treated largely in silence. Mints may or may not deal with his view; Palyi seems to deal with it only in passing. And Friedman seems not to as well. He is too busy inventing what he wants that tradition to be.

In partial summary, therefore, it is not clear that 'an' oral tradition existed at Chicago by 1932–1933 with the substance initially identified by Friedman. If one clearly existed (and it is not certain that one did), it likely was different from and more complex, and likely more ambiguous, than what Friedman proposed.

It would be difficult for me to come up with a greater serendipitous coincidence. I had unwittingly agreed to review a collection at the same time I was publishing archival material directly bearing on the problem of the collection. Taylor Ostrander was a graduate student at Chicago during 1933–1934 and became friends with Friedman's future wife, Rose Director, and her brother, Aaron Director, and numerous other eventually famous economists; indeed, it was Aaron Director who brought Ostrander to Washington, D.C., by offering him a job. Ostrander recalls first meeting Friedman in 1936 in Chicago when Taylor was running the Works Progress Administration there.

Yet I have two other coincidences, ones albeit not so serendipitous. While also working on this chapter, I was transcribing Ostrander's notes from Economics 5, Money and Banking, given by Walter B. Smith. In his discussion of the types of business cycle theories, within four lines of notes there are references to two men. One 'Hexter' must be Maurice Beck Hexter, whose notes from Frank Williams Taussig's course in economic theory, 1921–1922, I am editing for eventual publication. Under the 'Psychological' type of theory, the notes read, 'Marriages and births (Hexter) – some degree of analysis', and go on to mention Pigou. The next type of theory is labeled 'Uncertainty, ignorance (Hardy)' – and it is notes from Hardy's course which are cited above.

The Ostrander and other collections of class notes

I have been involved in the publication of several sets of notes taken in classes of important economists (and others) at important universities – although the first of these sets did not commence publication until AS 6 in 1997. The first published were notes taken by Victor E. Smith, my late colleague at Michigan State University (MSU), while a graduate student at Northwestern during the years prior to the award of his doctorate in 1940. The courses were those taught by his major professor, William Jaffé, a highly esteemed and distinguished historian of economic thought. The second set to be published is the notes taken by F. Taylor Ostrander, already referred to above. These notes were taken in courses given at Williams College, Oxford University, and the University of Chicago during 1930–1934. The next two sets are, coincidentally, also from Chicago and Northwestern. The notes taken by Glenn Johnson, my recently deceased colleague in Agricultural Economics at MSU, date from 1946 to 1948 at Chicago. Those from Mark Ladenson were taken at Northwestern.

I had commenced work on Victor Smith's notes shortly before his death in 1995. He had agreed to my publishing all his notes from Jaffé's courses, which were, I believe, the only ones he had retained. In AS 6 (1997) I published Smith's notes from Jaffé's lectures on the history of economic thought from Plato to Adam Smith. The printed notes run to about 105 pages. They are the second set of lecture notes on the history of economic thought. The first, the sole document in AS 3 (1992), was notes from Edwin R. A. Seligman's lectures at Columbia during 1927–1928. Also in AS 6 I published Smith's 1937 graduate-student paper on the theory of rent. It is a comprehensive account of rent theory, and is about 90 printed pages in length. Since then I have published, in 21-C (2003), Smith's notes from Jaffé's lectures on general equilibrium and on Keynes as well as from seminars and lectures he attended at Oxford during the 1954–1955 academic year. The courses were given by Nicholas Kaldor, John R. Hicks, Lawrence Klein, Richard Goodwin, and Michael James Farrell. The subjects include value and distribution, welfare economics, personal savings, dynamic economics, and problems in econometrics. Each of the three materials in AS 21-C run to about 50 pages.

Awaiting publication are Smith's notes from Jaffé's 1937 course on Marshallian theory. Alfred Marshall, the partial-equilibrium theorist, and Leon Walras, the general-equilibrium theorist, represent the two principal approaches to microeconomics in the late 20th century. Jaffé is the translator and interpreter of Walras. Here is Jaffé, whose lectures on general equilibrium were published in 21-C, lecturing on Marshall.

F. Taylor Ostrander, who is 94, had attended a dinner for John Maynard Keynes in Washington, D.C., in 1941 and had written a memorandum about the affair. He much later wrote to Donald Moggridge about the memorandum. Don suggested that he show it to me. He did so, and I published it in the regular volume 20-A (2002). Through emails

and telephone conversations I learned of his education and subs
career – and also that he had kept his notes from Williams (
Oxford, and Chicago. This is serendipity raised to a high power!

Williams College, one entry requirement of which was mastery of
Latin, provided its students with a marvelous education. This finding is
only one of the results of publishing Taylor Ostrander's comprehensive
and detailed notes from his courses.

In 22-B (2004) I published, in addition to a brief biography of Taylor,
his notes from the three courses he had in the history of economic
thought. These courses were given by David Taggart Clark at Williams,
Redvers Opie at Oxford, and Frank H. Knight at Chicago. Volume 23-B
(2005) has three groups of Taylor's notes. One group of notes is from
Knight's courses on economic theory, current tendencies, and institutional economics. Included with the notes from the economic theory
course is Taylor's research paper on the meaning of cost. The second
group of notes is from two courses given by Henry Simons, price theory
and public finance. The notes from the price theory course are those
of Taylor and another student, Helen Hiett, and are accompanied by
Kirk D. Johnson's comparison of the 1933–1934 and 1946 versions of
Simons's Syllabus, the latter version published earlier by Gordon Tullock.
The third group of notes is from Melchior Palyi's courses on monetary
theory, business cycle theory, and the European banking system.

Volume 23-C has Ostrander's notes from John U. Nef's courses on
European economic history and on French industrial history since the
Reformation (Economics 221 and 322, respectively); Hardy's course on
money and banking, already mentioned; and Chester Whitney Wright's
courses on the economic history of the United States (Economics 220
and 320).

Remaining to be published are Ostrander's notes from a number of
other economics courses and from several other fields. The economics
courses include Principle, Money and Banking, and the Senior Seminar. The non-economics courses include Comparative Government,
Comparative National and Local Government, Public Opinion, and
Review of Political Theory. The professors in these courses were Peter
H. Odegard, later at University of California, Berkeley, and president of
the American Political Science Association; Telford Taylor, successor to
Justice Jackson at the Nuremburg Trials and promoter of an international
court of criminal justice; and Sir George Young, diplomat, educator, and
professor.

Also to be published are Glenn Johnson's notes taken in courses at
the University of Chicago during 1946–1948. These include courses

given by Tjalling Koopmans (statistics), Mints (Money and Banking), Theodore W. Schultz (Resource Administration and Policy, Agriculture in the Political Economy), Milton Friedman (Economic Theory), D. Gale Johnson (Income and Welfare), Knight (History of Economic Thought, Economic Theory), Jacob Marschak (Mathematical Economics), Nef (English Economic History), Layton S. Thompson (International Economic Arrangements to Stabilize Primary Products), Charles M. Hardin (Politics of Agriculture), W. Allen Wallis (Statistical Methods), and Don Patinkin (Mathematical Statistics). Obvious comparisons between 1933–1934 and 1946–1948 will be limited but possible. The Old Chicago and the New Chicago compared but likely the material needs to be combined with much else.

The other set of graduate economics notes on hand is that of Mark Ladenson at Northwestern. They are as yet not fully organized, though I have determined, with the aid of a consultant, that the mathematical economics courses do not warrant publication.

Other major groups of individual notes

To a large extent, the publication of materials in the archival supplements has been ad hoc, depending on the combination of availability – of materials on hand and newly acquired materials – and my selection. That accounts for volume-by-volume variation, except for the sets discussed in the previous section. Nonetheless, the materials already published fall into several groups.

One group is notes and other materials from courses on the history of economic thought. In addition to Smith's notes from Jaffé, AS 6 (1997), and Ostrander's notes from Clark, Opie, and Knight in 22-B (2004), the following have been published: Edwin R. A. Seligman, from 1927 to 1928 at Columbia, the sole contents of AS 3 (1992); Roswell Cheney McCrea, from 1927 to 1928 also at Columbia, in AS 5 (1996); and C. H. Hull's 1895 Syllabus on the history of economic theories and my notes from James S. Earley's year course, from 1954 to 1955, both in 21-B (2003). Richard T. Ely's *The Story of Economics in the United States*, his hitherto unpublished manuscript and not student notes, nonetheless belongs in this group; it was published in 20-C (2002). Other history-of-economic-thought materials include Edwin Cannan's unsuccessful Cobden Prize Essay on political economy and socialism, in 22-B (2002); and two sets of introductory notes to the history of economic thought; in 22–23 (2004) and 23-A (2005).

Largely but not entirely due to Edwin Witte's thoughtfulness, a second group of materials concerns the Wisconsin branch of institutional economics. Some relates to institutionalism as such, some to individual institutionalists. AS 4 (1994) includes materials from early institutional economics by John R. Commons and Selig Perlman. AS 5 (1996) includes a reader's guide to *Commons's Legal Foundations of Capitalism*, not archival but useful; and further early materials from Commons. AS 7 (1998) is wholly occupied by Commons's *Investigational Economics*, the early version of his *The Economics of Collective Action*, and two comparisons, one between the two versions and another between the *Legal Foundations of Capitalism* and *The Economics of Collective Action*. AS 8 (1999) is wholly occupied by notes taken in Selig Perlman's courses on American labor history and on capitalism and socialism; on Perlman's additional chapters written for his *History of Trade Unionism*, correspondence between Commons and Perlman, and some additional documents from Perlman. Volume 18-B (2000) includes further documents from Commons and Perlman. Volume 21-C (2003) includes Martin Glaeser's autobiographical notes. Volume 22-C (2004) includes notes from Edwin Witte's and Robert Lampman's courses on Government and Business and on the Role of Government in the economy. Volume 23-C (2005) publishes correspondence of Selig Perlman, and notes from Edwin Witte's course on Government and Labor.

Relevant to Wisconsin are two sets of notes from courses given by Hans Gerth – on democratic and totalitarian societies and on mass movements (AS 6 (1997) and 23-C (2005)) – and two documents, one a report on the *Journal of Economic Issues* and the other an exploration of the meaning of institutional economics (21-C (2003)); and a roundtable on the historiography of institutional economics (22-A (2004)).

Other materials have been published relevant to non-Wisconsin institutionalism. These include AS 5 (1996), the correspondence between Clarence Ayres and Waldo Emerson Haisley; AS 6 (1997), a bibliography of Japanese studies on Veblen; AS 9 (1999), a set of references to Thorstein Veblen, from 1983 to 1996. Volume 19-B (2001) is a collection of writings of Edward Everett Hale plus several on Hale. Volume 22-B (2004) published Jacob Warshaw's memorandum on Veblen.

The largest group of materials separately published is documents in, though in some cases on, the history of economic thought. AS 2 (1991) is entirely devoted to such documents: Frank A. Fetter on the present state of economics in the United States (1927); Knight's famous but hitherto unpublished 'The Case for Communism, from the Standpoint of an Ex-Liberal' (1932); Jacob Viner on the search for an ideal common-wealth (1914); the philosopher Lewis Zerby's 'You, Yourself, and Society'; John Maynard Keynes on the 1914 financial crisis; and Abba Lerner on Israel and the economic development of Palestine. Also in this group are Henry C. Simons on banking and currency reform and on the long-term objectives of monetary management, Alfred Marshall's early philosoph-ical writings, and the correspondence between Irving Fisher and Benito Mussolini (AS 4 (1994)); Anthony Crosland's missing chapter on the managerial revolution (AS 6 (1997)); the correspondence between John Bates Clark and Franklin H. Giddings (18-B (2000)); the correspondence of Alfred Eichner and Joan Robinson, the correspondence of Wesley C. Mitchell, Henry Schultz on quantitative method, and Arthur F. Burns on scientific method and business cycles (18-C (2000)); a collection of Henry George's writings on the United Kingdom (20-B (2002)); the correspon-dence of Frank Knight and John Maurice Clark on marginal productivity theory and, with Morris Copeland, on behaviorism in economics (21-A (2003)); an 1880 list of references and outlines for his Principles course by Walton H. Hamilton and a bibliography of F. Y. Edgeworth (21-C (2003)); a report and a critique of the Buchanan colloquium on the status of the status quo (22-A (2004)); Eli Ginzberg on the economists' neurosis (22-B (2004)); 19-C (2001) is entirely devoted to notes from Edwin R. A. Selig-man's course on Public Finance at Columbia, 1927–1928; and papers from a conference on the history of heterodox economics in the 20th century (22-C (2004)).

The most unusual item published is the collection of portraits of great economists originally provided to me by Frank W. Fetter (AS 4 (1994)). The original collection now resides at Duke University.

A number of people have been helpful to me in the creation of this archival collection. In addition to Edwin Witte and my eventual co-editors, before and after they became co-editors, Jeff Biddle and Ross Emmett, they include individuals who have provided and/or edited archival materials and/or performed other invaluable services. These include Pier Francisco Asso, Alberto Bassini, Bradley Bateman, Luca Fior-ito, Richard Gonce, Daniel Hammond, Douglas Irwin, Glenn Johnson, Kirk D. Johnson, Marianne Johnson, Douglas Kinnear, Judy Klein, Mark Ladenson, Frederic Lee, Steven Medema, Don Moggridge, Norman Obst, Taylor Ostrander, Mark Perlman, Ronnie J. Phillips, Tiziano Raffaelli, David Reisman, Malcolm Rutherford, Allan Schmid, Victor Smith, Toshi-hiro Tanaka, Harry Trebing, Charles J. Whalen, Felicity Wasser, Solidelle Wasser, and Kenneth Wenzer. In addition, invaluable assistance has been provided by the many individuals who have refereed manuscripts and by the members of the editorial board who have done many helpful things.

Preparation of documents for publication

I will say a few things about document preparation, though the best way to comprehend the complications is to examine the paragraphs in various introductory materials which discuss them.

The first task subsequent to the decision to seek publication is to acquire the right to publish from whoever has rights or control. This can be a difficult matter. In some cases, the editor must take as authoritative the word of a manuscript librarian or other source. In a few cases, I have consulted legal counsel (the MSU attorney's office, my publisher's legal department) regarding potential problems. Where I know or can find out who has control over someone's materials – their literary executor – I seek their permission. To date I have been turned down only once. I have also once had to walk gingerly among descendents, with strained relations among them, for permission. At least one of them wondered about how much money the publication of their ancestor's work would be worth. The person accepted my word that my income from the sale of the volume in which it appeared would not repay my personal out-of-pocket expenses (to which my income tax forms will attest!). A major expense is proofreading.

The next step is to transcribe the document onto the computer. Scanning can help with this but old, typed documents do not scan well (one can try to scan from originals or Xerox copies). In any event, documents in longhand must be entered by hand, as is done for most typed documents. These then have to be proofread. Here three alternatives are possible: one is to hire a pair of graduate students (sometimes three, as in the case of Commons's posthumous book which involved the precursor text (which I was publishing), the final already-published version, and the page-proof of my precursor text). Two are needed in order to compare the original with either the computer printout of my transcription or the page-proof, or both. A second is to do it yourself (I used to do it myself or with my wife). A third is to have the author or the author's wife, son, or other relative – two of them – do the proofreading. In the case of Victor Smith's notes, his wife, Margaret, and son, Michael, undertook the proofreading; I once joined Margaret. In the case of Glenn Johnson, his son Mark and Mark's wife Marilyn have proofread. In the case of Taylor Ostrander, he, his wife Ruth, his daughter and son-in-law, and several hired helpers have done the proofreading. In these cases, the proofreading that matters is the comparison of my computer printout with the original notes. They had to not only correct my mistakes but answer my questions about what was indecipherable to me. To Taylor, for example, I shipped his original notes, a Xerox copy on which I had marked legibility problems in yellow, and a copy of the computer printout of my transcription of his notes. He returned the latter two with suggested corrections and answers.

Two final matters. The notes (and other materials) are prefaced with commentary placing the notes in critical and historical perspective. Limited annotations are provided, principally where I cannot assume that most readers will know who or what is mentioned. More complete annotations would be desirable, but require additional resources.

Acknowledgments

I am indebted to Ross Emmett, Jerry Evensky, Steven G. Medema, Leonidas Montes, and A. Allen Schmid for helpful comments on an earlier version of this chapter. I am also indebted to Robert Dimand, David Laidler and F. Taylor Ostrander for comments on various manuscripts pertinent to this one, especially to Robert Leeson for the fact that Friedman was at Columbia during 1933–4.

Reference

Leeson, R. 2003, *Keynes, Chicago and Friedman*. 2 Vols (London: Pickering & Chatto).

3
Frank H. Knight and *The Economic Organization*[1]

Ross Emmett

> There can be few contemporary works on economics which, without ever having been regularly published, have achieved such wide circulation and fame as Frank H. Knight's *The Economic Organization*. For nearly a generation the various typed and mimeographed editions have been extensively used and drawn up. It is really to be welcomed that this influential essay is now at last made available in permanent form.
>
> F. A. Hayek (From the dust jacket of the 1951 edition)

In 1951, Augustus M. Kelley published a short book bearing the title *The Economic Organization (EO)*. The title page indicated that an additional article was included – 'Notes on Cost and Utility'[2] – and that the author was Frank H. Knight, of the University of Chicago. On the reverse, copyright was attributed to Knight, with the dates 1933 and 1951. The table of contents listed four chapters: 'Social Economic Organization,' 'The Price System and the Economic Process,' 'Demand and Supply and Price,' and 'Distribution: The Pricing of Productive Services Individually.' The text of these four chapters totals 119 pages. Hayek's remark was the only one provided on the dust jacket.

These bare facts hide the fascinating story of Knight's little textbook. Begun as a part of a longer textbook project, chapters included in *EO* were used by Knight in his classrooms at the universities of Chicago and Iowa as early as 1924–1925. By 1925, the text of the material contained in the second, third, and fourth chapters of *EO* had stabilized. The adoption in 1932 of the four chapters as part of the required reading for the new undergraduate general social science course at the University of Chicago gave Knight's material a wider audience (University of Chicago Social

Science Staff, 1932), resulting in the reprinting of the four chapters a year later as a separate booklet under the title *The Economic Organization* (Knight, 1933).

And now the story gets interesting, for the manuscript Knight intended for his students' use had achieved a life of its own, independent of its author and his intentions. By the time the booklet was reprinted, Knight had begun to think his way through economic theory once again, and he came to conclusions that were inconsistent with some of the views expressed in *EO*. Attempts to have additional notes added to the text in the social science course reader were to no avail; Knight had to settle for the addition of a very short note in the open space provided at the end of the second chapter of the booklet. Because a committee in the College of the University of Chicago controlled the selection of readings for the general social science courses, various combinations of chapters were used over the years. In the economics department at the University of Chicago, Henry Simons expected students to have a copy of the booklet and used various portions of it in conjunction with his syllabus (Simons, 2002). Students who did not have Knight as a professor but wanted to understand the economics being taught in the Chicago economics department obtained copies, as did professors and students at other universities (someone at Yale University had a copy as early as 1934[3]). As Jim Buchanan has pointed out, *EO* 'contains the elements of theory that helped to establish for Chicago its eminence in neoclassical economics' (Buchanan, 1968, 425). Everyone who sought to understand Chicago economics wanted a copy.

Meanwhile, Knight himself went on with the task of writing an economics textbook. Before the reprinting of the booklet, in May 1933, he corresponded with Harcourt Brace regarding a new sophomore-level textbook that could replace Richard Ely's *Outlines of Economics* (Ely and Hess, 1937) and articulate an approach to social control of the economy that would challenge Sumner Slichter's *Modern Economic Society* (Slichter, 1931).[4] A year later H. T. Warshow inquired whether Knight would be willing to write a textbook for Adelphi (Warshow to Knight, 16 May 1934, FHK Papers, Box 58, Folder 2). Although no contract with either company was signed, Knight continued to work on a textbook throughout the 1930s; the last version in his papers is dated 1943–1944. The chapters in *EO* had no place in the later versions of the textbook.

The separation of text from author became complete in 1951, when Kelley published *EO* (Knight, 1951). Years later, Knight wrote of *EO*:

these chapters were prepared for local use – looking forward to completion as a text-book, but were never 'published'. That is, not 'legitimately'; one August Kelley Inc. [*sic*] put the material between covers, with some other stuff, without authorization; (in 1951). It carried notice, copyright by me, which was a pure invention; to my knowledge, it never has been covered by copyright.

(Frank H. Knight to Elisabeth Ann Jakab, Harper & Bros., 6 January 1962, FHK Papers, Box 60, Folder 4)

Yet, despite Knight's obvious displeasure in Kelley's reprinting of *EO*, the book made widely available material that previously had been difficult to obtain. Within a few years, the Kelley reprint of *EO* appeared in over 500 university libraries around the United States.[5] Its popularity was enhanced by the connections between Knight's chapters and the new wave of textbooks in economics published in the early 1950s. Obvious borrowings from *EO*, such as the definition of the basic functions of an economy and the circular-flow diagram (see section 'The Economic Organization and its Children' below), reflected respect for Knight's pioneering approach, which departed substantially from popular early-twentieth-century American textbooks. In 1961, a Spanish translation of the book appeared – again without Knight's knowledge and permission (Knight, 1961) – followed shortly by Harper & Row's paperback edition in 1965 (Knight, 1965a), and Kelley's second reprint of the book as part of his Reprints of *Economics Classics series* in 1967 (Knight, 1967a).[6]

The story of *EO* has long intrigued me, especially as I began to see that the book had a history separate from, and perhaps even in tension with, its author. The purpose of the rest of this paper is to unpack the brief story told above through what might well be called a genealogical investigation of *EO*. Where did this text come from? What is its history? What essays and manuscripts are its predecessors? Was the text stable over time or did it change? If it changed, what happened? And what may have prompted the changes? What copyright date, if any, should be assigned to *EO*? Answers to these questions will also help to contextualize the book, both in its time and in relation to Knight's other work. Table 3.1 provides an overview of the history of *EO* as it will be presented in this chapter. And we can also ask about *EO*'s children. How did it influence the transformation of economics textbooks during the mid-twentieth century?

Table 3.1   History of *The Economic Organization*

1918	'The Economic Organization of Society' (textbook outline)
1920	'Social Organization: A Survey of Its Problems and Forms from the Standpoint of the Present Crisis' (essay)
1922	Untitled Annotated Textbook Outline
1924–25	Course materials, including 'The Price System and the Economic Process,' 'Demand and Supply and Price,' and 'Distribution: The Pricing of Productive Services Individually'
1925	'Social Economic Organization' (in three chapters)
1932	Adoption of 'Social Economic Organization,' 'The Price System and the Economic Process,' 'Demand and Supply and Price,' and 'Distribution: The Pricing of Productive Services Individually' for General Social Sciences
1933	*The Economic Organization*
1938	Addition of note regarding capital theory and tripartite division of factors of production
1951	Post-1938 version published by Augustus M. Kelley, with 'Notes on Cost and Utility'
1961	Spanish translation completed in Puerto Rico
1965	Paperback edition with 'Notes on Cost and Utility' published by Harper & Row, Harper Torchbook, The Academy Library
1967	A. M. Kelley reissue in *Reprints of Economics Classics series*

The *EO* and its predecessors

Knight worked on a textbook on economics for almost 30 years, from the late 1910s until the mid-1940s. He produced several different versions, none of which were published in their entirety. Instead, four chapters of material written for classroom use and possible inclusion in a textbook were incorporated into classroom materials for an undergraduate general social sciences course at the University of Chicago in 1932, and 'published' as *EO* shortly thereafter. In order to tell the story of *EO*'s predecessors, we need to begin by looking more closely at its four chapters (see Table 3.2).

Table 3.2   Chapters in *The Economic Organization* (1933)

1. Social Economic Organization
2. The Price System and the Economic Process
3. Demand and Supply and Price
4. Distribution: The Pricing of Productive Products Individually

Note: A complete outline of the book, based on Knight's headings, is in the Appendix.

The four chapters of *EO* divide into two sections. However, there are two different ways that one can divide the sections. The first division follows the observation that Chapters 3 and 4 comprise the essence of price theory. Chapter 3 introduces the basics of demand and supply theory, elasticity, and discusses the problem of time in connection with the determination of price. Chapter 4 examines the problem of imputation, and then addresses the determination of wages, interest, rent and profit from a price-theoretic framework. Thus, from a price theory perspective, Chapters 3 and 4 are the core of the book, and the first two chapters are introductory. When the College staff teaching the social sciences courses revised their syllabus in 1936, they followed this division, removing the last two chapters and keeping the two introductory chapters. No doubt the vast majority of economists have also approached *EO* from this perspective.

However, if one adopts an organizational perspective, rather than a price theoretic one, *EO*'s chapters divide differently. In the first chapter, Knight argues that all economies perform the same functions, but that their forms of organization differ. The second, third, and fourth chapters then go on to examine the functioning of the free-enterprise form of economic organization, which operates through the price system. Chapter 2 provides a bridge between the first chapter and the last two chapters, introducing the price system as the mechanism used in the free-enterprise form of economic organization. From the perspective of social organization, *EO* divides into two sections, with Chapter 1 comprising the first section. The latter division will be used here to help with the interpretation of the textual lineage of *EO*. The price theory section will be discussed first, followed by an examination of precursors to 'Social Economic Organization.'

The history of the price theory chapters

The second section of *EO* (the last three chapters) was written and mimeographed for distribution to students in connection with Knight's lectures on price theory in the 1924–1925 academic year. However, the price theory chapters had several precursors. Knight's initial treatment of price theory was, of course, the first half of *Risk, Uncertainty and Profit* (Knight, 1921a), which he began to revise when teaching at the University of Chicago between 1917 and 1919, and finished after taking up an appointment at the University of Iowa. But even before he finished *Risk, Uncertainty and Profit*, Knight had begun to think of writing a textbook. In 1918, he wrote a 25 page annotated outline of a text, bearing the title

Table 3.3 'The Economic Organization of Society' (1918)

Book 1	The Scope, Aims and Method of Economic Study
Book 2	Consumption, Demand, Exchange, Markets, Price
Book 3	Production in Relation to Demand Under Given Conditions
Book 4	Free Enterprise and Social Progress
Book 5	Criticism of the Competitive System. Economics and Welfare

Source: Knight (1918).

'The Economic Organization of Society' (Table 3.3).[7] The proposed text bears a strong resemblance to *EO*, especially in its prominent coverage of price theory in the second, third, and fourth 'books.' Knight's move to Iowa pre-empted further work on the text, and it was several years before he picked up the task again.

When Knight moved from Chicago to Iowa in 1919, he began an eight-year span of teaching elementary economics to undergraduate students.[8] Between 1919 and 1924, he wrote two items that bear directly on the three chapters that eventually appeared in *EO*. The first was his reconstruction of Marshall's interpretation of short- and long-run supply curves in 'Costs of Production and Price over Long and Short Periods' (Knight, 1921b). The attention paid in the third chapter of *EO* to different periods of time in the determination of price, particularly in regard to the shape of the supply curve, comes from the 1921 article.

The second was another annotated outline of a potential textbook (Knight, 1922) (Table 3.4). Although the outline began with Chapter 3, a note at the beginning of the third chapter indicated that the first chapter introduced the reader to the notion that 'the study of free enterprise centers in the phenomenon of price' and the second chapter was organized around the differentiation between time periods that Knight had recently introduced in his 1921 article. From that point, the outline

Table 3.4   Untitled annotated outline of textbook (1922)

Chapter 3	General Principles of Price Fixation
Chapter 4	The Demand for Consumption Goods
Chapter 5	The Supply of Consumption Goods
Chapter 6	Monopoly and Competition
Chapter 7	Distribution in the Static State
Chapter 8	Social Criticism of Free Enterprise

Source: Knight (1922).

of Chapters 3–7 covered the same ground as the final two chapters of *EO*. Once again, however, the actual production of the text was postponed.

In November 1924, Knight closed a letter to Allyn A. Young with the comment 'I am wrestling with the Principles of Economics course with unusual vigor this year and have plenty to do.' He was teaching the course with the 1923 edition of Ely's text (Ely *et al.*, 1923), in which Young himself had written the price theory section. But Young's treatment of price theory was always in tension with Ely's own resistance to its use (see Mehrling, 1997, 22–23), and Knight was disappointed with the result. Prompted by his disappointment, Knight suggested to Young that he might prepare a 'brief discussion of theory' (Frank H. Knight to Allyn A. Young, 18 November 1924, FHK Papers, Box 62, Folder 24). The result was the three-part, seven-chapter, set of materials identified in Table 3.5. Young's encouragement of the project was followed later by his comments on the three chapters included in Part II.[9] These three chapters are the same chapters that appear in *EO*. Apart from the change in title from 'Demand and Supply: The Prices of Consumption Goods' to 'Demand and Supply and Price,' the second section of *EO*, therefore, was complete by the end of the 1924–1925 academic year.

But what about 'social economic organization'?

The reader will no doubt have noticed that the first chapter of *EO*, and its subject matter, is conspicuously absent from the various textbook outlines and class materials discussed under the previous sub-heading. Despite various comments by Knight that the chapters in *EO* were written in the 1924–1925 academic year, 'Social Economic Organization' does not appear in any list of material produced that year, and it is absent from the group of chapters that Young commented on. Nevertheless,

Table 3.5 1924–1925 course materials

Part I	Utility as Fact, Force, End, Value: Science and Criticism in Economic Theory
Part II	The Price System and the Economic Process
	Demand and Supply: The Prices of Consumption Goods
	Distribution: The Pricing of Productive Products Individually
Part III	Social Interpretation and Criticism
	Limitations of Competitive Individualism, A: Mechanical Limitations
	Limitations of Competitive Individualism, B: Ethical Considerations (outline)

Sources: Emmett (1999a, b).

there is good reason to believe that the first chapter of *EO* was written no later than 1925, and circulated with the price theory chapters to students at the University of Iowa.

The primary justification for the belief that 'Social Economic Organization' was written at about the same time as the price theory chapters is textual. Knight built the second chapter of *EO*, 'The Price System and the Economic Process,' around the functional approach to economic organization developed in 'Social Economic Organization.' For example, the 'wheel of wealth' – the circular-flow diagram – in Chapter 2 is introduced to illustrate how the price mechanism in a free-enterprise economy simultaneously solves the social functions that an economic organization must provide, rather than to demonstrate macroeconomic flows, as is more often the case (see section 'The Economic Organization and its Children').

Additional support for the belief that the first chapter of *EO* was written at approximately the same time as the rest of the chapters also comes from the text of the second chapter. At two points in that chapter, Knight makes explicit reference to the preceding chapter. The first reference points to the first chapter's outline of the social functions of economic organization (Knight, 1951, 33). The second cites the first chapter's dissolution of economic progress into changes in the 'givens' of price theory: resources, technology and wants (Knight, 1951, 64–65). Obviously, Knight had 'Social Economic Organization' at hand when he drafted 'The Price System and the Economic Process.'

But what version of 'Social Economic Organization' was in his hand as he wrote the price theory chapters? There are two reasons to believe that the version was not exactly the same as the one which appears in *EO*. The first comes from a deliberate omission on my part in the previous paragraph's mention of the second chapter's reference to 'Social Economic Organization.' Knight's exact words are 'As explained in previous *chapters*' (emphasis added) and 'the discussion of earlier *chapters*' (emphasis added). Although generations of readers of *EO* may have simply skimmed over the plural form of 'chapter,' thinking it a typographical error, it is not. In fact, one copy of the material in *EO* contains six chapters, the first three of which are the three sections of 'Social Economic Organization' (see Table 3.6 and the Appendix).[10] Although this copy of *EO* has no date attached to it, we may reasonably conclude that it was prepared at approximately the same time as the 1924–1925 classroom materials, because 'The Price System and the Economic Process' is identical in the two versions. The mimeograph also indicates that the first chapter of *EO* was created by merging the three chapters of the

Table 3.6 The first version of *EO*

---

3. Social Economic Organization and Its Five Primary Functions
4. Advantages and Disadvantages of Organized Action
5. Types of Social Organization: Economics and Politics
6. The Price System and the Economic Process
7. Demand and Supply and Price
8. Distribution: The Pricing of Productive Services Individually

---

Source: Untitled mimeograph in FHK Papers, Box 30, Folders 15–17.

earlier material into one, with a title borrowed from the first title of that material.

The second reason to believe that 'Social Economic Organization' was not the same at the time the second chapter of *EO* was written is also a minor textual point, but one that suggests that the writing of 'The Price System and the Economic Process' may have led Knight to alter the text of 'Social Economic Organization' as well. Careful readers of 'The Price System and the Economic Process' may have noticed another problem in it. At the end of the chapter, after introducing the circular-flow diagram, Knight discusses how the simultaneous determination of the prices of consumption goods and productive services in a free-enterprise economy fulfils the social functions of any economic organization. In that discussion, he indicates that there are *four* social functions (Knight, 1951, 62). In the first chapter, however, five functions are listed.

This apparent discrepancy is resolved if we look more closely at the discussion of the five functions in 'Social Economic Organization.' The fifth function is clearly a late addition to the chapter. In the text, only four functions are included in the introduction to the section 'The Five Functions of an Economic System,' and these four functions are subsequently numbered 1–4. The fifth function ('To adjust consumption to production within very short periods') is not prefaced by a number, but rather by the words 'A Fifth Function' (Knight, 1951, 7–15). The late addition of a fifth function to 'Social Economic Organization' is supported by the *inclusion* of a discussion of how the price theory adjusts consumption to production in short periods of time as *point 5* in the outline of the last section of 'The Price System and the Economic Process.' That is, despite indicating that there are only four functions, Knight concludes his treatment of the price system's fulfillment of the required social functions with a discussion of the fifth function. Whether he revised 'Social Economic Organization' after writing the last subsection of 'The Price System and the Economic Process' or revised both chapters simultaneously at a later date is not known.

What we can conclude, however, is that the text of the first chapter of *EO* was complete at about the same time as the text of the price theory chapters. In the mid-1920s, these chapters formed part of a larger textbook project, as evidenced by the chapter numbering in the undated, untitled mimeograph identified in Table 3.6. They were assembled, apparently for the first time as four chapters, in 1932 for use in the Chicago social science reader.

Precursors to 'social economic organization'

We now know that the text of the first chapter of *EO* was also completed in the mid-1920s. But we have not yet answered the same question about the origins of that chapter that we answered for the price theory chapters. We turn now to that task.

Despite the similarity in title, 'The Economic Organization of Society' (Knight, 1918), which was mentioned earlier, bears little resemblance to the first chapter of *EO*. In particular, the 1918 textbook outline is not organized around the functional approach to economics that Knight uses to integrate price theory with the theory of social economic organization in *EO*. The absence of earlier references to functional approaches is reinforced when we compare 'Social Economic Organization' with a 1920 essay that Knight considered submitting to the *Journal of Political Economy*, entitled 'Social Organization: A Survey of Its Problems and Forms from the Standpoint of the Present Crisis' (Knight, 1920), and the last chapter of *Risk, Uncertainty and Profit*, which was written about the same time.

The 1920 essay 'Social Organization' highlights many of the same themes as the chapters in *EO* regarding the social usefulness of a free-enterprise form of economic organization. But the focus of the essay is not the benefits of the price system. Instead, Knight argues that despite free enterprise's positive attributes, its ethical limitations should encourage us to pursue its replacement.

> In the existing system, the serpent's tail is always in his mouth; all the inequalities of the system aggravate themselves cumulatively around an unbreakable vicious circle. It is supposed to give us a social value scale made up of individual desires, but in reality the purchasing-power factor in demand ever more overtops the desire or need factor; in the agitators' phrase, the money is placed ahead of

the man. In addition, as we have already noticed, the system places a high premium on the corruption of tastes; and this also works cumulatively. And at the same time that the progress of civilization is throwing men closer together and calling ever more insistently for an enlightened social consciousness and conscience, competitive business breeds individualism, narrowness and selfishness of outlook....

The first step in any progress toward this grand consummation is to replace our present so-called system which directs a large part of its energies to the corruption of mankind with some sort of more truly social order under which attention can be directed toward the improvement instead of the degradation of tastes and ideals....

... our last word must be to reiterate that we *cannot* continue to do as we are now doing; the present system is self-defeating and impossible as well as intolerable, and we *must learn* to construct and operate a better one. The sooner we put our minds and hands to the task the better it will be in every way.

(Knight, 1920)

Readers more familiar with Knight's later defense of free enterprise may be surprised by the tone of the essay, but similar sentiments are found in muted form in the last chapter of *Risk, Uncertainty and Profit*, written at the same time as the 1920 essay, and, most memorably, in the 1923 *Quarterly Journal of Economics* article 'The Ethics of Competition' (Knight, 1999a).[11] Furthermore, every outline of a textbook Knight worked on during the 1920s includes a section of social and ethical criticism, for which the 1920 and 1923 essays served as models. For example, the 1922 untitled annotated outline of a textbook mentioned earlier in the discussion of the precursors to the price theory chapters of *EO* specifically identifies 'The argument of the paper I am sending to the *Q.J.E.*' as the material to be covered in the final chapter, entitled 'Social Criticism of Free Enterprise' (Knight, 1922).

The absence of social and ethical criticism of free enterprise from 'Social Economic Organization,' and in fact from *EO* generally, reinforces Knight's argument that the chapters were intended to become part of a larger textbook. The larger project would probably conclude, like the 1922 outline, with an ethical criticism of laissez-faire. Ironically, when the Social Science Staff in the College chose to remove the third and fourth chapters of *EO* from the social science reader in 1938, they replaced them with 'The Ethics of Competition.'

Knowing that Knight drafted several essays during the early 1920s that dealt not only with his treatment of the price system but also with the theory of social and economic organization does not, however, answer the fundamental question about the origins of 'Social Economic Organization.' When did Knight begin to construct the functional approach to economic organization that shapes the entire argument of *EO*? None of the previously mentioned essays and textbook outlines adopts the approach that made *EO* famous. In fact, the first place where Knight's functional approach appears is in the first chapter of the untitled mimeograph mentioned above (see Table 3.4); in other words, *EO* introduces Knight's functional approach. Where did it come from?

The obvious answer is, 'from functionalist approaches in sociology.' Here we have to be careful because Knight was critical of the classical functionalist approach of Durkheim. A closer kinship would be with the structural functionalism of Talcott Parsons, with whom Knight was friendly in the late 1920s and early 1930s. But we have already established that Knight's functionalist account was introduced about 1925, which pre-dates his friendship with Parsons. That leaves us with Max Weber, whose *General Economic History* was translated by Knight into English in the mid-1920s (Weber, 1927). Knight encountered Weber's work ten years earlier in Heidelberg, while on a postgraduation tour of Europe. The commonality of their approaches to social science, and Knight's strong interest in Weber during the 1920s suggests that Weber's functionalism informed Knight's decision to employ a similar model in approaching the problem of social economic organization.

Knight's reading of Weber provided a contrast to the functionalist approach to economic organization incorporated in a 1921 book by Leon Carroll Marshall, who was the head of the political economy department at the University of Chicago from 1918 to 1929. Marshall compiled a variety of materials for introductory courses in economics at Chicago, and published *Our Economic Organization* in 1921 for use in introductory economics courses (Marshall and Lyon, 1921). Marshall's functionalism is closer to Durkheim's than Weber's and Knight's, but Knight was familiar with it because of his close ties to the Chicago department during his tenure in Iowa City.[12] When Knight told Young that he was adopting a functionalist approach, Young told him,

I have a perfectly irrational prejudice against the word "functional," possibly because of a way in which I think Marshall has been inclined to abuse the term in the organization of his work at Chicago. But I shall reserve any specific criticisms until I see just what you mean by it.

> (Allyn A. Young to Frank H. Knight,
> 11 March 1927, FHK Papers, Box 62, Folder 24).[13]

Young would not have been disappointed to discover that the functionalist approach Knight adopts in *EO* stands in sharp contrast to the organicist, descriptivist approach Marshall used.

Our reviews of the history of both sections of *EO* lead us to the same point: the academic year 1924–1925. The price theory chapters were certainly finalized at that point. 'Social Economic Organization' was probably written at that point, or shortly thereafter. Both sections have predecessor material, and the functionalist approach adopted in the first chapter was the last addition.

The life of the *EO*

The reprinting of the four chapters under the title *EO* does not end our story. Indeed, the introduction suggested that we might think of 1933 as the birth date of a book whose story diverges from that of its author. Four aspects of the divergent stories will be examined in this section. The first is the evolution of the use of *EO*'s four chapters in the course reader for general social science courses at the University of Chicago. The first two essays were used in every edition of the Social Science II reader from 1932 to 1941. The third and fourth essays were dropped from the reader during the revision of the reading list and syllabus in 1936. In 1942 Social Science II was renumbered to Social Science III with a new reader (University of Chicago Social Science Staff, 1942), but the edition numbering from the Social Science II reader was maintained (the first Social Science III reader was identified as Edition 10). The first two essays by Knight remained in the Social Science III reader from 1942 to 1946 (Editions 10–12); they were not used in the second- or third-year courses in the post-war period. However, after an absence of 13 years, the first two essays returned in the course readers for Social Sciences 112 and 113, the first-year social science course sequence, in 1958 and 1959. They continued to be used in the first-year courses, albeit sporadically, as late as 1964.[14]

The second aspect of the story is related to the first. One often noticed, but soon forgotten, fact about the booklet version of *EO* is that each page has a header that includes 'F. H. Knight' and the chapter number, expressed as a roman numeral. The odd thing is that the roman numerals start at VII and proceed to X. Why is the first chapter of *EO* numbered Chapter 7? Providing the answer requires remembering that creating reproducible material in the 1930s was expensive, and that it was often easier to use a pre-existing reproducible copy. The pre-existing copy of *EO* was the one prepared in 1932 for the preliminary edition of the Social Science II reader. There 'Social Economic Organization' was numbered as Chapter 7. It remained at that spot in the reader through-out the 1930s. Thus, in 1933, when the University of Chicago printed a separate version of *EO*, they simply used the same reproducible copy that had been prepared for the reader. The only change made was a renumbering of the pages (one could probably be excused for overlooking the fact that the page numbers in the booklet are printed in a different typescript than the text).[15]

The third unfinished part of the story is Knight's revision of the text of *EO* in the late 1930s. After the Social Science Staff removed the third and fourth essays from the course reader, Knight revisited the text and suggested a correction. As indicated in the section 'The Economic Organization and its Predecessors' above, Knight had revised his understanding of capital and economic resources generally during the latter part of the 1920s and early 1930s and no longer agreed with the interpretation of 'productive resources' contained in 'The Price System and Economic Progress.' In 1938, he wrote two statements he intended to have the Social Science Staff include with the first two chapters of *EO* in the course reader. These statements explained the reason for Knight's disagreement with the argument the students would read in the second chapter, and suggested what his newer understanding would be. Neither of these statements was included in the course reader. However, Knight was able to insert a short note in the empty space on the last page of Chapter 2 in the reprinted booklet version of *EO* (identified by the same principle as that employed above in explaining the numbering sequence of the chapters). The note in the booklet not only stated Knight's disagreement with the 'orthodox' version he had espoused in the late 1920s, but added that his new understanding was compatible with the understanding of the interest rate and the supply side of distributive theory contained later in *EO*. Every printing of the booklet *EO* after 1938 contains this note, but the chapters included in the social science course reader did not.

Finally, we can add the addition to *EO* of 'Notes on Cost and Utility.' 'Notes' was the English version of a two-part article originally published in German in 1935. As mentioned earlier, Knight frequently reprinted versions of his writings for use by students, sometimes adding material that had been deleted from the published version. 'Notes' is no exception. A mimeograph of the English version was produced, and a footnote added: 'In the published translation section 13 and the last paragraph of section 17 were deleted and have been here restored, a few minor revisions as compared with the translation have also been made.' 'Notes' was often circulated among students with *EO* and other significant articles for Chicago price theory.[16] More importantly, 'Notes' works out the details of the change in Knight's thinking alluded to in the note he added in 1938. Hence, the inclusion of 'Notes' in *EO* is entirely appropriate.

When did Knight grant permission for publication?

Augustus M. Kelley's 1951 edition of *EO* bears the following copyright information: 'Copyright 1933, 1951 by Frank H. Knight.' However, as we saw earlier, when Harper & Row contacted Knight to request permission to republish *EO* as a Harper Torchbook paperback in the Academic Library, Knight replied that Kelley had not obtained his permission to publish the book. In fact, he described the 1951 publication as illegitimate. What is the copyright status of *EO*?

Before looking at Kelley's publication of *EO*, we need to return to its original publication by the University of Chicago for classroom use. The booklet version of *EO* bears the following copyright information: 'Copyright 1933, by The University of Chicago.' Unfortunately, the records of the Board of University Publications do not support that copyright designation. The only decision the Board made regarding Knight's material was the approval of the publication of the preliminary edition of the Social Sciences syllabus in 1932 (Minutes of the Board of University Publications, 23 January 1932, UCP Records, Box 21, Folder 5). Even here the copyright for Knight's material is murky because there is no identification in the minutes of the contents of the Social Sciences syllabus. Furthermore, no subsequent approval for separate publication of Knight's booklet occurred.

Knight's suggestion that any copyright date for *EO* is a 'pure invention' sounds better and better! We know he approved the printing of the class materials and the booklet for 'local use' in the 1930s. The statement 'Reprinted with permission of the author' on the cover of the Chicago booklet accords with this approval. Beyond that, no assignment of rights appears to have occurred in the 1930s.

We can now return to Kelley's reprint of *EO*. The problems with the copyright inscription in Kelley's reprint would be resolved if we knew that Kelley had obtained permission from the University. Unfortunately, there are no records on either side to confirm or deny an arrangement. Gus Kelley usually did obtain permission (often in conjunction with a one-time payment) for his reprints, so it is reasonable to assume that an arrangement was made in 1951.[17] But that arrangement did not include Knight.

When did Knight approve a reprinting of the book other than for local use at the University of Chicago? The answer to that question lies in the correspondence between Knight and Harper & Row. In the early 1960s, Harper & Row wrote to Knight asking permission to publish a paperback version of the Kelley reprint. After Knight informed the publisher that Kelley did not have his permission to publish, he signed a contract for publication with Harper & Row. However, the contract merely provided Harper & Row the right to publish a paperback edition for a limited period of years, with renewal rights. The paperback version bore the same copyright inscription as Kelley's 1951 reprint, but added the following: 'This book was originally published in book form by Augustus M. Kelley, Inc., New York, in 1951. It is here reprinted by arrangement with the Author.' The Harper & Row reprint was renewed once, in 1969, but not subsequently. No rights have been assigned since the 1970s.

Two footnotes to this history of copyright should be added. First, Kelley reprinted *EO* again in 1967 as one of the first items in his Reprints of *Economics Classics series*. No record exists that indicates a new arrangement with the copyright holder (either the University or Knight) was made. The copyright inscription remained the same as in his 1951 reprint.

Secondly, shortly after Knight's death in 1972, an Argentinean publisher contacted Knight's wife through Harper & Row, seeking permission to publish a Spanish translation of *EO* (see correspondence with Domingo Palombella and Marina Finn in FHK Papers, Box 60, Folder 4). Although we do not have a copy of Mrs Knight's response, a translation was not undertaken at that time. However, a translation had previously been done in Puerto Rico, without Knight's knowledge or permission. Only a single known copy of the translation remains, in the library of the University of Puerto Rico, where it was prepared for classroom use (Knight, 1961).

The *EO* and its children

More than a generation of students were introduced to economics at the University of Chicago through *EO*. When it was their turn to teach students economics, they naturally turned to the source that had taught them well. And when they wrote their own textbooks they modelled them, at least in part, on Knight's teachings. *EO's* children, then, are the textbooks that followed it.

The most famous of those is Paul Samuelson's *Economics: An Introductory Analysis*. Samuelson, who took Knight's course as an undergraduate at the University of Chicago, borrowed three key elements of *EO* for his textbook. The first was Knight's functional approach to economic organization. Samuelson boiled Knight's five functions down to three: (i) '*What* commodities shall be produced and in what quantities?'; (ii) '*How* shall they be produced?'; and (iii) '*For* whom are they to be produced?'. 'These three questions,' Samuelson adds, paraphrasing Knight, 'are fundamental and common to all economies' (Samuelson, 1948, 12–13). Although Knight is not cited at this point in Samuelson's first edition, he appears in the second edition, in a footnote which reads, 'This viewpoint, with minor adaptations, corresponds to that worked out some years ago by Frank H. Knight of the University of Chicago, a distinguished American economist. See his *Social Economic Organization* (syllabus for second-year course in the social sciences, University of Chicago Press, 1933, 2nd edn)' (Samuelson, 1951, 14).

Samuelson's second borrowing from Knight is the subsequent discussion, several chapters later, of how free enterprise fulfils the basic functions of any economy. Samuelson's discussion of the economic order that appears in a free-enterprise economy follows Knight's, but his discussion of problems with that order does not. Where Knight places emphasis on both 'mechanical' and 'ethical' limitations to perfect competition, Samuelson focuses almost exclusively on the former category. Because some of Knight's other students (George Stigler and Milton Friedman, in particular) were able to show that the 'mechanical' arguments against free enterprise were not as damaging as one (perhaps even Knight) may have thought, we can see the rift between Samuelson and Chicago opening. That rift was never to close, despite Samuelson's own affection for Knight.

The third great debt to Knight in Samuelson's textbook – the use of Knight's 'wheel of wealth' – is more problematic. Knight introduces the 'wheel of wealth' as an illustration of the way in which free enterprise simultaneously fulfils all the functions of economic organization (Knight, 1933, 63). As Don Patinkin points out, this price theory use of the circular-flow diagram is unique to Knight: previous, and most subsequent (at least outside Chicago), uses of it are focused on macroeconomic flows (Patinkin, 1981b). Samuelson has used the circular-flow diagram in both ways. In the first three editions of his book, the circular-flow appears only in the context of macroeconomic flows. But starting from the fourth edition, Samuelson begins to use the circular-flow diagram in conjunction with his discussion of the organization functions of the price system (he then reintroduces it later in the macroeconomic chapters). Patinkin has a full discussion of Samuelson's indebtedness to Knight and his use of the wheel of wealth (Patinkin, 1981a, b).

Within the Chicago tradition, *EO* eventually came to complement the textbooks that defined post-war 'Chicago economics': Stigler's *The Theory of Price* (1946) and Friedman's *Price Theory* (1962).[18] Stigler's book acknowledges the debt to Knight explicitly: *Risk, Uncertainty and Profit* appears in the lists of recommended readings for five chapters (even Marshall does not appear as often), and the third chapter ('The Functions of an Economic System') is identified as being 'based directly' on the first chapter of *EO* (Stigler, 1946, 32).[19] Stigler's reading of Knight's five functions is similar to Samuelson's: what shall be produced, how shall resources be allocated to produce it, and how shall the product be distributed? Stigler identifies Knight's third function – adjusting short-run consumption to a relatively fixed supply – as 'a special case' of the distributive function (Stigler, 1946, 32). He also places the fifth function – making provision for the long-term maintenance and expansion of the economic system – outside the scope of price theory, with the exception of the role of the interest rate (Stigler, 1946, 39–40). However, unlike Samuelson, Stigler follows Knight in utilizing the circular-flow diagram exclusively in conjunction with their explanation of the price system's allocative functions.

Chicago economists continue to acknowledge their intellectual debt to Knight's *EO* today. Each autumn quarter, Gary Becker and Kevin Murphy teach the price theory course required of all incoming graduate students – the famous Economics 301. Their syllabus for the autumn quarter of 2006 (Becker and Murphy) recommends that students read the first chapter of *EO* in conjunction with their required reading of Friedman's methodology essay (Friedman, 1966), and Becker's overview of 'The Economic Approach to Human Behavior' (Becker, 1976).

Stigler, Friedman, Becker and Murphy reflect the transmission of Marshallian theory through Knight to today, although all of them emphasize the predictive capacity of the theory more than Knight did. Stigler and Friedman (both students of Knight's) are well known for their versions of the argument that a theory based on a small set of assumptions that may appear unrealistic, but which prove to be analytically relevant, is the most useful one. Stigler and Becker (and now Murphy) are known for the argument that the analytics of price theory can explain a wide range of human behavior if we make the basic assumption that human preferences, values, and tastes remain constant over time and among individuals – *de gustibus non est disputandum* (Stigler and Becker, 1977). While Knight eventually came to defend the analytical side of their arguments (Knight, 1999d), he was always skeptical of the predictive capacity of economics, and rejected the *de gustibus* assumption. Stigler once said that Knight's understanding of the role of economic theory was to 'contribute to the understanding of how by consensus based upon rational discussion we can fashion liberal society in which individual freedom is preserved and a satisfactory economic performance achieved' (Stigler, 1987, 58). That larger role did not call for a focus on the prediction of key economic variables or the outcomes of regulatory controls; instead, it called for an understanding of how satisfactory economic performance can be achieved by reliance upon the price system's operation within a free-enterprise economy. In the end, the lasting legacy of *EO* is Knight's explanation of that contribution.

Appendix

The Economic Organization
Table of contents and outline of chapters

Social Economic Organization
  I. Social Economic Organization and Its Five Primary Functions
 II. The Five Main Functions of an Economic System
III. Advantages and Disadvantages of Organized Action
 IV. Types of Social Organization: Economic and Politics

The Price System and the Economic Process
   I. Modern Economic Organization, an 'Automatic' System
  II. Price, the Guide and Regulator. The Price System
 III. Principles versus Facts. Explanation versus Justification or Criticism
 IV. Subdivision of the Problem. The Notion of an Unprogressive Society or 'Static State'
  V. The Economic Process in a 'Static' View
 VI. The Elementary Concepts of Economics
VII. Wants and the Direct Means of Satisfying Wants

Notes

1. The assistance of the following individuals is gratefully acknowledged: Jeff Biddle, Mary Caldera (Archivist, Yale University), Fred Cheesman (A. M. Kelley), Dan Meyer (Archivist, University of Chicago), David Mitch, Jerry Nordquist, Warren Samuels, Hugh Van Dusen (HarperCollins), and Peter Yu. Permission for the use of materials from the Frank H. Knight Papers and the University of Chicago Press Records has been granted by the University of Chicago Archives.

2. The article was another manuscript published by Knight for classroom use (Knight, 1936). *Notes* was originally published in German as a two-part article (Knight, 1935a, b).

3. The Yale copy is the earliest known copy outside the University of Chicago, and is now in the Yale Library. It is a reprint of the original version of the chapters from the 1932 Social Science II reader (paginated as in the reader rather than in the 1933 booklet), dated 1934. Archivists at Yale have found

no indication of *EO*'s use in general education classes during the 1930s. Contradictory bibliographic information makes it difficult to know how it arrived there. The copy itself indicates that it was reproduced in 1934 by the Yale Cooperative Corporation, which regularly produced course readers. Information in the online catalog, however, suggests that it is a photocopy made in the early 1980s.

4. The letter from James M. Reid (Harcourt Brace) to Frank H. Knight, 10 May 1933, is in the FHK Papers, Box 60, Folder 4. The Harcourt Brace editors had read Knight's review of Slichter's book (Knight, 1999b). Reid says,

> As we understand it, you believe in control and to that extent you are sympathetic with Slichter. You insist, however, ... on analyses of the economic factors upon which 'control' must be based, which are at least comparable in thoroughness and logic to the analyses of economists like Frank Marshall [sic] and Ely. We realize, of course, that the kind of analyses that are suitable for comprehension by college sophomores will necessarily modify and control the development of your arguments in the projected textbook.

5. Information on the spread of Knight's book to North American libraries gathered from *The National Union Catalog (Pre-1956 Imprints)* and WorldCat.

6. Portions of *EO* were also anthologized. Chapter 1 was the most popular excerpt, appearing (in its entirety or in part) in Knight (1953, 1958, 1965b, 1967b, 1968). A portion of Chapter 2 was also included in Knight (1953).

7. Knight taught Political Economy 14 (Advanced Economic Theory) at Chicago with John Maurice Clark during the summer quarters from 1918 to 1920, and prepared 'The Economic Organization of Society' in conjunction with the course. Advanced Political Economy followed Principles of Political Economy in the curriculum at Chicago in the early 1900s. Alfred Marshall's *Principles of Economics* was a standard textbook in the course (Marshall, 1916).

8. Jerry Nordquist compiled Knight's teaching responsibilities from the *State University of Iowa Schedule of Courses*.

9. Young's comments on the chapters from *EO* are in the FHK Papers, Box 54, Folders 6, 9, and 11. The chapters Young read were numbered 3, 4, and 5. This numbering of the chapters does not correspond to any version of Knight's textbook material preserved in the FHK Papers. A year-and-a-half later, in September 1926, Young wrote back after reading some additional text-related material that Knight had sent him. From Young's comments, it is clear that the second group of chapters he read were not ones included in *EO*. Unfortunately, we do not know exactly what manuscript Young read in 1926 (see the letter from Young to Knight, 9 September 1926, FHK Papers, Box 62, Folder 24).

10. No indication has been found of what the first two chapters of this book were. But Chapters 3–8 comprise the entirety of the material used in 1932 at the University of Chicago.

11. In fact, even at the time some of Knight's acquaintances were surprised. C. O. Hardy read the 1920 essay upon Knight's request, to judge whether it was ready for submission to the *Journal of Political Economy*. Hardy replied,

> I am returning your article, 'Social Organization' because I feel that you ought to read it again before I pass it around to the editorial circle. I have read it with mingled emotions, most of them painful. Had I received it from an utter stranger, I should merely have cursed him and we should probably have published it. But such a large part of it seems to me quite opposed to your views... that I don't feel justified in letting anybody else see it.
>
> (C. O. Hardy to F. H. Knight, 23 September 1920,
> FHK Papers, Box 31, Folder 6)

12. Marshall's tenure as department head began during the last year of Knight's first stint at Chicago (1918–1919). Over the next several summers, Knight returned to Chicago to teach courses for the department.
13. When he began to revise his textbook materials in the late 1930s, Knight wrote a defense of his functional approach (1938)
14. Information regarding the use of the essays in the Social Science readers was gathered from the copies held in the University of Chicago Library. For general information regarding Knight's place in the social sciences curriculum, see Orlinksy (1922).
15. The original page numbering in the Social Science reader ran as follows: Chapter VII: 125–154; Chapter VIII: 155–192; Chapter IX: 193–223; and Chapter X: 224–250.
16. Other favorites included Knight (1999c) and Viner (1932).
17. Information on Kelley's business practices and records come from a phone conversation with Fred Cheesman, a long-time employee of A. M. Kelley, on 10 March 2004.
18. Stigler's book was originally published as *The Theory of Competitive Price* in 1942. The 1946 version was enlarged to include consideration of the theory of imperfect competition. Friedman's book was assembled from David Fand's notes on his price theory course at the University of Chicago in the late 1940s. Roger Weiss, who was an instructor in the College of the University of Chicago during the 1960s and 1970s, wrote *The Economic System* with the intention of simplifying *EO* for use by beginning students, and broadening the range of coverage (Weiss, 1969).
19. Richard Leftwich, a pupil of Stigler's, also explicitly bases his discussion of the functions of an economic system on *EO* (Leftwich, 1955, 11).

References

FHK Papers, Frank H. Knight Papers, University of Chicago Archives.
UCP Records, University of Chicago Press Records, University of Chicago Archives.
Becker, G. S. 'The Economic Approach to Human Behavior,' in *The Economic Approach to Human Behavior* (Chicago: University of Chicago Press, 1976), 3–14.

Becker, G. S. and K. M. Murphy. Economics 301 Reading List (Autumn 2006). home.uchicago.edu/~gbecker/econ301/Autumn%20Quarter%202006.pdf (accessed on October 15, 2006).

Buchanan, J. M. 'Frank H. Knight,' in *International Encyclopedia of the Social Sciences*, edited by D. Sills, vol. 3 (New York: Macmillan, 1968), 424–28.

Ely, R. T., T. S. Adams, M. O. Lorenz, and A. A. Young. *Outlines of Economics* (New York: Macmillan, 1923).

Ely, R. T. and R. H. Hess. *Outlines of Economics* (New York: Macmillan, 1937).

Emmett, R. B. 'Frank Hyneman Knight (1885–1972): A Bibliography of His Writings,' *Research in the History of Economic Thought and Methodology*, archival supplement 9 (1999a): 1–100.

—— 'Frank Hyneman Knight Papers 1910–1972: Finding Guide,' *Research in the History of Economic Thought and Methodology*, archival supplement 9 (1999b): 101–273.

Friedman, M. *Price Theory: A Provisional Text* (Chicago: Aldine, 1962).

—— 'The Methodology of Positive Economics,' in *Essays in Positive Economics* (Chicago: University of Chicago Press, 1966), 3–43.

Knight, F. H. 'The Economic Organization of Society,' FHK Papers, Box 37, Folder 18, University of Chicago Archives, 1918.

——. 'Social Organization: A Survey of Its Problems and Forms from the Standpoint of the Present Crisis,' FHK Papers, Box 31, Folder 6–7, University of Chicago Archives, 1920.

——. *Risk, Uncertainty and Profit* (Boston: Houghton Mifflin, 1921a).

——. 'Cost of Production and Price Over Long and Short Periods,' *Journal of Political Economy*, 29 (1921b): 304–35.

——. 'Untitled Outline of Textbook,' FHK Papers, Box 37, Folder 13, University of Chicago Archives, 1922.

——. *The Economic Organization* (Chicago: University of Chicago, 1933).

——. 'Bemerkungen über Nutzen und Koston 1: Kritisches und Dogmengeschichtliches,' *Zeitschrift für Nationalökonomie*, 6 (1935a): 28–52.

——. 'Bemerkungen über Nutzen und Koston 2: Versuch einer Neugestaltung der Kostentheorie,' *Zeitschrift für Nationalökonomie*, 6 (1935b): 315–36.

——. *Notes on Utility and Cost* (Chicago: University of Chicago, 1936).

——. 'A Functional View of the Study of Economics,' FHK Papers, Box 16, Folder 7, University of Chicago Archives, 1938.

——. *The Economic Organization, with an Article 'Notes on Cost and Utility'* (New York: A. M. Kelley, 1951).

——. 'Social Economic Organization,' in *Introduction to Social Science*, edited by A. Naftalin *et al.*, vol. 2: *Works* (Chicago: J.B. Lippincott, 1953), 57–71.

——. 'Social Economic Organization,' in *Selections in Economics*, edited by R. C. Epstein and A. D. Butler (Buffalo: Smith, Keynes & Marshall, 1958), 19–39.

——. *La Oragnizacion Economica* (Rio Piedras, Puerto Rico: Oficina de Publicaciones de Estudios Generales, Universidad de Puerto Rico, 1961).

——. *The Economic Organization, with an Article 'Notes on Cost and Utility'* (New York: Harper & Row, 1965a).

——. 'The Economic Organization,' in *Theories of Society: Foundations of Modern Sociological Theory*, edited by T. Parsons *et al.* (New York: Free Press, 1965b), 454–57.

——. *The Economic Organization, with an Article 'Notes on Cost and Utility'* (New York: A. M. Kelley, 1967a).

——. 'Social Economic Organization,' in *The Business System: Readings in Ideas and Concepts,* edited by C. Walton and R. Eels, vol. 1 (New York: Macmillan, 1967b), 333–43.

——. 'Social Economic Organization,' in *Readings in Microeconomics,* edited by W. Breit and H. H. Hochman (New York: Holt, Rinehart & Winston, 1968), 3–19.

——. 'The Ethics of Competition,' in *Selected Essays by Frank H. Knight,* edited by R. B. Emmett, vol. 1: *'What is Truth' in Economics?* (Chicago: University of Chicago Press, 1999a), 61–93.

——. 'The Newer Economics and the Control of Economic Activity,' in *Selected Essays by Frank H. Knight,* edited by R. B. Emmett, vol. 1: *'What is Truth' in Economics?* (Chicago: University of Chicago Press, 1999b), 172–210.

——. 'The Ricardian Theory of Production and Distribution,' in *Selected Essays by Frank H. Knight,* edited by R. B. Emmett, vol. 1: *'What is Truth' in Economics?* (Chicago: University of Chicago Press, 1999c), 237–89.

——. 'Realism and Relevance in the Theory of Demand,' in *Selected Essays by Frank H. Knight,* edited by R. B. Emmett, vol. 2: *Laissez Faire: Pro and Con* (Chicago: University of Chicago Press, 1999d), 243–83.

Leftwich, R. H. *The Price System and Resource Allocation* (New York: Rinehart, 1955).

Marshall, A. *Principles of Economics: An Introductory Volume* (London: Macmillan, 1916).

Marshall, L. C. and L. S. Lyon. *Our Economic Organization* (New York: Macmillan, 1921).

Mehrling, P. G. *The Money Interest and the Public Interest: American Monetary Thought, 1920–1970* (Cambridge: Harvard University Press, 1997).

Orlinsky, D. E. 'Chicago General Education in Social Sciences, 1931–92: The Case of Soc 2,' in *General Education in the Social Science: Centennial Reflections on the College of the University of Chicago,* edited by J. J. MacAloon (Chicago: University of Chicago Press, 1992).

Patinkin, D. 'Frank Knight as Teacher,' in *Essays on and in the Chicago Tradition* (Durham: Duke University Press, 1981a), 23–51.

——. 'In Search of the "Wheel of Wealth": On the Origins of Frank Knight's Circular-Flow Diagram,' in *Essays on and in the Chicago Tradition* (Durham: Duke University Press, 1981b), 53–72.

Samuelson, P. *Economics: An Introductory Analysis* (New York: McGraw-Hill, 1948).

——. *Economics: An Introductory Analysis,* 2nd edn (New York: McGraw-Hill, 1951).

Simons, H. C. 'The Simons' Syllabus,' in *The Chicago Tradition in Economics, 1892–1945,* edited by R. B. Emmett, vol. 8 (London: Routledge, 2002), 3–70.

Slichter, S. H. *Modern Economic Society* (New York: Henry Holt, 1931).

Stigler, G. J. *The Theory of Price* (New York: Macmillan, 1946).

——. 'Frank Hyneman Knight,' in *The New Palgrave: A Dictionary of Economics,* edited by J. Eatwell, M. Milgate and P. Newman, vol. 3 (New York: Stockton Press, 1987), 55–59.

Stigler, G. J. and G. S. Becker. 'De Gustibus Non Est Disputandum,' *American Economic Review,* 67 (1977): 76–90.

University of Chicago Social Science Staff. *Second-year Course in the Social Sciences* (Chicago: University of Chicago, 1932).

University of Chicago Social Science Staff. *Third-year Course in the Study of Contemporary Society: Selected Readings* (Chicago: University of Chicago, 1942).

Viner, J. 'Cost Curves and Supply Curves,' *Zeitschrift für Nationalökonomie*, 3 (1932): 23–46.

Weber, M. *General Economic History* (Chicago: Adelphi, 1927).

Weiss, R. *The Economic System* (New York: Random House, 1969).

4
Friedman in Washington (1941–1943) on Taxation and the Inflationary Gap

Enrico Sergio Levrero[1]

Introduction

In 1941 Milton Friedman was added to the Division of Tax Research of the Treasury Department[2] by Roy Blough on the recommendation of Carl Shoup, with whom Friedman was involved in the research project on taxation to prevent inflation which was financed by the *Carnegie Foundation* and the *Institute of Public Administration*. The Division was preparing a major revision of the tax system to which Friedman contributed greatly in the years 1941–1943.[3]

According to Friedman, his contribution in these fields had a distinct Keynesian flavour. As he wrote after rereading one of his statements made in 1942 before the US Congress, 'I had completely forgotten how thoroughly Keynesian I then was. I was apparently cured, or some would say corrupted, shortly after the end of the war' (cf. Friedman, 1998, 113). Whereas the 'cure' happened just when the climate surrounding J. M. Keynes's *General Theory* and its more radical policy implications began to change in the United States with the spread of the so-called 'Keynesian-neoclassical synthesis' forged by the works of J. R. Hicks (1937) and F. Modigliani (1944), Friedman's initial 'Keynesian illness', if true, had probably been facilitated, as he himself suggested, by the 'prevailing Keynesian temper of the times' (cf. Friedman, 1943a, 253). After the initial cold reception of *The General Theory*, thanks also to the 'Hansen conversion', the judgment about Keynes's work rapidly changed in the United States (at least in academic circles, because in practice it had already had a great influence). And besides A. H. Hansen, S. E. Harris and A. P. Lerner, there were many economists – like M. S. Eccles, J. Galbraith, L. Henderson, R. Nathan and W. Salant – ready to apply Keynesian ideas and particularly active in influencing the economic policy of the time.[4]

Unlike other aspects of his activity, only scant literature and debate exists on this initial 'Keynesian illness' of Friedman. One reason is that greater attention has been devoted to his later restatement of the quantity theory of money, as well as to his works on methodological themes and the consumption function. Another reason might be that assessing the Keynesian 'flavour' of his 1941–1943 writings is not easy due to both the peculiar economic situation of the time and the many (and to some extent ambiguous) meanings taken on over time by the term 'Keynesian theory' or 'Keynesian policies'.

Regarding the first aspect, in the period 1941–1943 the American economy was moving fast towards a condition of full employment of resources due to the huge increase in war expenditure. The short-term danger thus became inflation rather than a shortfall in effective demand, also because shortages in basic commodities were rapidly increasing.[5] As Eccles (1941b, 1284) was already stressing in 1941, when the utilisation of productive capacity was nevertheless still at 70 per cent,

> (t)oday our problem is to curb consumer demand and purchasing power so that they will not divert too much of our productive capacity to the manufacture of nonessentials (...). The country must undergo a rapid readjustment of its thinking in order to comprehend the meaning of shortages rather than surpluses in many fields.

As far as what is labelled as Keynesian is concerned, the idea itself of a Keynesian revolution (cf. L. R. Klein, 1949) is known to have been increasingly criticised in the last few decades (see, for instance, D. Laidler, 1999).[6] In the meantime, however, it has been recognised that 'many important elements of the new message which Keynes was trying to convey in 1936' were neglected 'by the IS-LM model' (Laidler, 1999, 4), thus concealing some of the main analytical innovations of Keynes regarding income determination and monetary analysis. When considering these elements – which have been developed (though in different ways) by the Cambridge economists nearest to Keynes, as well as to some extent by Lerner and Hansen in the United States during the period under examination – they permit us a sharper comparison between a Keynesian and the monetarist approach developed after the war by Friedman.

In particular, considering the arguments analysed herein, in order to evaluate Friedman's claim of an initial Keynesian flavour of his own work, we shall stress as a Keynesian feature the recognition of the possibility of a persistent under-utilisation of resources arising from the principle of effective demand. We will then (and consequently) outline as Keynesian the idea that an increase in the money-wage ratio will not necessarily lead to a rise in the aggregate demand due to a fall in the interest rate and/or an increase in the real value of wealth (the so-called 'Pigou effect'). Finally, on a methodological plane, we will consider as Keynesian a non-simultaneous determination of the money rate of interest (that is, of the equilibrium in the money market), on the one hand, and of the level of income (that is, of the equilibrium in the commodity market) on the other, which instead characterises Hicks and Modigliani's interpretation of *The General Theory* (namely the IS-LM model), but which Keynes himself seems to have refuted.[7] Though sometimes contradictorily, these and other assumptions as to what characterises a Keynesian theory appear to agree with elements that Friedman himself recognised as properly Keynesian.[8]

Having said this, the aim of the present work will be primarily to reconstruct Friedman's activity in the period 1941–1943, and then to attempt to understand to what extent it was influenced by a Keynesian view regarding income and prices determination. The section 'The activity in Washington: The Ruml Plan' will be devoted to summarising the debate on the pay-as-you-go system of taxation, which was highly technical and less interesting for our purpose, but which pointed to two elements that we often find in Friedman's writings of the period, namely the need to curb private purchasing power during the war years and the necessity of equity in taxation to support the war effort. We will then go on to analyse Friedman's works on the 'inflationary gap' and his writings on the spending tax, which are both central in evaluating Friedman's activity in his Washington phase. Finally, in the section 'Some final remarks' the content of Friedman's writings in the years 1941–1943 will be compared with those after the war with a view to assessing differences and similarities. Albeit as a first assessment, his initial 'Keynesian illness' will indeed appear to have been less serious and deep than Friedman himself feared.

The activity in Washington: The Ruml Plan

A large part of Friedman's activity in the years 1941–1943 was aimed at contributing to reform tax collection.

Prior to 1942 in the United States there was no collection at source and the tax on income received in one year was payable in quarterly instalments the next year. This raised few problems so long as the income tax was low and only a small fraction of the population was subject to the tax. By 1943, however, the top tax rate had risen sharply and the total taxes collected multiplied nearly 15-fold. It was thus time to adopt a pay-as-you-go system, and all the proposed solutions in the first year of adoption implied some degree of forgiveness of one of the two years' taxes which for a while overlapped and should otherwise be both paid in the same year.

The discussion of alternatives became very technical. The chief proposal other than that of the Treasury was presented to the Senate Finance Committee on July 27, 1942 by Beardsley Ruml, and most of the New York financial community strongly favoured it. The final version was signed into law on June 9 by President Roosevelt as the *Current Tax Payment Act* of 1943. It incorporated a modification of the Ruml Plan, cancelling one year's tax obligations of $50 or less and 75 per cent of the required tax on the lower of the 1942 or the 1943 incomes. The compromise was reached after a debate spanning one year.

Friedman was one of the architects of the Treasury's alternative which involved much less 'forgiveness' than the Ruml Plan. In particular the Treasury's proposal aimed to achieve a greater collection of revenue and control of consumer purchasing power than the Ruml Plan (Friedman, 1942b, 56). In the case of the latter, in fact, 'people who had accrued their tax liabilities' and 'felt they were relieved of that debt' would have been able to spend it. Consequently,

> The unmodified Ruml plan raises less in revenues, and it also involves a psychological effect of accrual, so that it is clear that the unmodified Ruml plan would have less of an effect in withdrawing purchasing power from the market for consumer goods than either of the others.
> (Friedman, 1942b, 58)

But there was also a matter of equity on which Friedman and the other American Treasury's advisers insisted. While Ruml's idea of equity was that of giving 'equal treatment to all taxpayers under a change in method of assessing taxes' (Ruml, 1943, 87), Friedman, R. E. Paul and others at the Treasury outlined that higher taxpayers 'have capital, and they are in a position to meet the extraordinary demands on the new revenue act' (Paul, 1942, 60), while 'the cancellation of the 1941 liabilities would constitute a windfall gain to persons whose income were abnormally high in 1941' thanks to 'the war effort' (Friedman, 1942b, 62. See also Paul, 1943).[9]

The debate on the inflationary gap

During the years 1941–1943 the aims of curbing consumer purchasing power and of equity in taxation were central also in the debates on the 'inflationary gap' and the effects of price inflation.

At the time there was a broad consensus that in conditions of full employment an excess of the nominal aggregate demand on aggregate supply could be 'closed' either by means of inflation or by means of taxation and direct price controls[10] and the rationing of consumer goods (see, for example, Eccles, 1941a; T. C. Koopmans, 1942, 53; Henderson, 1941; Morgenthau, 1941; A. Smithies, 1942).[11] Friedman himself, in his statement before the *Ways and Means Committee of the House of Representatives* on May 1942, while pointing out that '(t)he pressure to spend would be great enough (...) to break through any price control and rationing plan that could be devised without using a policing force so large as to constitute a serious drain on man power for industry and the armed forces' (Friedman, 1942a, 1–2), maintained that

> Taxation is not, however, the only method being employed to combat inflation. Price control and rationing, control of consumers' credit, reduction in governmental spending, and war bond campaigns are the most important other methods that are now being employed. But just as it does not seem feasible to prevent inflation by taxation alone, so these other methods cannot be relied upon in the absence of additional taxes.
>
> (Friedman, 1942a, 2)

The debate thus concentrated upon the effects of price inflation, the *relative* efficacy of the above-mentioned various possible measures to prevent it, and in this respect, the amount of taxes needed to close the 'inflationary gap', namely the difference between the *expected* expenditures and the value of goods expected to be available. In particular, even if all were supposedly using the same Keynesian tools, the estimates of the amount of taxes needed to prevent inflation differed markedly. For instance, those advanced in October 1941 by M. Friedman, R. P. Mack and C. Shoup in a preliminary mimeographed report titled 'Amount of Taxes needed in June 1942, to Avert Inflation' were greater than those advanced by OPA economists, which forecasted no serious inflation problem until the fiscal year 1944.[12]

Now, as already mentioned, Friedman's writings on these matters are crucial in evaluating his view on price inflation and income determination during his 'Washington phase'.

Friedman clearly distinguished between a cost-pull and a demand-pull type of inflation. With respect to the former, he noted that you can move along an *increasing* aggregate supply curve or you can have a *shift* in that curve. Thus Friedman (1943b, 4–5, my emphasis) wrote[13] that '(a)lthough time rates of wages remain unaltered' there may be 'a rise in labor cost per unit, and possibly in other unit costs also'. Otherwise costs can rise 'because the agents of production arbitrarily raise the price of their services by *concerted action*'. In both cases

> taxation is no cure (. . .). Whether the result were an increased money flow supported by an *expansible credit system*, or a decreased volume of production, or both, would depend in part on the tax policy that was adopted; but the rise in prices would be present in any case, in the absence of subsidies combined with rationing.

Friedman contrasted this case of cost inflation with that of a price rise 'touched off by something other than a rise in money costs'. The latter arises when

> (c)onsumers, for whatever reason, increase their spending, or the supply of goods and services available declines, or there is a combination of both. As a result, dealers find that they can raise their selling prices without having goods pile up on their shelves.

Indeed, according to Friedman (1943b, 4–5, my emphasis), at the beginning of the war effort an increase in aggregate demand would not necessarily lead to a rise in prices since there would probably be constant unit costs of production and 'the absolute amount of consumer goods and services may increase as *idle resources* are utilized'. Nevertheless, 'soon the scarcities become more general' and there will appear a stage in which 'total output and total money income stabilize'. At this point the rise in prices will become a necessity owing to 'the decline in consumer goods as more production is devoted to war'. Such a rise will produce 'windfall profits, *at least in the first instance*', and in these respects 'it differs from the price rise caused by increased difficulty of production'. Friedman refers to the former kind of inflation arising from 'money income' expanding 'more than in proportion to income-earning activity' as 'atomistic inflation' or 'deficit-induced inflation', citing A. C. Pigou (1941, 439, 442) as his main reference.

An initial Keynesian flavour?

Of course one is struck by the missing reference to Keynes in these works of Friedman, unlike those of Koopmans, Hansen, Harris and other American economists of the time, when analysing the causes of price increases. However, the analysis sketched out above contrasts to a great extent with Friedman's subsequent view on the determinants of the price level and its changes over time. For instance, as in Hansen (1941, 171), Friedman pointed out that no general statement can be made about the effects on prices of an increasing public debt (even when financed by money). In his writings of the period 1941–1943 there is thus at least no reference to what Hansen (1944, 39) called 'a hangover from a crude quantity theory of money', that is that an increase in the income stream due to a rise in the quantity of money and/or in its circular velocity will automatically lead to a rise in the general price level with no effect on relative prices and the real income. Moreover, unlike in his writings related to the restatement of the quantity theory of money (see, for example, Friedman, 1969, 172), Friedman did not now seem to consider the trade unions as affecting the general level of prices only in very short periods, while having no *direct* role (when not influencing money supply) in explaining its ample fluctuations or its long-run movements. Even if trade union action was to lead to 'a decreased volume of production' and therefore to labour unemployment (see p. 52 in this chapter), there is in fact still no reference in Friedman's 1941–1943 works to a forthcoming fall in money wages due to the pressure of competition in the labour market.[14]

In the next section we will outline some elements that distinguished Friedman's position from a Keynesian one already in the period 1941–1943. But a Keynesian flavour in his early writings on price inflation appears also when analysing what he called 'atomistic' or 'deficit-induced' inflation. On the one hand, Friedman, as mentioned above, not only maintained that such an inflation cannot arise if there are 'idle resources', but he seemed also to maintain that labour unemployment (other than frictional) can be, in actual fact, a normal phenomenon (see again Friedman, 1943b, 4–5). On the other hand, when considering a situation of full employment, as in wartime, he pointed out that if at an initial price level there is inconsistency between expenditure and the value of goods available for sale, it could be resolved by an increase in prices that raises 'the ratio of saving to spending, or the ratio of tax revenue to spending, or both' (Friedman, 1942d, 8. See also Friedman, 1942c, 316). He thus wrote,

> a price change does not involve merely a revaluation of goods and of incomes. Because of frictions and lags, price changes lead to *a redistribution of incomes* and to a change in spending–saving relationships. The initial increase in income from a rise in prices is likely to be concentrated in the hands of *recipients of profits,* a group that tends to receive fluctuating income and that is accordingly predisposed to save a disproportionately large part of any increase in income. Moreover, the receipt and spending of incomes are not simultaneous. All along the line, *it takes times* for recipients of higher incomes to readjust their spending patterns; it also *takes time to make competitive readjustments* of resource prices.
>
> (Friedman, 1943b, 11, my emphasis.
> See also Friedman, 1942d, 7–8)[15]

Such a change in income distribution as a way of closing the 'inflationary gap' by raising the ratio of saving to spending is of course similar to what was put forward by Keynes in his works *Social Consequences of Changes in the Value of Money* (1923) and *How to Pay for the War* (1940) – where Keynes,[16] after having considered the inability of *voluntary* savings to close the gap, advocated the need to obtain a 'forced saving' by means of a 'deferred wage' allocated in public bonds, instead of by means of an inflationary process leading to an income redistribution unfavourable to the labourers (or at least to the less-organised workers). On the other hand, changes in distribution as a consequence of price inflation in conditions of full employment were usually admitted at the time on both empirical and theoretical grounds,[17] and Friedman clearly shared such ideas. Like A. G. Hart (1942), Koopmans (1942) and Smithies (1942), Friedman thus saw the required fall in consumption in real terms as being achieved by wages lagging behind prices and leading to an increase in savings, as well as by the 'illusion behaviour' of income receivers basing their spending behaviour upon the assumption that current prices and income remain stable. Moreover, Friedman also seemed to refer to 'capital losses' inflicted by inflation as taken into account in planning current expenditure.

At this stage it therefore seems that two conclusions can already be advanced. The first is that in the years 1941–1943 the only 'methods of avoiding inflation' which Friedman mentioned 'in addition to taxation' were truly 'price control and rationing' (Friedman, 1998, 112), while he did not even mention 'money' or 'monetary policy'. Second, due perhaps to the influence of *How to Pay for the War* or to that of Keynes's *Treatise on Money* and the works on 'forced savings' of F. A. Hayek, Pigou and D. Robertson[18] (all having been debated in Chicago in the 1930s), in his 'Washington phase' Friedman emphasised that price inflation will have *real* effects in the form of changes in relative prices and income distribution. Except for a case outlined below (see p. 57), at no stage do we instead find any *clear* argument concerning money neutrality,[19] nor any analysis of the determinants of the demand for money on which he will then found his restatement of the quantity theory of money (cf. Friedman, 1956).[20] In this respect the real effects arising from price inflation we detect in his 1941–1943 writings should not be confused with those then sometimes (and to some extent, contradictorily) put forward by Friedman in terms of changes in the *rate of inflation* probably affecting capital accumulation by changing the desired real quantity of money and the allocation of wealth to the various activities.

But on theoretical grounds some distance from his subsequent works again appears when his calculations of the 'inflationary gap' and the amount of taxation needed to prevent inflation are analysed.

When dealing with the inflationary gap Friedman, like Keynes ([1941], 1971–1989, XXII, 291–292), stressed that at any given time there must of necessity be 'momentary equilibrium' between aggregate demand and supply, for the income of the public must always 'be equal to the sum of taxes plus consumption plus savings'. Furthermore, like Keynes, Friedman pointed out that the equilibrium to be maintained needed appropriate changes to be made in prices and in saving habits by placing obstacles in the way of consumption and so on. Thus he stressed that, while '(i)n retrospect, there can be no gap', in prospect 'there may well be a gap' (Friedman, 1943c, 131).

Now, the *ex ante* inflationary gap could be closed with taxation rather than inflation, and according to Friedman two methods were used to estimate the required amount of taxation. The first was that adopted by J. W. Angell (1941), who estimated the expansion in spending on the basis of the historical relation between changes in the stock of money and changes in income. The second method, adopted by R. V. Gilbert and V. Perlo (1942), referred to the historical relation between investment and the national income. In both cases the estimates of the expansion of aggregate demand were then compared with the estimated possible increases in output in order to determine the probable degree of price change (Friedman, 1943c, 114–115).

In this respect three elements characterised Friedman's position. First, the estimate method he used is similar to the second one mentioned above. He actually compared the expected increase in the real output and that in war expenditure in order to obtain the expected available *civilian* output. In order to obtain the consequent amount of decrease in the civilian aggregate demand needed to prevent inflation, he then subtracted from the (calculated) available civilian output the change in the demand for it that will occur if no new anti-inflationary measures were adopted. This latter change was estimated on the basis of the expected changes in the component parts of capital formation and in the propensity to consume assuming that disposable income and prices were the same as at the initial date.

The second element worth noting is that in his estimates Friedman (like Hansen, P. Samuelson and others at the time) linked the expected changes in capital formation to the expected changes in consumer spending, while he did not mention any influence of the rate of interest on the amount of investments. Thus he wrote,

> capital formation probably has some tendency to decline if an increase in consumer spending slackens appreciably. Though this result is not to be counted on invariably, it seemed to deserve some consideration in the present analysis.
>
> (Friedman, 1943b, 42)[21]

Finally, and more importantly, Friedman refuted Angell's method of estimating the expansion in spending on the basis of the relation between changes in the stock of money and changes in income when given the marginal circular velocity of money (that is, the ratio between a change in national income from one year to the next and the associated change in the stock of money). On the one hand, Friedman rejected taking the government deficit as equivalent to an increase in the stock of money, since it would mean both assuming that the stock of money does not change for any other reason, and neglecting that '(a) change in the deficit as a result of taxes levied solely on high incomes' might have a very different effect on spending 'from an equal change in the deficit as a result of taxes levied on very low incomes' (Friedman, 1943c, 117–118). On the other hand, Friedman noted that Angell's estimates were based on historical data which showed the actual changes in the stock of money, making no explicit allowance for the reactivation of formerly idle money as a way of financing the government deficit. This procedure 'implicitly assumes a constant relation between the changes in the total stock of money and the amount of reactivation of formerly idle money' which, according to Friedman (1943c, 117–118), was not supported by the data. In particular, the data did not support the conclusion that 'the marginal circular velocity of money may be considered as fairly stable'.

Some elements of a traditional view on income and price determination

Here Friedman was apparently rejecting a year-to-year explanation of income changes on the basis of a 'rude' quantity theory of money – an explanation which, though only in part, was supported by I. Fisher at the time,[22] but not, for instance, by Simons, who had outlined that the circular velocity of money can change even abruptly during the cycle (Simons, 1936, 164–165). However, Friedman (1943c, 119, my emphasis) also pointed out that the data used by Angell

> may be adequate for studying the *average* circular velocity of money or the relation between *long-period* changes in national income and the stock of money.

Hence on the whole he already seems to share elements of the 'Chicago tradition' that afterwards were to characterise his monetary analysis, where money will usually appear to be neutral in the long run, even if not in the short run (see, for example, Friedman, 1982, 60; 1987, 250).[23] Although in fact there are no other traces in his 'Washington period' writings of the idea that the equilibrium of the money market can be reached by making changes in the price level given the *real* income and a *stable* desired quantity of money in *real* terms, the context of the above quotation reveals to us a causal chain which in the long run goes from changes in the nominal supply of money to changes in money income thanks to a stable circular velocity of money.[24]

We thus begin to find a first element of a traditional determination of income and prices which might help us to explain Friedman's rapid 'conversion' against a Keynesian approach just after the war. This is not, however, an isolated element, and shows us that Friedman was still largely shaping his thinking in the period 1941–1943. He thus maintained that there exists a 'monetary veil that obscures and at times conceals the physical realities of the economic system' (Friedman, 1943a, 50, my emphasis), which clearly contrasted with Keynes's emphasis on the *intrinsic* monetary nature of the economic relations in the market economies that led him to construct a 'monetary theory of production' (cf. Keynes, [1933], 1971–1989, XXIX, 81–82). Moreover, when analysing the effects of a cost-push inflation, as has already been seen (see p. 52) Friedman stated that it will lead to '*a decreased volume of production*' unless 'an increased money flow supported by an expansible credit system' occurs. Quite mechanically, cost-push inflation could therefore easily be transformed into being temporary in character unless it is followed by an expansion in the quantity of money.[25] Finally, when discussing the estimates by OPA economists of the inflationary gap, Friedman rightly observed that in a changing world their hypothesis 'that ex ante saving next year is equal to ex post saving this year' has 'little basis in either theory or fact'. But after himself having simplified the analysis by assuming an unchanged disposable income in calculating the inflationary gap, he further stated against Salant (1942) that the breakdown of the inflationary gap 'among broad *classes* of output' is impossible[26] since '(t)he composition of the gap is determinate only at specified relative prices for different classes of goods' and 'it can be anything at all if relative prices are permitted to vary' (Friedman, 1942c, 319, my emphasis).

At least on theoretical grounds, if not in practice, Friedman thus stressed the existence of a strict relation between relative prices and outputs. We do not know whether in this respect he was influenced by his previous works on the demand curves of commodities (see, for instance, Friedman, 1935), or by F. Knight and H. Schultz, who had taught Friedman in the 1930s and kept the general equilibrium analysis alive in Chicago. Certainly, Keynes never emphasised the effects of changes in relative prices on the composition of output. While admitting in Chapter 20 of *The General Theory* that changes in the aggregate demand might lead to changes in relative prices and the composition of production, as a first necessary step in the analysis he considered that composition as given in determining the real income.[27] In view of the uncertain effects of the changes in relative prices and the rate of interest on consumption and the propensity to save, Keynes, on the other hand, made extensive reference to social and institutional factors (as well as to the different income levels earned by the workers and the capitalist class) in determining the composition of output and the propensities to consume of the different groups of society (see, for instance, Keynes [1936], 1971–1989, VII, Chapter 8). And he saw those factors as relatively stable and given when determining the amount of employment using the income multiplier and the level of the aggregate demand.[28]

To sum up, Friedman's analysis of the inflationary gap undoubtedly contained many Keynesian elements but also traces of a traditional approach which can help to explain his 'conversion' just after the war. Indeed, also his observation (put forward when analysing 'how the fraction of resources used to produce goods not available for current consumption adjusts to the fraction of income that individuals wish to save') according to which '(n)o judgement is intended on the crucial issue separating the Keynesians and anti-Keynesians as to whether there is an automatic tendency for such an adjustment to be made at a level of full employment' (Friedman, 1943a, n. 2) appears to move in that traditional direction if only one considers the 'prevailing Keynesian temper of the time'.

The proposal of the spending tax

Although in a different domain, a break with a Keynesian approach emerges even when we examine Friedman's proposal of a spending tax as a measure of avoiding inflation.

It is a fact that in *How to Pay for the War* Keynes proposed a plan of compulsory savings to avoid inflation, as it was not possible to cover the whole cost of the war by taxation. According to him, '(b)y such a plan (...) the wage and salary earner can consume as much as before and in addition have money over in the bank for his future benefit and security, which would belong otherwise to the capitalist class' (Keynes [1940], 1971–1989a, IX, 375).[29] The plan was debated in the United States, and an appeal for its adoption appeared in 1941[30] arguing that combining compulsory lending with taxation was the method of war finance 'best suited to satisfy the requirements of equity' (cf. Fellner, 1942, 11). The plan was instead opposed by those who feared that compulsion would kill the 'voluntary spirit', and to some extent by the trade unions, which were suspicious of the request to stabilise wages.

During the summer of 1942, however, the US Treasury developed a different proposal for a spending tax as a supplement to the income tax, and presented it to the Senate Finance Committee in September 1942. While Keynes had considered such a tax as theoretically sound but impossible in practice, perhaps heeding Pigou's warning of the likelihood of the upper classes and savers thus escaping taxation to a great extent (cf. Kaldor, 1955, 12), the direct reference of the Treasury's proposal was Fisher's (1942) works on a progressive spending tax. Indeed, the proposal of the Treasury combined Keynes's plan and the spending tax, using spending as the basis for extracting funds from the public, and treating some of the funds raised as compulsory savings instead of taxes. The proposal was thus received as a plan for enforced savings[31] and opposed by the Finance Committee and the financial community (see *NYT*, September 1, 4, 5, 6, 7, 8, 1942).[32] Also due to the fact that it was presented without Roosevelt's support and so late in the tax hearings that the plan would either be quickly discarded or prolong the tax bill deliberations further, five days after its presentation the Finance Committee rejected the plan by 12 votes to none (some members abstaining), and it was never heard of again.

Friedman supported and in part elaborated the Treasury's proposal (though refusing to treat part of the taxes raised as compulsory savings). As in the case of Keynes's plan the background to Friedman's proposal was the disruptive effects of inflation, which he deemed to be in conflict with the utilisation of the product for war purposes, a fair income distribution and post-war stability. But Friedman thought that neither rationing nor compulsory savings could be effective in this regard. In the former case it would not be possible, according to Friedman, to get individuals to consume scarce goods in specified amounts and proportions.[33] In the latter case the problem would be that compulsory lending may be satisfied with previous savings without decreasing the consumption of those who live on capital (Friedman, 1943a, 60). Furthermore, Friedman pointed out that it would be 'impossible in principle' to enforce compulsory savings 'since income and expenditures are never definitely known until after the end of a period' (Friedman, 1943a, 52).

As in Fisher's analysis of taxable capacity, in supporting his alternative proposal of a spending tax, Friedman first of all divided the individual income into two shares, a subsistence share and a surplus share. Thus he wrote (Friedman, 1943a, 58),

> As a resource, much of what (an individual) consumes is an intermediate product, a cost of production, like the food to livestock. As a consumer, what he consumes is a final product, designated to satisfy the wants of the prime mover of the production process. In ordinary times, the consumer aspect of the individual is dominant. He is an end, not a means (....). In wartime, values change (...). The individual becomes a means, not an end.

It is thus in order to avoid workers receiving 'less than they need for health and efficiency' (Friedman, 1943a, 58) that tax has to be progressive. However, the marginal tax rate could in this case be so great as in turn to impair efficiency, so that

in order to achieve a more efficient distribution of the available consumer goods and at the same time maintain the incentive value of
income as much as possible, fiscal methods involving the withdrawal
of income must be supplemented by savings-inducement methods,
that is, by methods that impinge directly on spending, rather than
on income.

(Friedman, 1943a, 61)

This kind of taxation must reduce 'types of spending that are least necessary for the maintenance of output in general and war output in
particular'. In the case of spending on commodities that use resources
specially adapted to war production, special excises could to some extent
be the appropriate remedy. For the rest, 'the maintenance of output calls
for restraining all spending in excess of a basic minimum' (Friedman,
1943a, 61) and the result can be achieved by 'a progressive spending tax
that exempts a basic minimum and imposes a higher rate of tax, the
larger the excess of spending over the basic minimum'.

Indeed in Friedman's arguments in favour of the spending tax[34] the
need to minimise any intervention imposing a limit on individual
choices and the market mechanisms was central. In both wartime and
in peace taxation can in fact, according to Friedman, modify the control over current output granted by income without, however, seriously
impairing the 'function of income in organizing the use of resources'.
Moreover, in wartime the amount of income above the basic minimum
can still be permitted 'to serve as a claim to future output', while 'even
the separation of income from control over current output need not be
complete' (Friedman, 1943a, 56).

Friedman thus viewed the spending tax as the best measure for stimulating savings and preserving them on a voluntary basis, as well as
for '*minimizing* the role of government intervention into the details of
the economic system' in the transition from war to peace (Friedman,
1943a, 62, my emphasis).[35] Therefore, unlike Keynes's compulsory saving plan, Friedman did not try to avoid the claim on resources after the
war being concentrated in the hands of the capitalist class alone. On
the contrary, while curbing purchasing power, Friedman wanted to preserve savings as an individual effort to ameliorate one's future condition
when income exceeds a certain minimum level. The emphasis is thus
placed on an individual choice between present and future consumption which seems to clash with Keynes's view of different social classes
that are structurally characterised by different propensities to consume
and thereby affected by the war in such a way that the wage-earning

class 'in spite of the extra-work done' will run the risk, in the absence of any intervention, of owning 'nothing, having lost the right to consume now and having gained no rights to consume hereafter' (Keynes [1941], 1971–1989, XXII, 145).

Some final remarks

Summing up, while there is an apparent Keynesian flavour in Fried-man's early writings, in the years 1941–1943 he appears to have to some extent already differentiated himself, under the influence of the Chicago tradition, from the 'Keynesian prevailing temper of the times'. This differentiation emerges more clearly after the war, particularly when he returns to Chicago in 1946. But already in 1944, in reviewing Alt-man's book, Friedman spoke in quite worried tones of a 'Keynesian saving-investment theory' which 'has had such vogue in recent years' (Friedman, 1944, 101). More important, immediately in 1946 in his remark that 'OPA alone cannot prevent inflation' Friedman observed that '(a) major effect of OPA price control has been to disguise rather than prevent increases in price', and

> We can and must take measures now to control the basic causes of inflation by limiting the supply of cash and bank deposits.
> (Friedman, 1946, A2209)[36]

Friedman consequently advocated minimising public expenditure and raising taxation, as well as increasing the bank's reserve requirements and the rate of interest.[37]

While Friedman's monetarist 'counter-revolution' took on a definitive shape some years later (see Friedman, 1956), just after the war he thus took up and developed those aspects which were present in Mints and Simons[38] against any obstacles to the market mechanisms and any active policies. Friedman's scanty previous Keynesian background and the now changed economic conditions of course favoured such a conversion. He thus outlined early that

> (e)conomists now tend to concentrate on cyclical movements, to act and talk as if any improvement, however slight, in control of the cycle justified any sacrifice, however large, in the long-run efficiency, or prospect of growth, of the economic system.

and he wanted instead to assure 'both sets of objectives simultaneously' (Friedman, 1948, 133) by reforming the monetary and banking system in order to eliminate both the private creation or destruction of money and the discretionary controls over the quantity of money by the central bank authority. Moreover, he advocated automatic stabilising mechanisms during the cycle by means of a progressive tax system and a fiscal policy determining the volume of government expenditures entirely on the basis of the community's desire, need and willingness to pay for public services.

At the beginning the 'conversion' vis-à-vis a Keynesian approach mainly took the form of an insistence on the rigidities in prices as a cause of unemployment (see also Patinkin, 1948) and on the time lag in the response by active policies against cyclical movements as a reason to abandon those policies (see, for example, Friedman, 1947, 413–414). As immediately stressed by P. Neff (1949), it assumed the idea of an automatic and rapid tendency of the market economies towards conditions of full employment, since otherwise even in a flexible price world at least a *discretionary* counter-cyclical policy would appear necessary. It was, on the other hand, the firm belief in the absence of any automatic tendency towards full employment that led Keynes, against any laissez-faire ideas like those advanced by the 'Chicago school', to advocate using active policies to maintain a state of quasi-expansion and adopting measures to increase the propensity to consume and to socialise a share of investment.

Notes

1. I wish to thank R. Leeson, C. Marcuzzo and M. Pivetti for their comments. The usual disclaimer applies.
2. On his life, see M. Friedman and R. Friedman (1998) [hereafter only Friedman, 1998].
3. As Friedman (1998, 113) told us, in those years he wrote numerous memoranda, reports and letters that have been 'buried somewhere in the files of the Treasury Department'. My research at the US National Archives did not succeed in discovering them, though having given me access to materials that I have used in this work. I have also utilised materials conserved in the Friedman Archives in the Hoover Institution, Stanford University, as well as publications of the US Congress and articles published at the time in *The Wall Street Journal*, *The New York Times* and *The Washington Post* (hereafter respectively *WSJ*, *NYT* and *WP*). I thank Professor Milton Friedman for permission to use the materials conserved in his Archive in Stanford.
4. When Keynes went to the United States in May 1941 he met a lot of these economists. He also spoke with D. W. Bell, H. Morgenthau, L. Currie and New Dealers as Harry White. H. Simons, reviewing Hansen's book on fiscal policy, summarised the climate of the time as follows: 'His book (...) may well become the economic bible for that substantial company of intellectuals,

following Keynes and recklessly collectivist, whose influence grows no less rapidly in academic circles than in Washington' (Simons, 1942, 185).

5. On the movements of prices, real wages and the real income in the United States in those years see W. L. Crum, J. F. Fennelly and L. H. Seltzer (1942), J. S. Early and M. Stein (1942), W. Fellner (1942), A. Rees (1959). The unemployment rate decreased from 17.2 per cent in 1939 to 1.2 in 1944.

6. Indeed, it is his unprejudiced observation of facts and the ability to pick up and coordinate elements scattered in the interwar economic literature on the adjustment of savings to investments and the peculiarity of a monetary economy which represented one of Keynes' contributions to the economic theory, and built up an analytical framework to which those who stressed the need of fiscal and monetary active policies to assure full employment could refer.

7. See, for instance, Keynes ([1936], 1971–1989, VII, Chapters 14, 18 and 21; 1937, 251). On the 'linear' causal chain running from the money market to the commodity markets which characterises Keynes's analysis see p. 58, note 28, in this chapter and L. Pasinetti (1974). The presence in *The General Theory* of traditional elements such as the notion of the marginal efficiency of capital, as well as some limits of Keynes's monetary theory, facilitated the reabsorption of his analysis within the neoclassical theory. Contrary to what is argued in Chapter XIX of *The General Theory*, it thus became possible to maintain that on average, a fall in money wages would be capable of bringing the rate of interest to its 'natural' value, namely that guaranteeing full employment of resources (see P. Garegnani, 1978–1979).

8. Thus Friedman (1969, 97; 1987, 256) maintains that the main proposition (or 'error') of Keynes is the idea that stable unemployment equilibria do not arise from wage rigidity, which is instead considered a 'rational answer' to those equilibria (see also Laidler, 1999, 265). However, in the meantime Friedman interpreted Keynes's work as a half-revolution which took place within the framework of the quantity theory of money by only emphasising that during the cyclical phase of depression the liquidity preference might become infinite and/or investments might be inelastic to the rate of interest. According to Friedman (1987, 257), Keynes viewed this situation as a limiting case, while his disciples viewed it as a normal case.

9. On the other hand, cancelling 'the first bracket normal and first bracket surtax' of 1941 liabilities 'would relieve entirely from any problem of excess payments approximately over 18 million out of fewer than 20 million taxpayers in 1942', thus resolving the problems for the average man (Friedman, 1942b, 62).

10. They were organised by the Office of Price Administration (OPA), which was created in the spring of 1941 and headed by Henderson. The Emergency Price Control Act signed on January 30, 1942, gave the OPA the authority to fix maximum prices, and OPA action had some success in controlling prices, which rose less than in other countries (see H. Rockoff, 1985). However, OPA's activity was characterised by great contrasts, as in the cases of the Chrysler Corporation and Aircraft builders' opposition to the price ceilings (see, for example, *WSJ*, June 27, 1941, and July 8, 1942). Moreover, as in the case of agricultural produce, there were many exceptions to price freezing which reduced the chances of its success, e.g. by fomenting requests for wage increases (see Fellner, 1942, 123).

11. See also *WSJ* (July 15 and 30, 1941) which reported the positions of H. A. Wallace and F. D. Roosevelt.
12. The discrepancies in those estimates persisted afterwards but were opposite in sign. According to Friedman (1998, 111), this happened because while in the process of lobbying Congress for the price control act OPA had argued that price controls were the only way to stop inflation, after February 1942 its interest changed and '(t)he Treasury (...) became an ally, not a competitor' in controlling prices. However, even before 1942 Henderson and other OPA officials stressed the need for taxation to prevent inflation, while Friedman (1943c, 136) himself stressed that 'the question of exactly what constitutes an inflationary gap is extremely difficult to answer'. It is also worth noting that Keynes believed that Salant and other OPA economists had overestimated supply and underestimated demand. Thus he wrote to J. M. Clark on July 26, 1941: 'I have tried to persuade Gilbert and Humphrey and Salant that they should be more cautious' (Keynes, 1971–1989, XXIII, 192).
13. Note that in the Foreword of the book written by Friedman with Shoup and Mack it is specified that '(t)he outlines of the approach that is taken in Part I were developed first by Milton Friedman'.
14. In this respect Friedman did not seem to follow Pigou (1941, 440), according to whom inflation can only come about as a concomitant of an increase in the stock of money or an increase in the proportion of money income to the stock of money. Thus Pigou stated that, in wartime, it is only because money is continuously created that wage inflation does not kill itself by leading to labour unemployment but it produces a 'vicious price spiral'.
15. Note that according to Friedman, if there is no change in the ratio of saving to spending, inflation would close the gap only temporarily. For instance, if there is no business saving, no taxes, no stocks of consumer goods, and the government needs half a production value of 100$, while the consumers always want to spend 70 per cent of their received income, then the 'primary consumer expenditure gap' will be 20$ in the first period, 24$ in the second period and so on, while money income will rise from 100$ to 120$, to 144$ and so on. Hence the price response to the 'inflationary gap' will change according to the circumstances, depending on whether, when profits rise, labour is quick to obtain higher wages, or consumers are quick to interpret rising prices as a forerunner of further price rises, and so on (cf. Friedman, 1942d, 9).
16. See also Keynes ([1941], 1971–1989, XXII). With respect to the long run, as it is known, the idea that an increase in the rate of accumulation will lead to an increase in the amounts of savings per unit of capital through a fall in the real wage is an essential aspect of the post-Keynesian theory of distribution. However, as argued by Garegnani (1992), the needed increase in savings per unit of capital can be obtained in the long run by a change in the degree of capital utilisation and (as a consequence of it) by an increase in the amount of productive capacity, without any need for a change in distribution. This does not exclude that in special cases, such as the one considered here, there may ultimately be no room for further increases in civilian production, thus arriving at a redistribution of income to profits.
17. See, for instance, H. W. Spiegel (1942, 112 and 123) and F. Machlup (1943).
18. See Robertson (1926) and Pigou (1929, 146 and 153).

19. Indeed it is not clear if in his 1941–1943 writings Friedman considered those real effects of price inflation as being only temporary in character. Surely he viewed the redistribution of incomes as necessary for stabilising the level (or the rate of change) of prices, if resources are fully utilised.

20. Note that it might nevertheless be wrong to ascribe to Friedman an initial 'Keynesian flavour' by only emphasising his 1941–1943 analysis of the real effects of price inflation, since it was common to many (also non-Keynesian) economists of the time. However, it is a sign that, in that period, he had not yet elaborated his own definitive monetary explanation of price inflation.

21. The idea of Simons (1938, 23) that 'saving may be a real affliction during a depression' since it may 'aggravate hoarding and thereby aggravate mal-adjustments between the flexible and sticky prices' may have influenced Friedman in this regard. The effect of consumption on investment was, on the other hand, usually recognised at the time and at the Division of Tax Research. Thus Blough (1944, 6) wrote, 'since a businessman is a practical and prudent person he must have the assurance of a consumer market to induce him to invest and expand; accordingly the road to high employ-ment is a high level of consumer purchasing power, for consumption gives employment directly and also creates investment, thus giving employment indirectly (. . .)'.

22. Thus in his statement on the Revenue Revision of 1941 Fisher (1941, 1976, our emphasis) noted that 'there are those who doubt the possibility of con-trolling inflation by controlling the volumes of money because, they say, you would have to control the velocity of money too'. But 'these people are badly misled. Velocity in its important sense is one of the most nearly invariable magnitudes known in statistics (. . .). The really significant velocity is not that "transaction velocity" including, as it does, speculative transactions where the same property, stocks or real estate, is bought and sold over and over again, but "income velocity" which is centered on the spending of income and ultimate consumption, after the steady normal progress of commodities from farm and mine through successive manufacturing and marketing pro-cesses (. . .). 'It must be noted, however, that in order to explain the Great Depression, Fisher (1933) himself had maintained that over-indebtedness arising during the ascending phase of the cycle can lead to liquidation trig-gering distress selling, a fall in prices, a slowing down of velocity of circulation and so on. See also Laidler (1991, 300–301) on Fisher's analysis for the trade cycle.

23. On the origins of Friedman's monetary analysis see D. Patinkin (1969), S. Weintraub (1971) and G. S. Tavlas (1998). He seems to have been influ-enced by both the Chicago and the Cambridge tradition. In the latter a greater emphasis was placed on the desire and utility of keeping money (see Levrero, 1999. For an assessment see Leeson, 2003).

24. It is worth noting that in his subsequent works Friedman, while never telling us what money is (cf. J. Tobin, 1965, 465), admitted that changes in its quan-tity can be determined by changes in the money income during the cycle (cf. Friedman, 1969, 269). However, he denied it could happen in the long run, as instead was argued, for instance, by N. Kaldor (1982) on the basis of the results of the Radcliffe Report.

25. Indeed Friedman does not specify whether he considers as a normal state of affairs the existence of room for changes in the amounts of bank deposits in response to changes in the level of activity – something which would point us towards an endogenous determination of the quantity of money. Nor is it clear why, even if the quantity of money remained the same, the rise in prices would lead to a fall in production, since, as we have seen, Friedman at the time seemed to link the amount of investments to changes in real income, and he did not emphasise any Pigou effect on consumption.

26. Probably Friedman's aim was to deny the possibility to avert inflation only by rationing or some direct price controls or indirect taxes.

27. When considering unit constant costs in the case of unused productive capacity, and thus a constant real wage when employment varies, this assumption is of course strengthened.

28. In other words, Keynes adopted a two-stage argument in approaching economic phenomena. Taking as given the state of the long-term expectations, the techniques, the available productive capacity, the social structure and the main forces determining distribution other than those acting through the changes in the level of output, Keynes in fact first determined 'in isolation' the level of employment by assuming as given the marginal propensity to consume, the marginal efficiency of capital and the rate of interest. He then went on to consider the possible reciprocal influences of the envisaged variations in those independent variables, as well as the effects of a change in income level on those variables, together with the influences of all the other changes in the social and economic situation possibly occurring in the meantime. According to Keynes, such a procedure is the only one possible in any serious investigation of the economic phenomena and to be preferred to seeking refuge in useless and empty mathematical expressions (see, for example, Keynes [1936], 1971–1989, VII, 297–298. See also J. Schumpeter, 1954, 473).

29. In particular, '(t)he machinery of war finance will have operated by the rise in price diverting real purchasing power away from the consumer to the profit-earning class, who in turn will transfer a large part of these profits to the Treasury (. . .). It means (. . .) that at the end of the war it is the profit-earning class which owns, in the shape of holdings in the national war debt, a claim on future production; while the wage-earning class, in spite of the extra-work done, owns nothing, having lost the right to consume now and having gained no rights to consume hereafter' (Keynes [1940], 1971–1989b, XXII, 145).

30. See the Memorandum on 'Taxation for Defense', presented by S. E. Harris (1941) to the Ways and Means Committee.

31. See, for instance, *WSJ*, September 2, 1942; and *WP*, September 6, 1942.

32. Against the spending tax see also P. Haensel (1943, 219). While undoubtedly the tax was more complicated than the income tax, the difficulties associated with the proposal were not insuperable (cf. K. E. Poole, 1943 and C. L. Harriss, 1943), although the issues of determining the minimum subsistence to be exempted and of how to treat housing spending still remained unsolved.

33. Following W. A. Wallis (1942) and opposing Kalecki's Plan, Friedman also outlined that 'designating the precise number of dollars that each individual may spend involves either creating a new currency and providing a new machinery for distributing it or penalizing by fines, jail, sentences, or other penalties people who spend too much' (Friedman, 1943a, 58).

34. I take the occasion to correct an editorial error in Levrero (1999, 6), where 'taxing goods at consumption' appeared instead of 'taxing consumption expenditures', which seemed to identify the spending tax with a sales tax. Other minor editorial errors appeared in notes 20, 34, 43, 47, 50 and 56, although the true meaning is clear from the context of the notes.

35. Friedman admitted that the change in the composition of production after the war might generate unemployment, and maintained that, with no need for public intervention, the savings accumulated during the war 'can then provide the means for the repayment by bringing about the employment of resources that would otherwise be idle' (Friedman, 1943a, 57). Note also that according to Friedman (1943a, 62), in peace time a spending tax 'does not seem satisfactory'. He thus disagreed with Fisher in this regard, who saw any tax on savings as discouraging them and as merely a pre-tax on their yield. On the debate on the spending tax and taxable capacity see Kaldor (1955). Of course the spending tax stimulates savings and can be dangerous if the economy ever suffers over-saving in relation to investment opportunities.

36. The remark is included in an Extension of W. H. Judd at the House of Representatives, April 16, 1946.

37. The same policy proposals were to be stressed by L. W. Mints (1946) and G. Haberler (1946), who focused on the importance of the monetary policy versus the fiscal policy and on the crucial role of wage rigidity in explaining unemployment on the grounds of the Pigou effect and Modigliani's 1944 article. In this regard see, for instance, A Symposium on Fiscal and Monetary Policy by Mints, Hansen, H. S. Ellis, Lerner and M. Kalecki in the *Review of Economic Statistics*, May 1946. See also in the same review Haberler's (1946) assessment of Keynes's *The General Theory*. Hansen (1946, 324) argued against such views by observing that '(j)ust as cyclical price flexibility may intensify the cyclical problem because of the effect of such price changes upon business expectations, so sharp wage reductions are likely to be deflationary'. And indeed, according to Keynes, a fall in money wages could have a negative effect on employment by lowering the marginal propensity to consume and the marginal efficiency of capital, as well as due to the increasing difficulties of repaying debts in the presence of falling prices.

38. See, for instance, Simons (1934; 1936).

References

Angell J. W. (1941), 'Taxation, Inflation and the Defense Program', *The Review of Economic Statistics*, 23, 2, 78–82.

Blough R. (1944), 'Address before the National Tax Association at the Jefferson Hotel', September, in *National Archives Agency*, 'Central File of the Office of the Secretary of the Treasury 1933–1955', Entry 193, Box 198, Washington.

Crum W. L., Fennelly J. F. & Seltzer L. H. (1942), *Fiscal Planning for Total War*, NBER, New York.

Early J. S. & Stein M. (1942), *British Wartime Price Administration and Price Movements*, Office of Price Administration, February, US Government Printing Office, Washington.

Eccles M. S. (1941a), 'Statement before the Committee on Ways and Means House of Representatives', in Revenue Revision of 1941, *Hearings before the Committee on Ways and Means House of Representatives*, Seventy-Seventh Congress, First Session, April–May, US Government Printing Office, Washington.

Eccles M. S. (1941b), 'Statement before the Committee on Banking and Currency House of Representatives', in Price Control Bill, *Hearings before the Committee on Banking and Currency House of Representatives*, Seventy-Seventh Congress, First Session on H.R. 5479 (Superseded by H.R. 5990), 'A Bill to further the national defense and security by checking speculative and excessive price rises, price dislocations and inflationary tendencies, and for other purposes', Revised, Part 2, September–October, US Government Printing Office, Washington.

Fellner W. (1942), *A Treatise on War Inflation. Present Policies and Future Tendencies in the United States*, University of California Press, Berkeley & Los Angeles.

Fisher I. (1933), 'The Debt-Deflation Theory of Great Depression', *Econometrica*, 1, 4, 337–357.

Fisher I. (1942), *Constructive Income Taxation, A proposal for reform*, with Herbert W. Fisher, Harper and Brothers Publishers, New York & London.

Friedman M. (1935), 'Professor Pigou's Method for Measuring Elasticities of Demand from Budgetary Data', *Quarterly Journal of Economics*, 50, 1, 151–163.

Friedman M. (1942a), *Statement by Milton Friedman before the Ways and Means Committee of the House of Representatives*, May 7, Hoover Institution Archives, Stanford, California, Friedman's Archive, Box 37, Folder 17.

Friedman M. (1942b), 'Statement before the Subcommittee of the Committee on Finance United States Senate', in Withholding Tax. *Hearings before Subcommittee of the Committee on Finance United States Senate*, Seventy-Seventh Congress, Second Session on Data Relative to Withholding provisions of the 1942 Revenue Act, Wednesday, August 19, US Government Printing Office, Washington.

Friedman M. (1942c), 'The Inflationary Gap: II. Discussion of the Inflationary Gap', *The American Economic Review*, 32, 2, 314–320.

Friedman M. (1942d), *The Inflationary Gap*, Treasury Department, Division of Tax Research, July 23, Hoover Insititution Archives, Stanford, California, Friedman's Archive, Box 37, Folder 19.

Friedman M. (1943a), 'The Spending Tax as a Wartime Fiscal Measure', *American Economic Review*, 33, 1, 50–62, reprinted in M. Friedman, *Essays in Positive Economics*, 1953, Chicago University Press, Chicago.

Friedman M. (1943b), 'A Technique for Estimating the Amount of Taxation Necessary to Avert Inflation', with C. Shoup & R. P. Mack, in C. Shoup, M. Friedman & R. P. Mack, *Taxing to Prevent Inflation. Techniques for Estimating Revenue Requirements*, Columbia University Press, New York.

Friedman M. (1943c), 'Methods of Predicting the Onset of Inflation', in C. Shoup, M. Friedman & R. P. Mack, *Taxing to Prevent Inflation. Techniques for Estimating Revenue Requirements*, Columbia University Press, New York.

Friedman M. (1944), 'Review of "Saving, Investment and National Income" by Oscar L. Altman', *Review of Economic Statistics*, 26, 2, 101–102.

Friedman M. (1946), 'Opa alone cannot prevent inflation', in United States of America, *Congressional Records. Proceedings and Debates of the 79th Congress*, Second Session, Appendix, volume 92-Part 9, January 14 to March 8, US Government Printing Office, Washington.

Friedman M. (1947), 'Lerner on the Economics of Control', *The Journal of Political Economy*, 55, 5, 405–416.

Friedman M. (1948), 'A Monetary and Fiscal Framework for Economic Stability', *American Economic Review*, 38, 3, 245–264, reprinted in *Essays in Positive Economics*, 1953, University of Chicago Press, Chicago.

Friedman M. (1956), 'The Quantity Theory of Money: A Restatement', in M. Friedman (ed.), *Studies in the Quantity Theory of Money*, University of Chicago Press, Chicago.

Friedman M. (1969), 'The Optimum Quantity of Money', in M. Friedman (ed.), *The Optimum Quantity of Money and Other Essays*, Macmillan, London.

Friedman M. (1982), *Monetary Trends in the United States and the United Kingdom: Their Relations to Income, Prices and Interest Rates, 1867–1975*, with A. J. Schwartz, Nber Research Monograph, University of Chicago Press, Chicago.

Friedman M. (1987), 'Quantity Theory of Money', in J. Eatwell, M. Milgate & P. Newman (ed.), *The New Palgrave: A Dictionary of Economics*, Stockton Press-Macmillan, New York–London.

Friedman M. & Friedman R. D. (1998), *Two Lucky People. Memoirs*, University of Chicago Press, Chicago.

Garegnani P. (1978–1979), 'Notes on Consumption, Investment and Effective Demand: I–II', *Cambridge Journal of Economics*, 2, 4, 1978 and 3, 1, 1979.

Garegnani P. (1992), 'Some Notes for an Analysis of Accumulation', in J. Halevi, D. Laibman & J. Nell (Eds), *Beyond the Steady State*, Macmillan, London.

Gilbert R. V. & Perlo V. (1942), 'The Investment-Factor Method of Forecasting Business Activity', *Econometrica*, 10, 3/4, 311–316.

Haberler G. (1946), 'The Place of the General Theory of Employment, Interest and Money in the History of Economic Thought', *The Review of Economic Statistics*, 28, 4, 187–195.

Haensel P. (1943), 'Statement before the Committee on Ways and Means House of Representatives', in Individual Income Tax, *Hearings before the Committee on Ways and Means House of Representatives*, Seventy-Eight Congress, First Session on A proposal to place income tax on a pay-as-you-go basis, February, US Government Printing Office, Washington.

Hansen A. H. (1941), *Fiscal Policy and Business Cycles*, W. W. Norton & Company Inc, New York.

Hansen A. H. (1944), 'Inflationary potentialities of the public debt', in AA.VV, *Curbing Inflation through Taxation,* Symposium conducted by the Tax Institute, February 7–8, Books For Libraries Press, Freeport, New York.

Hansen A. H. (1946), 'Notes on Mints' Paper on Monetary Policy', *The Review of Economic Statistics*, 28, 2, 69–74.

Harris S. E. (1941), 'Statement before the Committee on Ways and Means House of Representatives', in Revenue Revision of 1941, *Hearings before the Committee on Ways and Means House of Representatives*, Seventy-Seventh Congress, First Session, April–May, US Government Printing Office, Washington.

Harriss C. L. (1943), 'Revenue Implications of a Progressive-Rate Tax on Expenditures, A Study of Selected Aspects of Irving Fisher's Proposal to Eliminate Savings From the Income Tax Base', *The Review of Economic Statistics*, 25, 3, 175–191.

Hart A. G. (1942), 'What it Takes to Block Inflation', *The Review of Economic Statistics*, 24, 3, 101–111.

Henderson P. H. (1941), 'Statement before the Committee on Banking and Currency House of Representatives', in Price Control Bill, *Hearings before the Committee on Banking and Currency House of Representatives*, op. cit., US Government Printing Office, Washington.

Hicks J. R. (1937), 'Mr. Keynes and the "Classics": A Suggested Interpretation', *Econometrica*, 5, 2, 147–159.

Kaldor N. (1955), *An Expenditure Tax*, Unwin University Books, London.

Kaldor N. (1982), *The Scourge of Monetarism*, Oxford University Press, New York.

Keynes J. M. (1937), 'Alternative Theories of Interest', *Economic Journal*, 47, 186, 241–252.

Keynes J. M. ([1933], 1971–1989), 'The Distinction between a Co-operative Economy and an Entrepreneur Economy', in *Collected Writings*, volume XXIX, 'The General Theory and After. A Supplement', Macmillan St. Martin Press for the Royal Economic Society.

Keynes J. M. ([1936], 1971–1989), ' The General Theory of Employment, Interest and Money', in *Collected Writings*, volume VII, Macmillan St. Martin's Press for the Royal Economic Society.

Keynes J. M. ([1940], 1971–1989a), 'How to Pay for the War', in *Collected Writings*, volume IX, 'Essays in Persuasion', Macmillan St. Martin Press for the Royal Economic Society.

Keynes J. M. ([1940], 1971–1989b), 'The United States and the Keynes Plan', in *Collected Writings*, volume XXII, 'Activities 1939–1945, Internal War Finance', Macmillan St. Martin Press for the Royal Economic Society.

Keynes J. M. ([1941], 1971–1989), 'The Theory of the Gap', in *Collected Writings*, volume XXII, 'Activities 1939–1945, Internal War Finance', Macmillan St. Martin Press for the Royal Economic Society.

Keynes J. M. (1971–1989), *Collected Writings*, volume XXIII, 'Activities 1940–1943, External War Finance', Macmillan, Cambridge University Press for the Royal Economic Society.

Klein L. R. (1949), *The Keynesian Revolution*, Macmillan, New York.

Koopmans T. C. (1942), 'The Dynamics of Inflation', *The Review of Economic Statistics*, 24, 2, 53–65.

Laidler D. (1991), 'The Quantity Theory is Always and Everywhere Controversial – Why?', *The Economic Record*, December, 67, 4, pp. 289–306.

Laidler D. (1999), *Fabricating the Keynesian Revolution. Studies of the Inter-war Literature on Money, the Cycle, and Unemployment*, Cambridge University Press, Cambridge.

Leeson R. (Ed.) (2003), *Keynes, Chicago and Friedman*, Chatto and Pickering Publishers, London.

Levrero E. S. (1999), 'Milton Friedman', *Studi Economici*, 68, 2, 5–79.

Machlup F. (1943), 'Forced or Induced Savings: An Explanation into its Synonyms and Homonyms', *The Review of Economic Statistics*, 25, 1, 26–39.

Mints L. W. (1946), 'Monetary Policy', *Review of Economic Statistics*, 28, 2, 60–69.

Modigliani F. (1944), 'Liquidity Preference and the Theory of Interest and Money', *Econometrica*, 12, 1, 45–88.

Morgenthau H. (1941), 'Statement before the Committee on Banking and Currency House of Representatives', in Price Control Bill, *Hearings before the Committee on Banking and Currency House of Representatives*, Seventy-Seventh Congress, op. cit., US Government Printing Office, Washington.

Neff P. (1949), 'Professor Friedman's Proposal: Final Comment', *American Economic Review*, 39, 5, 955–956.

Pasinetti L. (1974), 'La teoria economica della domanda effettiva', in L. Pasinetti, *Sviluppo economico e distribuzione del reddito*, Il Mulino, Bologna.

Patinkin D. (1948), 'Price Flexibility and Full Employment', *American Economic Review*, 38, 4, 543–564.

Patinkin D. (1969), 'The Chicago Tradition, the Quantity Theory, and Friedman', *Journal of Money, Credit and Banking*, 1, 1, 46–70.

Paul R. E. (1942), 'Statement before the Subcommittee of the Committee on Finance United States Senate', in Withholding Tax. *Hearings before Subcommittee of the Committee on Finance United States Senate*, Seventy-Seventh Congress, Second Session on Data Relative to Withholding provisions of the 1942 Revenue Act, Wednesday, August 19, US Government Printing Office, Washington.

Paul R. E. (1943), 'Statement before the Committee on Finance United States Senate', in Current Tax Payments Act of 1943, *Hearings before the Committee on Finance United States Senate*, Seventy-Eight Session, H.R. 2570, An Act to Provide for the Current Payment of the Individual Income Tax, and for other Purposes, Revised May 6 and 7, 1943, United States, US Government Printing Office, Washington.

Pigou A. C. (1929), *Industrial Fluctuations*, 2nd rev. edn, Macmillan, London.

Pigou A. C. (1941), 'Types of War Inflation', *Economic Journal*, 51, 204, 439–448.

Poole K. E. (1943), 'Problems of Administration and Equity under a Spending Tax', *The American Economic Review*, 33, 1, 63–73.

Rees A. (1959), ' Patterns of Wages, Prices and Productivity', in *Wages, Prices, Profits and Productivity: Background papers and Final report of the 15*. American Assembly, Columbia University, New York.

Robertson D. H. (1926), *Banking Policy and the Price Level*, Macmillan, London.

Rockoff H. (1985), *Drastic Measure. A History of Wage and Price Controls in the United States*, Cambridge University Press, Cambridge.

Ruml B. (1943), 'Statement before the Committee on Income', in Revenue Act of 1943, *Hearings before the Committee on Income*, United States Senate, Seventy Eight Congress, US Government Printing Office, Washington, 1943.

Salant W. S. (1942), 'The Inflationary Gap: I. Meaning and Significance for Policy Making', *American Economic Review*, 32, 2, 308–314.

Schumpeter J. A. (1954), *History of Economic Analysis*, Oxford University Press, Oxford–New York.

Shoup C., Friedman M., & Mack R. P. (1943), *Taxing to Prevent Inflation. Techniques for Estimating Revenue Requirements*, Columbia University Press, New York.

Simons H. C. (1934), 'A Positive Program for Laissez Faire: Some Proposals for a Liberal Economic Policy', University of Chicago Press, reprinted in H. C. Simons, *Economic Policy for a Free Society*, The University of Chicago Press, Chicago, 1948.

Simons H. C. (1936), 'Rules versus Authorities in Monetary Policy', *Journal of Political Economy*, XLIV, 1, February, 1–30, reprinted in H. C. Simons, *Economic Policy for a Free Society*, The University of Chicago Press, Chicago, 1948.

Simons H. C. (1938), *Personal Income Taxation. The Definition of Income as a Problem of Fiscal Policy*, The University of Chicago Press, Chicago.

Simons H. C. (1942), 'Hansen on Fiscal Policy', *Journal of Political Economy*, L, 2, April, 161–196, reprinted in H. C. Simons, *Economic Policy for a Free Society*, The University of Chicago Press, Chicago, 1948.

Smithies A. (1942), 'The Behavior of Money National Income Under Inflationary Conditions', *Quarterly Journal of Economics*, 57, 3, 113–127.

Spiegel H. W. (1942), *The Economics of Total War,* D. Appleton-Century Company Incorporated, New York–London.

Tavlas G. S. (1998), 'Was the Monetarist Tradition Invented?', *Journal of Economic Perspectives*, 12, 4, 211–222.

Tobin J. (1965), 'The monetary interpretation of history – a Review Article', *American Economic Review*, 55, 3, 464–485.

Wallis W. A. (1942), 'How to Ration Consumer Goods and Control Their Prices', *American Economic Review*, 32, 3, 501–512.

Weintraub S. (1971), 'Keynes and the Monetarists', *The Canadian Journal of Economics*, 4, 1, 37–49.

5

The Department of Economics of the University of Chicago: A Memoir

Thomas Gale Moore

After leaving the Navy in 1955 I enrolled at George Washington University, where I majored initially in foreign affairs. In my junior year, I discovered that there were no jobs in that field, so I switched to economics, a practical subject, I thought. As I neared graduation in 1957, I realized that economics, at least with only a BA, was also less than practical and that I needed graduate work.

The University of Chicago accepted me as they did most applicants. They took people from all types of backgrounds; but, as opposed to Harvard or MIT, which, when they accepted a student, all but guaranteed graduation, Chicago was more ruthless. True, even students without a formal undergraduate degree or a high school diploma who could do well on the graduate record exam were admitted. Many of them, however, flunked out in their first year.

I remember one student – later he became one of my best friends – who had had a checkered education. He was caught up in the Holocaust and came very close to being killed as his parents had been. He used to sit at the back of the class and ask what I thought were the stupidest questions in an effort, I later realized, to fill in the blanks. Given the opportunity he overcame his spotty education and did well at Chicago.

In 1957, when I was admitted, my ideology was very far to the left. I believed that socialism was the best system; I even had certain sympathies for communism. I chose Chicago because the University had a reputation for being very left wing, which shows that I had virtually no knowledge of the Department of Economics. Within six months, the Department had changed my orientation from flaming socialism to flaming libertarianism.

In my first year, I took a course on statistics in the business school from W. Allen Wallis, who was then Dean. Like its approach to students, the University put little stock in degrees. Wallis had never finished his dissertation, but he was still hired by the University. My understanding is that his thesis committee at the University of Minnesota wanted him to change some point in his dissertation, which he refused to do. He later went on to become Chancellor of the University of Rochester. During the first year, I also took a course in labor economics from George Shultz, who later went on to become US Secretary of Labor, Treasury, and State. While he was in the latter post in the Reagan Administration, he recommended me for the position of Member of the Council of Economic Advisers.

When I arrived at Chicago I had a small 'GI Bill' payment and an even smaller scholarship as the child of a World War I veteran. Needing money, I worked for Gregg Lewis on a major study of labor unions.[1] That fall, I took the basic microeconomics class, taught that quarter by Arnold Harberger since Milton Friedman, who usually taught the course, was on leave at Stanford. His presence, however, was palpable; we used a draft copy of a micro text written by Friedman. It was probably that course that changed me from a lefty to a libertarian.

Carl Christ taught the macro course, even when Friedman was in residence. Although he explained Keynesian thought, he raised questions about its long-run validity. Those courses prepared me well for the upcoming prelim exams, which I passed at the PhD level. The methodology of the exams was, I believe, unique to Chicago. All the questions were 'True, False, and **Why**.' You were graded on the '**Why**.'

After I did very well on both the winter quarter prelims that covered micro and macro economics and the summer exams that dealt with specialized fields, I was awarded an Earhart Foundation Fellowship for my second year, 1958–1959.

My intention had been simply to get an MA in Economics and then go to work in business. Gregg Lewis pointed out that I might as well spend a little extra time and get a PhD. He convinced me and I spoke with Theodore Schultz about writing a dissertation on the economics of marriage. (I had just become engaged.) I was recommended for a Ford Foundation scholarship, which was typically awarded to the best student. The Foundation executives, however, felt that the subject was too far outside the mainstream of economics. I was too early; Gary Becker would pioneer the field later.

Thrashing around for a dissertation topic, I talked to George Stigler. He had recently arrived at Chicago and was ensconced in the Business School as the Charles R. Walgreen Distinguished Service Professor. Stigler and I discussed various topics; but he was most interested in why governments, state and local, regulated some professions and not others. Friedman had laid out the effects of regulation on the professions in the 1930s; but why did state governments continue to regulate doctors, lawyers, dentists, and such occupations as beautician. My thesis committee consisted of Stigler as chairman, Milton Friedman, and Aaron Director, who was pioneering the field of public choice before it was so named.

In December 1959, the Department held a Christmas party at which we graduate students put on a short skit during which we presented Milton Friedman with a worker's box lunch, labeled 'a Free Lunch.' He promptly pulled out a dime and gave it to the presenters, saying, 'This is not a "Free Lunch."' A good time was had by all.

While at Chicago, I participated in the Industrial Organization Workshop, run by George Stigler. Chicago workshops were unusual. Every participant was expected to have read the paper being discussed and to have prepared questions designed to destroy the study. I remember giving a workshop held in the law school building in a room with seats raked sharply upward around the paper giver, he being at the bottom of a well. You were lucky to get your first sentence out before someone challenged you.

In my second year as a graduate student, I often participated in a poker game held at Arnold Harberger's carriage house. Hyde Park at the turn of the century had been a very fashionable neighborhood and it was scattered with beautiful old mansions and carriage houses. As I remember, Larry Sjastaad, a fellow graduate student, also participated.

I left Chicago in June 1960 to join Chase Manhattan Bank. I had remained committed to working in industry, even though George Stigler tried to talk me out of it. I hadn't quite finished my thesis but did so over the next eight months in New York. Stigler then recommended me to the Carnegie Institute of Technology (later it became Carnegie Mellon University) for a position. The Graduate School of Industrial Relations (GSIA) had received a grant from the Mellon Foundation to finance a study of the economics of the theater in the United States. Thus my first year at Carnegie was spent on leave in New York doing research on Broadway and off-Broadway economics.

The University of Chicago changed my life and gave me a career. I have taught at several universities and visited many others, but the University of Chicago is the most intellectual university in the world. It is a place of ideas, hotly debated by scholars, with no constraints on subject or approach. Political correctness has never been politically correct at Chicago. As long as Stigler and Friedman remained there it maintained that approach. Even today, it still appears to be a truly academic institution in the best sense of the word.

Note

1. 'The Effects of Unions on Industrial Wage Differentials,' 1962, in *Aspects of Labor Economics*, W. G. Lewis, editor.

6

Friedman's Methodology Essay in Context

J. Daniel Hammond

> *I have devised seven separate explanations, each of which would cover the facts as far as we know them. But which of these is correct can only be determined by the fresh information which we shall no doubt find waiting for us.*
>
> Sherlock Holmes, *The Adventure of the Copper Beeches*

Milton Friedman's methodology is built from a presumption that the goal of economic science is theory 'that yields valid and meaningful (i.e., not truistic) predictions about phenomena not yet observed' (1953, p. 7). Toward this goal Friedman argued in 'The Methodology of Positive Economics' that the only relevant test of the validity of theory is 'comparison of its predictions with experience' (1953, pp. 8–9). A half century after Friedman published the essay methodologists are still trying to uncover its meaning and coherence or lack thereof. This essay uses evidence of the context from which Friedman wrote to call into question the standard interpretation of the essay's central message.

A nutshell summary of Friedman's essay likely to come to mind for people familiar with it is, 'unrealistic assumptions do not matter while predictive success is all that matters in assessing a theory.' Mark Blaug (1992) and others have parsed what Friedman might have meant by unrealistic assumptions: (1) abstract, in being less than fully descriptive; (2) assigning motives that are not comprehensible; or (3) in conflict with directly perceived evidence of behavior. Paul Samuelson (1963, 1964) famously dubbed Friedman's argument about assumptions the 'F-twist,' which he argued was

> fundamentally wrong in thinking that unrealism in the sense of factual inaccuracy even to a tolerable degree of approximation is

anything but a demerit for a theory or hypothesis (or a set of hypotheses). Some inaccuracies are worse than others, but that is only to say that some sins against empirical science are worse than others, not that a sin is a merit or that a small sin is equivalent to a zero sin.

(1963, p. 233)

The lack of importance and even necessity of unrealistic assumptions is certainly an important part of Friedman's message in the essay. Why did Friedman think this was an argument he should make?

Among the reasons that Friedman wrote the essay as he did was a series of articles arguing that lack of realisticness of its assumptions rendered neoclassical price theory irrelevant to real-world economic problems. Critics such as R. A. Lester (1946) and R. J. Hall and C. J. Hitch (1939) called for greater realism in assumptions. They thought businessmen did not and could not make decisions the way neoclassical theory assumed. Other critics pointed out that real-world markets are unlike those portrayed by the models of perfect competition and perfect monopoly. Defending neoclassical theory, Fritz Machlup (1946, 1947) and George Stigler (1947) argued that the theory was realistic. Friedman chose not to join this defense but rather to argue that both the critics and the defenders were falling prey to methodological error. The charges of unrealisticness were not wrong, but they were irrelevant. He argued that realisticness of assumptions does not matter so long as the theory predicts well, that is so long as there is realisticness in the theory's implications.

Readers of the essay have taken this as its central message, and the message certainly is prominent in the essay. Furthermore, the essay seems to say that less realistic assumptions make a theory better! Samuelson saw this as the extreme version of the F-twist, although he was somewhat coy about whether he attributed this version to Friedman.[1] I believe this interpretation is a distortion of Friedman's actual claim. He was merely arguing that simple theory is preferable to complex theory. To suggest, as Friedman did, that 'the more significant the theory, the more unrealistic the assumptions' does not imply that making assumptions less realistic necessarily makes theory more significant. He meant only that significant theories will necessarily have unrealistic assumptions. But even putting this aside, I will argue that what remains as the standard summary of Friedman's thesis is based on a thin interpretation. The interpretation is thin in that it gives excessive weight to the choice between testing via assumptions and testing by implications. If the weight given to this choice is excessive, what is underweighted in the standard interpretation? I believe this is the choice between testing theory empirically and not doing so, that is *whether* to test empirically. Both testing by the realisticness of assumptions and testing by the success of predictions are means of testing empirically. The alternative that Friedman most opposed was foregoing empirical testing altogether.

Friedman himself must shoulder some of the blame for exaggerating the importance of *how* to test empirically. This question takes up a large portion of the essay's text. Readers' first encounter with the argument that realisticness of assumptions does not matter is six pages into the essay, where Friedman writes,

> Viewed as a body of substantive hypotheses, theory is to be judged by its predictive power for the class of phenomena which it is intended to 'explain.' . . . As I shall argue at greater length below, the only relevant test of the *validity* of a hypothesis is comparison of its predictions with experience.
>
> (1953, p. 8, emphasis in original)

After explaining what he means by predictions, and discussing the difficulty of obtaining the appropriate data outside controlled laboratory settings, he says there are two alluring escapes from the difficult task of testing by predictions. The first is 'a retreat into purely formal or tautological analysis' (p. 11). Dealing with this escape in the space of only two paragraphs, he argues that this retreat is misguided, for it reduces economics to disguised mathematics. Then, having established, however briefly and partially, that it is important to bring empirical evidence to bear on theory, Friedman moves to the question of where in the theory this should be done. First he distinguishes use of evidence to test theories from use of evidence to construct theories. Then, 12 pages into the 41-page essay, we come to the second escape from the difficulty of obtaining evidence for testing predictions, which is testing theory by the realisticness of its assumptions. Friedman devotes the remainder of the essay to this topic.

So it is not surprising that readers have taken Friedman's central message to be that testing theory by the realisticness of assumptions is inappropriate; the accuracy of predictions is the only legitimate test. But here I part company with many other readers. Notwithstanding the textual evidence from the essay, I believe this issue was less important to Friedman than it has become in the life of the essay since 1953. If I may borrow the metaphor of 'links in a chain' from Tom Mayer's *Truth Versus Precision in Economics* (1993), the argument that realisticness of assumptions does not matter is one link in Friedman's methodology. It is the largest and shiniest link in the essay. Friedman made it thick and put a high polish on it. So it is not surprising that this link has drawn so much attention. But this has distracted us from the rest of the chain.

My assertion that the realisticness argument is not as central as it appears flies in the face of Friedman's revealed preference. Why, you might ask, would he devote so much attention to this if it was not in fact the most important issue? Why make this link so prominent? One reason is that Friedman was reacting to debates in the literature at the time he wrote the essay. He began writing it in late 1947, probably finishing the first draft in the summer of 1948.[2] Through the two years prior to his starting the essay there were several articles in the *American Economic Review* criticizing and defending the assumptions about business practice that underlay marginal analysis of the firm.[3] Friedman joined this debate with the idea that the critics and defenders of marginal analysis alike were making a methodological error. So, when he began the essay the issue on the table was realisticness of assumptions, and he made that the central focus of the essay. But at a more fundamental level this was only part of what bothered Friedman about contemporary methodological trends.

In the 1948 draft, as in the published essay, Friedman gave a second example of what he considered flawed methodology. This was the move to replace perfect competition and monopoly with monopolistic competition. He dealt with the marginalism issue first, saying that it was the clearer example, but stated that he regarded the push for monopolistic competition more important. This is a hint of what we will find by digging further into the foundations of the essay.

Friedman's first forays into methodology were two book reviews (1940, 1941), written while he was a full-time staff member of the National Bureau of Economic Research and on the faculty of the University of Wisconsin. The reviews were of Jan Tinbergen's *Business Cycles in the United States of America, 1919–1932*, and Robert Triffin's *Monopolistic Competition and General Equilibrium Theory*. In the review of Tinbergen, Friedman makes a distinction between uses of data to test and to derive hypotheses. His main criticism is that Tinbergen did not test his business cycle model with data other than those used to estimate the equations. Tellingly, the two references in the review are W. C. Mitchell, *Business Cycles, The Problem and Its Setting* (1927), and A. F. Burns and W. C. Mitchell, *Methods of Measuring Business Cycles* (1946).[4] The authors of these references were former teachers, and at the National Bureau, colleagues of Friedman.

Robert Triffin sought to reorient the theory of monopolistic competition away from the Anglo-American tradition of Marshallian analysis toward continental Walrasian analysis. To him this meant dispensing with the concept of industry and moving the orientation simultaneously in two directions, inward toward the single firm and outward toward the 'whole economic collectivity.' Triffin wrote,

> The appearance of monopolistic competition assumptions has been a new step in the historical process of purification and formalization of economic theory. The analysis loses in content, while gaining in generality....
>
> On the other hand, we shall find that an increasing number of situations elude the grip of the traditional weapons of pure economics. This raises the question of whether we should not, reversing the historical process of growing generalization just mentioned, enlarge the present box of assumptions of pure theory so as to enable us to tackle these cases; again, the required assumptions should be chosen on an empirical basis, and a price will have to be paid in the form of a lesser generality for the ensuing analysis.
>
> (1941, pp. 15–16)

Friedman's reviews of these two books portend much of what he wrote later on methodology. In one review (of Tinbergen) he acknowledges that observed facts have their place at both ends of theory, in deriving theory and in testing it. He insists that testing has to be with data other than those from which the theory is derived. In the other review Friedman does not contest Triffin's assertion that the logic of monopolistic competition implies that one not group firms into Marshallian industries. He agrees with this. He rejects Triffin's choice of monopolistic competition over Marshallian industry analysis. And he does so because he thinks most of the practical problems for which economists want to use theory are at the level of industries, not at the level of firms or of the 'whole economic collectivity.' If industries have no place in monopolistic competition, then monopolistic competition must go.

In March 1943, Friedman joined the staff of the Statistical Research Group (SRG) at Columbia University as Associate Director. While there he wrote a review (1944) of a Temporary National Economic Committee publication by Oscar Altman, *Saving, Investment, and National Income* (1941). This book was a Keynesian analysis including empirical data on savings and investment. Friedman's criticism was that the data were not of the type that could be used to test the theory. Apart from the data's value as a record of savings and investment, Friedman found that they added little value to Altman's analysis. The data served only as window dressing for a mechanical application of the Keynesian savings–investment apparatus to the problem of full employment level of income.

> The theoretical analysis in Altman's monograph is set against an extensive factual background of data on saving and investment to which the bulk of the monograph is devoted. This comprehensive compilation of data on the aggregate volume of investment, the size of various components of saving and investment, their concentration in various groups in the economy, and the like, is excellent and of considerable interest in its own right as a description of one aspect of our economy. But it is presented as if it had direct relevance to the theoretical analysis, as if it directly substantiated the assertions about the conditions under which full employment is attainable which are the major *raison d'etre* of the monograph. Yet the relation between the figures and the theoretical analysis is nowhere considered.
>
> (1944, pp. 101–2)

It is significant that Friedman wrote with this emphasis on bringing data into contact with theory while at the SRG. In the two and a half years that he was with the SRG he did work on the relative effectiveness of conventional antiaircraft shells and shrapnel shells; the design of fuses for antiaircraft rockets, and alloy specifications for turbines. He contributed to almost 100 reports and memos on topics for which speculative analysis, unchecked by facts, was simply not acceptable. Lives of Allied soldiers and sailors and the outcome of the war were at stake.[5]

In another book review that Friedman wrote just prior to joining the University of Chicago faculty, he criticized Oscar Lange's use of what he called 'taxonomic theorizing' (1946). The distinguishing marks of taxonomic theorizing are that a formal theoretical model is specified in form only, not in content, and is used to speculate on various scenarios that might follow a change in policy or prices. Lange's concern was with the effects of a decline in the price of an underemployed factor of production. He considered direct effects of the change along with indirect effects that may reinforce or counteract the direct effects. This kind of theorizing, in and of itself, dispenses with factual analysis. According to Friedman,

> The basic sources of the defects in Lange's theoretical analysis are the emphasis on formal structure, the attempt to generalize without

first specifying in detail the facts to be generalized, and the failure to recognize that the ultimate test of the validity of a theory is not conformity to the canons of formal logic but the ability to deduce facts that have not yet been observed, that are capable of being contradicted by observation, and that subsequent observation does not contradict.

(1953 [1946], p. 300)

Friedman argued that notwithstanding their emphasis on formal theory, neither Lange nor anyone else employing this approach was content to rely on formal theory alone, without consideration of facts. They invariably brought facts into the analysis to rule out some of the countless theoretical possibilities. Thus, striving for formal completeness bred empirical ad hocery.

A man who has a burning interest in pressing issues of public policy, who has a strong desire to learn how the economic system really works in order that that knowledge may be used, is not likely to stay within the bounds of a method of analysis that denies him the knowledge he seeks. He will escape the shackles of formalism, even if he has to resort to illogical devices and specious reasoning to do so. This is, of course, a poor way to escape the shackles of formalism. A far better way is to try to devise theoretical generalizations to fit as full and comprehensive a set of related facts about the real world as it is possible to get.

(1953 [1946], p. 300)

Shortly after writing the review of Lange's book Friedman criticized Abba Lerner's *The Economics of Control* along similar lines. He saw the work as formal theorizing void of the quantitative and institutional details required for the analysis of countercyclical policy. He argued that without these details policy prescriptions turn out to be nothing more than tautologies and admonitions to do the right thing. To Friedman,

for our present purpose the relevant question is whether the discussion of 'functional finance,' besides being a logical exercise, is also a prescription for public policy. The answer, it seems to this reviewer, is clearly negative. Once again, what looks like a prescription evaporates into an expression of good intentions. . . .

To make this into a prescription to 'produce full employment,' Lerner must tell us how to know when there is 'insufficient total demand,' whether this insufficiency is a temporary deficiency in the process of being corrected or the beginning of an increasing deficiency that, if left alone, will lead to a drastic deflation. He must tell us how to know what medicine to use when the diagnosis has been made, how large a dose to give, and how long we may expect it to take for the medicine to be effective.

(1953 [1947], pp. 313–14)

These reviews written before 'The Methodology of Positive Economics' portray Friedman's ideas more fully than the essay alone. He opposed testing theory by assumptions, but did so within the broader context of arguing that theory should be fact-imbued, from beginning to end, soup to nuts. What are the implications for how we view the 1953 essay? By my reckoning this leaves us with two perspectives for locating Friedman's essay on the mid-twentieth-century methodological landscape. On the one hand, the essay is an argument with those who, like Friedman, believed that theories should be made with the aid of empirical facts and judged on the basis of their consistency with empirical facts. It is within this group that the argument over testing assumptions versus testing predictions is joined. On the other hand, the essay is an argument with those who would make theory from stuff other than empirical facts and judge theory on grounds other than the consilience of its predictions with facts. The argument here was with formalists.

'We have got to the deductions and the inferences,' said Lestrade, winking at me. 'I find it hard enough to tackle facts, Holmes, without flying away after theories and fancies.'

'You are right,' said Holmes demurely; 'you do find it very hard to tackle the facts.'

Inspector Lestrade and Sherlock Holmes,
The Boscombe Valley Mystery

Commentators have been puzzled by Friedman's different claims about the role of assumptions, claims that are not entirely mutually consistent. Friedman argued that the only relevant test of the validity of a hypothesis is the consistency of its predictions with experience. However, he then acknowledged the appeal of testing assumptions and admitted that 'there is too much smoke for there to be no fire' (1953, p. 23). He devoted an entire section of the essay to 'the significance and role of the "assumptions" of a theory,' which includes facilitating indirect tests of hypotheses. Up to this point at least Friedman had a clean straightforward thesis, with which one may or may not agree. Why did he extend the discussion in a way that seems to muddle his argument? Friedman did so because his friends, George Stigler and Arthur Burns, urged him to.

Friedman began discussions with Stigler as he started writing the essay. Their conversation was prompted by Edward Chamberlin's review (1947) of Stigler's, *The Theory of Price* (1946). In his textbook Stigler wrote that monopolistic competition was 'impracticable' because of the infinite variety of possible departures from the conditions of perfect competition and monopoly, and because of economists' ignorance of the facts necessary to choose among the multitude of possible assumptions. Chamberlin's review said that the textbook revealed Stigler's 'confusion and misconception in rare degree as to what "imperfect" and monopolistic competition theories are all about' (1947, p. 417). Undecided about writing a response for publication, Stigler asked Friedman for advice. He sent along a copy of a letter he wrote to Chamberlin.

Friedman's reply to Stigler:

> I have gotten involved for various irrelevant reasons in a number of discussions of scientific methodology related to the kind of thing you are talking about. In the course of these I have been led to go further than I had before in distinguishing between description and analysis and in discarding comparisons between assumptions in reality as a test of the validity of a hypothesis. I should like to offer the general proposition that every important scientific hypothesis almost inevitably must use assumptions that are descriptively erroneous. It is of the very nature of a really important scientific generalization that it provides a simpler rationalization of a mass of facts than was available before. It is likely to obtain its objective by an inspiration about the particular basic elements of the situation that are important and by discarding what after the event can be shown to have been irrelevant complicating assumptions. In a way, the better the hypothesis the greater the extent to which it simplifies, the more sharply will its assumptions depart from reality.
>
> (MF to GS, [November 19, 1947], in Hammond and Hammond, 2006, p. 65)

Friedman then stated his point differently by asking how one knows whether assumptions correspond closely to reality, illustrating the question with the physics problem of a body's rate of fall, with which we are now familiar.[6] He enclosed with his letter a reprint of his review of Triffin's *Monopolistic Competition and General Equilibrium Theory*.

By the summer of 1948 Friedman had completed the first draft of his methodology essay. He sent it to Stigler, whose reaction is given below:

> Personally I would like it published.... But I keep feeling that you arouse skepticism and opposition by stopping where you do. Because surely in some sense an assumption can be more promising than another.... It is surely possible to say something about some assumptions being more promising than others, and yet not to take back any of the things you are saying at present. If you can pierce this muddy frontier of your article, it would be a great improvement.
>
> (GS to MF, [September 1948], in Hammond and Hammond, 2006, pp. 89–90)

Friedman answered that his strictures applied to only the third of a four-part scientific enterprise, testing hypotheses. Three other parts that were not his concern were collecting data from which to draw generalizations, deriving hypotheses to generalize uniformities observed in the data, and using the hypotheses. He asked Stigler if his point was the same that Arthur Burns argued the previous summer, and said that, if so, it applied not to testing theory but to choosing among hypotheses that have not yet been tested. Friedman suggested that assumptions do play a role in this indirect testing. One has confidence in untested hypotheses that are related by their assumptions to others that have proven successful. He also suggested that something akin to the realisticness of assumptions matters at the first stage of the scientific enterprise, in which empirical regularities are observed. Realisticness matters in that good theories are more likely to be produced from actual facts than from false facts.

Shortly afterwards Stigler made a suggestion that turned out to be consequential. He wrote,

> I like your general position but want you to enlarge it, – precisely as you are enlarging it in your letter to me. While some elaboration along these lines will take some of the paradox out of your thesis (and in a certain sense weaken its message unless you write very carefully), it will create sympathy for and receptiveness to your thesis and make the paper much more influential.
>
> (GS to MF, [October 1948], in Hammond and Hammond, 2006, p. 94)

Friedman's essay was in gestation for a long time, no doubt in part because he took Stigler's advice. Four years later Stigler read a second draft of the essay, and they still had not settled their differences.[7] Stigler wrote,

> I'm inclined to go along with you on the use of a theory, but what do you think of the following reformulation:
>
> 1. After a theory has been developed and tested and much used, its applicability to certain classes of problems becomes established. These classes of problems may be completely specific or objective, as in the use of engineering formulas. Or they may be more loosely specified.
> 2. At all times there will also be many questions that do not clearly fall within or without the domain of the theory, and only further experiment can tell us whether a given problem should be handled by a given theory.
>
> (GS to MF, [November 30, 1952], in Hammond and Hammond, 2006, p. 130)

Stigler suggested that he was thinking primarily of class one, routine scientific work, and Friedman of class two, improvements in science. So the impetus to Friedman's discussions of methodology with George Stigler was the challenge posed by Walrasian monopolistic competition to Marshallian industry analysis. But Stigler thought that Friedman's argument against testing by the realisticness of assumptions was overly restrictive, as did Arthur Burns, and repeatedly urged him to find something positive to say about the urge felt by so many economists to choose theories on this basis.

> *As to Holmes, I observed that he sat frequently for half an hour on end, with knitted brows and an abstracted air, but he swept the matter away with a wave of his hand when I mentioned it. 'Data! data! data!' he cried impatiently. 'I can't make bricks without clay.'*
>
> Dr. Watson, *The Adventure of the Copper Beeches*

Friedman, Stigler, and Burns were close friends. But more than that, they shared a professional experience that shaped their methodological views. This experience was that the three were on the Research Staff of the National Bureau of Economic Research. Friedman's methodology was made from ideas that he acquired first as a student of Burns and Wesley C. Mitchell, and then as a member of the National Bureau staff. Just as monopolistic competition appeared poised in the 1940s to replace

Marshallian value theory, so Keynesian macroeconomics was poised to replace National Bureau–style business-cycle analysis.

In June 1946 Arthur F. Burns made his first annual report for the National Bureau, having replaced Mitchell, who retired as Director of Research the previous October. Burns's essay in the report was 'Economic Research and the Keynesian Thinking of Our Times.' He compared Keynesians to Ricardians, both groups believing that they had solved the mystery of the economic problem of their time. Burns judged that they had not done so. He wrote,

> The opinion is widespread that Keynes has explained what determines the volume of employment at any given time, and that our knowledge of the causes of variation in employment is now sufficient to enable governments to maintain a stable and high level of national income and employment within the framework of our traditional economic organization. If this opinion is valid, the solution of the basic problem of democratic societies is in sight, and the National Bureau would do well to reconsider its research program. Unhappily, this opinion reflects a pleasant but dangerous illusion.
>
> (1946, p. 5)

The research program of the National Bureau emphasized producing economic facts and fact-based analysis. The Keynesians, like the Ricardians before them, thought that 'speculative analysis' based on the master's theory was sufficient for the job.

Paul Samuelson was a prominent Keynesian at the time. His writings on Keynesian economics provide a sharp contrast with the view of the state of economic knowledge and methods for enlarging knowledge that characterized the National Bureau. Samuelson contributed an essay to Seymour E. Harris's *The New Economics* (1947), in which he wrote that *The General Theory* 'caught most economists under the age of 35 with the unexpected virulence of a disease first attacking and decimating an isolated tribe of south sea islanders' (1947, p. 146). According to Samuelson, Keynesian theory was sweeping aside Say's Law of Markets, the classical theory of employment, with good reason. Samuelson explained why

> The classical philosophy always had its ups and downs along with the great swings of business activity. Each time it had come back. But now for the first time, it was confronted by a competing system – a well-reasoned body of thought containing among other things as

many equations as unknowns, in short, like itself, a synthesis; and one which could swallow the classical system as a special case.

(1947, p. 148)

He also thought that in addition to being 'complete,' the theoretical system in *The General Theory* was 'relatively realistic' (1947, p. 151).

Samuelson's other writings from the period that have to do with Keynesian analysis are filled with the logic of theoretical models but empty of quantitative data and estimates. There are statements of fact, but no evidence of gathering or exploring facts. For instance, in 'The Theory of Pump-Priming Reexamined' (1940), Samuelson wrote,

> It is necessary in the beginning to set forth explicitly the basic features of the private economy forming the environment within which governmental action must take place. No attempt is made to justify the characteristics stressed beyond the assertion that in the recent business cycle literature they are regarded as fundamental.
>
> (1940, p. 492)

Samuelson asserts without evidential support several of these fundamental characteristics of the private economy: 'the possibility of, if not a definite tendency toward, cumulative movements of a disequilibrating kind' (1940, p. 492), and 'the fact that *even in a perfect capital market there is no tendency for the rate of interest to equilibrate the demand and supply of employment*' (1940, p. 493, his emphasis). Further along in the article he states,

> First, consider a downturn due simply to the giving out of investment opportunities....
>
> The reader will perhaps recognize in this example some of the features characteristic of the Great Depression of 1929.
>
> (1940, p. 496)

So Samuelson wrote as if the important macroeconomic facts were known. All that was required for economists was to apply Keynesian theory to the facts.

Samuelson wrote in another piece, 'Fiscal Policy and Income Determination' (1942), that his purpose was 'carrying forward the analysis of important theoretical and empirical factors, usually assumed constant or neglected in the oversimplified versions of the theory [of multiplier analysis]' (p. 575, emphasis added). On the basis of this theoretical and, as he suggested, empirical investigation he drew inferences about primary, secondary, and tertiary effects of public spending, and about their implications for the relative merits of public works and consumption expenditures. He also drew inferences about 'the vitally important comparison of the "multiplier hypothesis" and the "velocity-of-money hypothesis"' (1942, p. 575). However, despite the promise to analyze empirical factors, the article's sole empirical content is a table of estimates of tax revenue yields at different levels of income from the 1940 Report of the Secretary of the Treasury.

> *'This is indeed a mystery,' I remarked. 'What do you imagine that it means?'*
> *'I have no data yet. It is a capital mistake to theorize before one has data.*
> *Insensibly one begins to twist facts to suit theories, instead of theories to*
> *suit facts.'*
>
> Dr. Watson and Sherlock Holmes, *A Scandal in Bohemia*

As Milton Friedman wrote the first draft of the methodology essay in the winter and spring of 1948 Paul Samuelson was putting the finishing touches to *Economics: An Introductory Analysis* (1948). Parts of Samuelson's opening chapter are consistent with themes in Friedman's essay; some even look as if they could be a brief for the National Bureau research program.[8] Samuelson wrote that

> It is the first task of modern economic science to describe, to analyze, to explain, to correlate these fluctuations of national income. Both boom and slump, price inflation and deflation, are our concern. This is a difficult and complicated task. Because of the complexity of human and social behavior, we cannot hope to attain the precision of a few of the physical sciences. We cannot perform the controlled experiments of the chemist or biologist. Like the astronomer we must be content largely to 'observe.'
>
> (1948, p. 4)

Writing about economic theory and practice, he continues,

> The economic world is extremely complicated. Furthermore, it is usually not possible to make economic observations under controlled experimental characteristics of scientific laboratories.... As a result of

this limitation and many others, our quantitative economic knowledge is far from complete. This does not mean that we do not have great amounts of accurate statistical knowledge available. We do.

(1948, p. 7)

A statement about simplification resembles Friedman's:

Even if we had more and better data, it would still be necessary – as in every science – to *simplify*, to *abstract* from the infinite mass of detail. No mind can apprehend a bundle of unrelated facts. All analysis involves abstraction. It is always necessary to *idealize*, to omit detail, to set up simple hypotheses and patterns by which the mass of facts are to be related, to set up the right questions before we go out looking at the world as it is. Every theory, whether in the physical or biological or social sciences, distorts reality in that it over-simplifies. But if it is a good theory, what is omitted is greatly outweighed by the beam of illumination and understanding that is thrown over the diverse empirical data.

(1948, pp. 7–8)

Samuelson states clearly that formal features of theory are subordinate to empirical success:

Properly understood, therefore, theory and observation, deduction and induction cannot be in conflict. Like eggs, there are only two kinds of theories: good ones and bad ones. And the test of a theory's goodness is its usefulness in illuminating observational reality. Its logical elegance and fine-spun beauty are irrelevant. Consequently, when a student says, 'That's all right in theory but not in practice,' he really means 'That's not all right in theory,' or else he is talking nonsense.

(1948, p. 8)

However, one looks in vain through the collected works of Samuelson for systematic attempts to bring illumination to 'diverse empirical data,' and to accumulate 'quantitative knowledge' of booms and recessions or other economic phenomena. One looks in vain for empirical tests of theory, either by theory's predictions or by its assumptions. He paid lip-service to the empirical tradition of science and to the prudent dictum for everyday life to get the facts straight before coming to a judgment. But he practiced economics straight from the formalist script. In 1946

Friedman anticipated where the formalist script would lead economists, to 'formal models of imaginary worlds, not generalizations about the real world' (1946, p. 283).

Acknowledgments

For comments I thank Robert Leeson, Kevin Hoover, David Laidler, and participants at the History of Economics Society meeting, June 2004, and 'Milton Friedman's Essay at 50' conference, University of Rotterdam, December 2003.

Notes

1. See Samuelson (1963, pp. 232–3) and (1964, p. 736).
2. The title of this draft is 'Descriptive Validity vs. Analytical Relevance in Economic Theory' [1948].
3. Lester (1946, 1947), Machlup (1946, 1947), Stigler (1947), Oliver (1947).
4. The Burns and Mitchell volume was not then published. Thus the difference in the title given by Friedman and the book's actual title.
5. See Friedman and Friedman (1998), Chapter 8.
6. Friedman's example was oblique, referring to 'how rapidly a body will fall in a vacuum,' but without the equation that appeared in the essay. Of the several physical phenomena used in the essay this is the one he first used to explain his point to Stigler. This may not be mere chance, for the compact ball dropped from 30,000 to 20,000 feet in the essay appears as a bomb dropped from 40,000 to 30,000 feet in his letter. When he wrote the letter Friedman was two years away from his work on ordinance for the SRG.
7. The title of this draft is 'The Relevance of Economic Analysis to Prediction and Policy' [1952].
8. Samuelson (1963) later criticized Friedman's position on unrealistic assumptions, labeling it the 'F-twist.'

References

Altman, O. L. *Saving, Investment, and National Income*. Washington: U.S.G.P.O, 1941.

Blaug, M. *The Methodology of Economics, or How Economists Explain*, 2nd edn, Cambridge and New York: Cambridge University Press, 1992.

Burns, A. F. 'Economic Research and the Keynesian Thinking of Our Times', in *Twenty-Sixth Annual Report of the National Bureau of Economic Research*. New York: National Bureau of Economic Research, June 1946.

Burns, A. F. and Mitchell, W. C. *Measuring Business Cycles*. New York: National Bureau of Economic Research, 1946.

Chamberlin, E. H. 'Review of *The Theory of Price* by G. Stigler'. *American Economic Review*, 37 (June 1947): 414–18.

Doyle, A. C. *The Adventures of Sherlock Holmes*. Boulder, CO: NetLibrary. http://www.netlibrary.com.

Friedman, M. 'Review of *Business Cycles in the United States of America, 1919–32* by J. Tinbergen'. *American Economic Review*, 30 (September 1940): 657–60.

Friedman, M. 'Review of *Monopolistic Competition and General Equilibrium Theory* by R. Triffin'. *Journal of Farm Economics*, 23 (February 1941): 389–90.

Friedman, M. 'Review of *Saving, Investment, and National Income* by O. L. Altman'. *Review of Economics and Statistics*, 26 (May 1944): 101–2.

Friedman, M. 'Lange on Price Flexibility and Employment: A Methodological Criticism'. *American Economic Review*, 36 (September 1946): 613–31. Reprinted in *Essays in Positive Economics*, pp. 301–19.

Friedman, M. 'Lerner on the Economics of Control'. *Journal of Political Economy*, 55 (October 1947): 405–16. Reprinted in *Essays in Positive Economics*, pp. 277–300.

Friedman, M. 'Descriptive Validity vs. Analytical Relevance in Economic Theory'. Mimeo, Box 43, Milton Friedman Papers, Hoover Institution, Stanford University, undated [1948].

Friedman, M. 'The Relevance of Economic Analysis to Prediction and Policy'. Mimeo, undated [1952], Box 43, Milton Friedman Papers, Hoover Institution, Stanford University.

Friedman, M. 'The Methodology of Positive Economics', *Essays in Positive Economics*, pp. 3–43, Chicago: University of Chicago Press, 1953.

Friedman, M. and Friedman, R. D. *Two Lucky People: Memoirs*. Chicago and London: University of Chicago Press, 1998.

Hall, R. J. and Hitch, C. J. 'Price Theory and Business Behavior'. *Oxford Economic Papers*, 2 (May 1939): 12–45.

Hammond, J. D. and Hammond, C. H. (eds). *Making Chicago Price Theory: Friedman-Stigler Correspondence 1945–57*. London and New York: Routledge, 2006.

Harris, S. E. (ed.). *The New Economics: Keynes' Influence on Theory and Public Policy*. New York: Knopf, 1947.

Lester, R. A. 'Shortcomings of Marginal Analysis for Wage-Employment Problems'. *American Economic Review*, 36 (March 1946): 62–82.

Lester, R. A. 'Marginalism, Minimum Wages, and Labor Markets'. *American Economic Review*, 37 (March 1947): 135–48.

Machlup, F. 'Marginal Analysis and Empirical Research'. *American Economic Review*, 36 (September 1946): 519–54.

Machlup, F. 'Rejoinder to an Antimarginalist'. *American Economic Review*, 37 (March 1947): 148–54.

Mayer, T. *Truth versus Precision in Economics*. Aldershot, UK and Brookfield, VT: Edward Elgar, 1993.

Mitchell, W. C. *Business Cycles: The Problem and Its Setting*. New York: National Bureau of Economic Research, 1927.

Oliver, H. M. Jr. 'Marginal Theory and Business Behavior'. *American Economic Review*, 37 (June 1947): 375–83.

Samuelson, P. A. 'The Theory of Pump-Priming Reexamined'. *American Economic Review*, 30 (September 1940): 492–506.

Samuelson, P. A. 'Fiscal Policy and Income Determination'. *Quarterly Journal of Economics*, 56 (August 1942): 575–605.

Samuelson, P. A. 'The General Theory', in S. E. Harris (ed.), *The New Economics: Keynes' Influence on Theory and Public Policy*, pp. 145–60, New York: Knopf, 1947.

Samuelson, P. A. 'Problems of Methodology – Discussion'. *American Economic Review*, 53 (May 1963): 232–6.

Samuelson, P. A. 'Theory and Realism: A Reply'. *American Economic Review*, 54 (September 1964): 736–9.

Stigler, G. J. *The Theory of Price*. New York: Macmillan, 1946.

Stigler, G. J. 'Professor Lester and the Marginalists'. *American Economic Review*, 37 (March 1947): 154–7.

Triffin, R. *Monopolistic Competition and General Equilibrium Theory*. Cambridge: Harvard University Press, 1941.

7
Mythical Expectations

Robert Leeson and Warren Young

According to the conventional account, economists have relied on three types of expectations: static (contained in the original Keynesian Phillips Curve); adaptive (introduced by Milton Friedman in the course of his Monetarist counter-revolution) and rational (part of Robert Lucas's natural rate New Classical counter-revolution). This chapter argues that there is a fourth expectational type: the myths associated with these natural rate counter-revolutions.

The conventional chronology regarding the relationship between expectations and the Phillips Curve is that Friedman's 1967 AEA Presidential Address (Friedman, 1968a) transformed macroeconomics by focusing on the *neglect* of expectations in the Keynesian Phillips Curve. However, the archival evidence reveals this conventional account to be both inadequate and inaccurate. In this chapter, it will be shown that Phillips allocated a more destabilising role to inflationary expectations than did Friedman and that the adaptive expectations formula used to undermine the original Phillips Curve was actually provided to Friedman by Phillips.

In the late 1940s, Phillips (a sociology undergraduate) came to the attention of his economics teachers at the London School of Economics (LSE) by suggesting how a figure in Kenneth Boulding's (1948, 117, Fig. 9) *Economic Analysis* could be extended (Barr, 2000; Dorrance, 2000). The figure represented the process by which prices rise in response to excess demand, measured by the change in stocks in response to flow disequilibrium. Boulding's 'liquid' model led to one of the first physical (and highly 'liquid') macroeconomic models: the Phillips Machine (CW 2000 [1950], Chapter 10).

Phillips' (CW 2000 [1950], 73, 76–77) first appearance in the literature involved a brief discussion of the destabilising influence of expectations about prices:

> This simple model could be further developed, in particular by making a distinction between working and liquid stocks, introducing lags into the production and consumption functions, and linking the demand Curve for liquid stocks to the rate of change of price through a co-efficient of expectations. Each of these developments would result in an oscillatory system. They will not be considered further here...

The 'simple model' assumed that prices were constant, or that values were measured in 'some kind of real units'. Phillips demonstrated that it was possible to 'introduce prices indirectly into the system', allowing real and nominal magnitudes to be considered (and graphed) separately.

Dennis Robertson 'practically danced a jig' when he saw the Phillips Machine in operation. When the Chancellor of the Exchequer and the Governor of the Bank of England attended a dinner at LSE, they adjourned to the Machine room where the Chancellor was given control of the fiscal levers and the Governor control of the monetary ones (Dorrance, 2000).

The correspondence between Phillips and Robertson on the efficacy of the 'Phillips Machine' provides a good illustration of the significance of 'the essential stuff' of archival research in economics. In reply to Robertson's critique of the treatment of prices' and the 'multiplier formula' in the 'Phillips Machine approach' (cited in Robertson to Meade, 27 August 1950), Phillips wrote to Robertson (19 September 1950):

> I agree entirely with your criticism of the multiplier formula under conditions of full employment... But the machine will deal with Curves of any shape... If the price rise is so great that confidence in the monetary system is lost altogether, savings will actually drop to zero... If now income rises beyond the region of full employment, the slopes of the Curves, and therefore of the multiplier change. When the stage is reached at which, for a given increase in income, investment increases more than savings, the process becomes 'explosive'... Machines could be designed by a competent engineer (but not by me!) to deal with far more complex price effects than this, if economists could agree on what they wanted to happen.

In fact, what can be termed 'the theoretical Phillips curve' was, as Phillips related, an extension of the unfinished research program that emanated from his 'Machine' (Yamey, 2000). Early on, Phillips (CW 2000 [1954], 187) had criticised Michel Kalecki's *Theory of Economic Dynamics* (1954) for attaching 'no causal significance ... to price movements'. The opening sentence of the theoretical Phillips Curve (CW 2000 [1954], 134) addressed Robertson's letter: the method of

> comparative statics ... does not provide a very firm basis for policy recommendations [because] the time path of income, production and employment during the process of adjustment is not revealed. It is quite possible that certain types of policy may give rise to undesired fluctuations, or even cause a previously stable system to become unstable, although the final equilibrium position as shown by a static analysis appears to be quite satisfactory. Secondly, the effects of variations in prices and interest rates cannot be dealt with adequately with the simple multiplier models which usually form the basis of the analysis.

Thus Phillips' academic career was, from the start, associated with the attempt to explain the instabilities and discontinuities associated with rising prices. As David Vines (2000) put it in his discussion of the 'Phillips tradition', there is 'more in the Machine ... than is allowed for in macroeconomic conventional wisdom'.

Phillips enrolled for a PhD under James Meade. His LSE colleagues turned to him for assistance with the analysis of inflationary expectations. Henry Phelps Brown, for example, acknowledged a specific debt to Phillips for 'the form of the argument' about inflationary expectations and profit expectations – the situation where

> the price level itself is taking the initiative, and moving under the influence of a preponderant expectation about the likelihood and feasibility of rises and falls in product prices, which has itself been built up by such factors as changes in ... 'the market environment' ... [which impart] a gentle but continuing motion to the price level.
>
> (Phelps Brown and Weber, 1953, 279)

In recognition for his contribution to macroeconomic analysis (including presumably the analysis of inflationary expectations), Friedman (1955, no specific date) wrote to offer Phillips a visiting position in

Chicago: 'I only know how stimulating I would myself find it to have you around for a year; and I venture to believe that the change in environment might be stimulating to you as well.' Friedman hoped that Phillips would teach a course in economic fluctuations and added that the theoretical Phillips Curve (CW 2000 [1954], Chapter 16) was

> a stimulating prologue. The difficulty is that it could be a prologue to a number of different lines of work and I am led to wonder which of these you are in the process of pursuing. This is highly relevant from the point of view of its possible relation to various research undertakings in process here.

In a letter to Friedman (22 January 1955), Phillips declined on the grounds that he hoped to get 'a small group together under Professor Kendall, to review the problems involved in obtaining better empirical knowledge of behaviour responses'. It was Kendall who edited the volume in which Phillips first outlined his econometric policy evaluation critique.

Friedman tried to recruit Phillips again in 1960. In his answer to Friedman, Phillips (25 January 1961) once again declined. He wrote,

> The reason is that the theoretical work I have been doing over the last three or four years on dynamic processes and statistical estimation still progressing and absorbing most of my energy and I have been forced to realise that I cannot do this intensive theoretical work alongside anything substantial in the way of empirical research. It will probably take another three or four years to push the theoretical work as far as I am capable of doing and I hope then to use it to get to grips with real problems in the way you are doing. I should like to do the two types of work together but physical and mental limitations prevent it, so I had better clear up what I can in the one field before having a try at the other.

Phillips described Chicago as a 'notable ... centre of empirical research in economics', which Friedman, in his reply (14 February 1961), appeared to take exception to: 'Heaven preserve us if Chicago should not offer as hospitable an environment for theoretical as to empirical research, and conversely.'

One of the reasons that Friedman was keen to recruit Phillips was that Friedman had just launched his Workshop in Money and Banking (1953), and Phillips had just solved a problem for Friedman concerning the analysis of inflationary expectations. At least one of the economists – pivotal to the second-generation Chicago School – had previously despaired of the theory of expectations. In a review of Albert Hart's *Antici-pations, Uncertainty and Dynamic Planning*, George Stigler (1941, 358–359) referred to expectations as 'the promised land to some economists and a mirage to others. The reviewer must admit that he leans towards the latter view: much of the literature on expectations consists of obvious and uninformative generalisations of static analysis.' With respect to 'the revision of anticipations... progress depends much more on the accu-mulation of data (of a type almost impossible to collect!) than on an increase in the versatility of our technical apparatus'. Friedman himself (1953 [1946], 277–300) had attacked Oskar Lange on similar grounds:

> An example of a classification that has no direct empirical counterpart is Lange's classification of monetary changes... An explicit monetary policy aimed at achieving a neutral (or positive or negative) mone-tary effect would be exceedingly complicated, would involve action especially adapted to the particular disequilibrium to be corrected, and would involve knowledge about price expectations, that even in principle, let alone in practice, would be utterly unattainable.

Robbins invited Friedman to deliver two lectures at the LSE on 1 and 6 May 1952 assuring him that 'I think you find that there are so many people here who have questions to put to you that if you are will-ing to sit about and talk you'll never find any difficulty in filling the rest of your days' (4 March 1952). Friedman (correspondence to one of the authors, 25 August 1993) had questions to ask as well, raising with Phillips the question of 'how to approximate expectations about future inflation'. Phillips then wrote down the adaptive inflationary expecta-tions equation, which would later transform macroeconomics. At the time, economists were in no doubt about Phillips' implicit assumption about inflation: 'Implicitly [emphasis added], Phillips wrote his article for a world in which everyone anticipated that nominal prices would be stable' (Friedman, 1968a, 8). Friedman (correspondence to one of the authors 25 August 1993) explained that 'the "implicitly" is really needed... Phillips himself understood that his analysis depended on a particular state of expectations about inflation... Phillips' (CW 2000 [1954], Chapter 16) *Economic Journal* article made a very real impres-sion on me. However, his discussion of inflationary expectations in that article is very succinct.'

In 1952 Friedman returned to Chicago, where he provided Phillip Cagan with the adaptive inflationary expectations formula. Cagan (1956), Mark Nerlove (1958, 231) and Arrow and Nerlove (1958, 299) used this formula to transform economic analysis. This formula is generally known as the Friedman–Phelps formula; but Cagan (2000) calls it 'Phillips' Adaptive Expectations Formula'. It was this formula that Friedman (1956, 19–20) predicted would transform whole sections of economics: Cagan's

> device for estimating expected rates of change of prices from actual rates of change, which works so well for his data, can be carried over to other variables as well and is likely to be important in fields other than money. I have already used it to estimate 'expected income' as a determinant of consumption (Friedman, 1957) and Gary Becker has experimented with using this 'expected income' series in a demand function for money....

The final and most crucial subsections of Phillips' stabilisation model (CW 2000 [1954], 153–157) were 'Inherent Regulations of the System' and 'Stabilisation of the System', which began like this: 'Some examples will be given below to illustrate the stability of this system under different conditions of price flexibility *and with different expectations concerning future price changes*' [emphasis added]. The theoretical Phillips Curve was then tested against a variety of scenarios: inflationary expectations being a crucial factor in determining whether the system has satisfactory outcomes or not:

> Demand is also likely to be influenced by the rate at which prices are changing, or have been changing in the recent past, as distinct from the amount by which they have changed, this influence on demand being greater, the greater the rate of change of prices...The direction of this change in demand will depend on expectations about future price changes. If changing prices induce expectations of further changes in the same direction, as will probably be the case after fairly rapid and prolonged movements, demand will change in the same direction as the changing prices...there will be a positive feed-back tending to intensify the error, the response of demand to changing prices thus acting as a perverse or destabilising mechanism of the proportional type.

Even if Phillips saw inflationary expectations as destabilising aggregate demand alone, this by itself would destroy the possibility of a stable trade-off because the expectation of further inflation 'tend[s] to introduce fluctuations':

> The strength of the integral regulating mechanisms increases with the increasing degree of price flexibility, while the total strength of the proportional regulating mechanisms decreases as demand responds perversely to the more rapid rate of change of prices, and both these effects tend to introduce fluctuations when price flexibility is increased beyond a certain point. When price expectations operate in this way, therefore, the system...becomes unstable... (CW 2000 [1954], 155).

Phillips' path-breaking contributions caught his contemporaries unaware: his work is a precursor to at least one expectations research project. Charles Holt, together with Franco Modigliani, John Muth and Herbert Simon, was working along similar lines to Phillips (Holt *et al.*, 1960). When Merton Miller left the LSE and joined the Carnegie Institute of Technology, he prompted Holt to contact Phillips. Holt (2000) subsequently spent 18 months working with Phillips at the LSE. The visit had been prompted by some correspondence:

> Many useful techniques have been developed in Electrical Engineering and the field of Automatic Control which could profitably be translated into the field of Economics. Since prior to coming into Economics my background was in the fore mentioned fields, I was interested in doing this job. However, in many instances you have anticipated me and thus saved me the trouble (Holt to Phillips, 6 July 1956).

Phillips (15 October 1956) replied to Holt:

> Your work on the control of inventories and production by individual firms and the relation between these decisions and aggregate economic relationships seems to me of major importance. I have very much neglected these matters so far in my own work and concentrated on the sort of problem that would face a central bank or other regulating authority in attempting to control the aggregates in a system. I think this is justified in the early stages of an investigation and we are, I feel sure, only at the beginning of systematic

research work in this field, but it will certainly be necessary to develop the analysis of the relation between micro- and macro-economic relationships.

Phillips did not go on to provide these microeconomic foundations, but the Phelps (1970) volume was a continuation – not a critique – of Phillips' research agenda.

In the early 1960s, Phillips spent six months at the University of Wisconsin with Holt. Phillips' (CW 2000 [1962], 218) policy proposal was to locate the economy in the low or zero 'compromise' zone, while 'trying to shift the relation' inwards through labour market reform. Thereafter he worked 'on the central theoretical problems' of the Ford Foundation–funded 'Project on Dynamic Process Analysis' (May 1956–April 1963). The objective was to specify and estimate models for the control of economic systems. In this period, he presented some empirical illustrations of his stabilisation proposals, while continuing to pursue the matter theoretically. The theoretical Phillips Curve was published in June 1954; in the three years to June 1957, Phillips became familiar with the Nyquist stability criterion and experimented with electronic simulations of stabilisation proposals using equipment at the National Physical Laboratory (NPL) and Short Brothers and Harland Ltd. From about 1952, Phillips interacted with Richard Tizard at the NPL; and, in 1956, Tizard resigned as Head of the NPL Control Mechanisms and Electronics Division to take up a two-year Fellowship at the LSE to work full-time with Phillips (Swade, 2000). These collaborations led Phillips (CW 2000 [1957], 169) to conclude that 'the problem of stabilisation is more complex than appeared to be the case'. An empirical agenda was needed: 'improved methods should be developed for estimating quantitatively the magnitudes and time-forms of economic relationships in order that the range of permissible hypotheses may be restricted more closely than is at present possible'. It seems likely that around June 1957, he began to work on the first empirical Phillips Curve (CW 2000 [1958], Chapter 25).

Having pioneered the destabilising effects of inflationary expectations, Phillips provided very little discussion of this topic in his 1958 empirical curve. His second explanatory variable (the rate of change of unemployment) in Phillips' (CW 2000 [1958], 243) model influenced wage changes through the expectation that the business cycle will continue moving upwards (or downwards). Lipsey (1960, 20) labelled this 'an expectation effect...the reaction of *expectations* [emphasis in text], and hence of competitive bidding, to changes in u'. But there is no systematic analysis of inflationary expectations. It is possible that Phillips instructed

Friedman, Phelps Brown and others how to model adaptive inflation-ary expectations in their empirical work, but decided to ignore it on his own. An alternative explanation is that Phillips was primarily interested in the low inflation 'compromise' zone, where inflationary expectations are not a dominating force.

There is a distinct continuity between the 1954 theoretical Phillips Curve, the 1958, 1959 and 1962 empirical Phillips Curves and his growth model. In a 'Simple Model of Employment, Money and Prices in a Growing Economy', Phillips (CW 2000 [1961], 201–202) described his inflation equation as being 'in accordance with an obvious extension of the classical quantity theory of money, applied to the growth equi-librium path of a steadily expanding economy'. His steady state rate of interest, *rs* ('the real rate of interest in Fisher's sense, i.e., as the money rate of interest minus the expected rate of change of the price level'), was also 'independent of the absolute quantity of money, again in accor-dance with classical theory'. His interest rate function was 'only suitable for a limited range of variation of *YP/M*'. With exchange rate fixity the domestic money supply (and hence the inflation rate) become endoge-nously determined; the trade-off operates only within a narrow low inflation band.

This was exactly how Phillips (CW 2000 [1961], 201) described the limits of his model: he was only 'interested' in ranges of values in which actual output (*Y*) fluctuates around capacity output (*Yn*) by a maximum of five per cent:

> In order to reduce the model with money, interest and prices to linear differential equations in x [$= Y/Y_n$], *yn* and *p* it is necessary to express log Y ... in terms of log Y_n and x. For this purpose we shall use the approximation
>
> $$\log Y \cong \log Y_n + (Y - Y_n)/Y_n$$
> $$= \log Y_n + x - 1$$
>
> The approximation is very good over the range of values of $(Y - Y_n)/Y_n$, say from -0.05 to 0.05, *in which we are interested* [emphasis added].

Since Phillips (CW 2000 [1961], 196) stated that these output fluctu-ations were 'five times as large as the corresponding fluctuations in the proportion of the labour force employed', this clearly indicates that Phillips limited his analysis to outcomes in the compromise zone of plus or minus one percentage point deviations of unemployment from normal capacity output. Phillips was restating the conclusion of his empirical work; normal capacity output (and approximately zero inflation) was consistent with an unemployment rate 'a little under $2^1/_2$ per cent' (CW 2000 [1958], 259).

Although Phillips drew an average curve representing the trajectory of the British economy as it swung from bust to boom and back again, at no stage did he suggest that *high* inflation would reduce unemployment for anything other than a temporary period. Yet Phillips' historical investigations had produced an average curve that encompassed 32 per cent wage inflation and 22 per cent unemployment (CW 2000 [1958], 253, Fig. 25.9). Wage inflation in excess of 27 per cent occurred in 1918 and this observation falls on Phillips' Curve. But Phillips' empirical analysis also reveals that 1918 was followed by two decades of extraordinarily high unemployment – hardly an augury of a stable high inflation trade-off. Phillips did not state or imply that any point on his average curve could be targeted for stabilisation purposes.

But underpinning the original Phillips Curve was the argument that 'One of the important policy problems of our time is that of maintaining a high level of economic activity and employment *while avoiding a continual rise in prices*' [emphasis added]. Phillips explained that there was 'fairly general agreement' that the prevailing rate of 3.7 per cent inflation was 'undesirable. It has undoubtedly been a major cause of the general weakness of the balance of payments and the foreign reserves, and if continued it would almost certainly make the present rate of exchange untenable.' His objective was, if possible,

> to prevent continually rising prices of consumer goods while maintaining high levels of economic activity... the problem therefore reduces to whether it is possible to prevent the price of labour services, that is average money earnings per man-hour, from rising at more than about 2 per cent per year... one of the main purposes of this analysis is to consider what levels of demand for labour the monetary and fiscal authorities should seek to maintain in their attempt to reconcile the two main policy objectives of high levels of activity and stable prices. I would question whether it is really in the interests of workers that the average level of hourly earnings should increase more rapidly than the average rate of productivity, say about 2 per cent per year.
>
> (CW 2000 [1959], 261, 269–280; [1962], 208; [1961], 201; [1962], 218; [1958], 259)

Like Phillips, Friedman (1968a, 9–11) described the initial expansionary effects of a reduction in unemployment. But when inflation became high enough to influence expectational behaviour, Friedman later argued that expansion 'describes only the initial effects'. Modern macroeconomics has several explanations for the existence of a temporary trade-off (involving monetary misperceptions and intertemporal substitution). Friedman's version of the Phillips–Friedman–Phelps Critique suggested a temporary trade-off between unanticipated inflation and unemployment lasting 'two to five years', taking 'a couple of decades' to return to the natural rate of unemployment. Friedman's mechanism involved real wage resistance in response to the initial 'simultaneous fall *ex post* in real wages to employers and rise *ex ante* in real wages to employees'. Thus real wage resistance plays an equilibrating role in Friedman's version.

Unlike Friedman, Phillips was highly sceptical about equilibrating forces. In a Robbins seminar paper on 'Stability of "Self-Correcting" Systems' (21st May 1957) Phillips examined a system in which the rate of change of prices was proportional to excess demand. Phillips concluded that 'If the "equilibrating forces" are too strong they will make the system unstable...The argument extends without difficulty to any system, in which there are "equilibrating" or "self-correcting" forces operating through time lags.'

Phillips' version of the Phillips–Friedman–Phelps Critique was a far more potent constraint on policy makers than Friedman's version: inflation had far more serious consequences for Phillips than for Friedman. For Friedman, the (purely internal) imbalance corrected itself through utility maximising labour supply adjustments, as inflation ceased to be incorrectly anticipated. Only a temporary boom would result, and would soon be eroded by real wage resistance. But in Phillips' model, external imbalance (driven by only minor inflation differentials) could be addressed by exchange rate adjustment, leaving the internal imbalance in need of still greater attention. In addition, the role Friedman allocated to inflationary expectation was benign, whereas the role allocated to inflationary expectations by Phillips (CW 2000 [1954]) was far more destabilising, denying the possibility of a stable target in the presence of such expectations.

Not only was there 'fairly general agreement' (Phillips, CW 2000 [1962], 207–208) that non-trivial (3.7 per cent) inflation was intolerable, but the assumption of low (but unspecified) and stable inflation rates was commonly invoked by model builders in the pre-stagflation era. For example, the Lucas and Rapping (1969, 748) model of 'Real Wages, Employment and Inflation' was assumed to hold 'only under reasonably stable rates of price increase. To define what is meant by reasonable stability, and to discover how expectations are revised when such stability ceases to obtain, seems to us to be a crucial, unresolved problem.' Friedman (1968a, 6; 1968b, 21) also stated that the 'price expectation effect is slow to develop and also slow to disappear. Fisher estimated that it took several decades for a full adjustment and recent work is consistent with his estimate.' Friedman presented evidence about the time it took for 'price anticipations' to influence behaviour that was 'wholly consistent with Fisher's'. Phillips' opposition to inflation was axiomatic: an expression of one of the eternal truths that separate economists from monetary cranks. Nevertheless, he clearly stated the assumptions under which small amounts of inflation could be traded off for small amounts of unemployment in the 'compromise' zone. He did not suggest that a permanent trade-off existed outside the 'compromise' zone.

In the 1950s, Philips was aware of an explicit examination of the process by which inflationary expectations shifts a 'Phillips curve'. John Black (1959, 145, n1), the author of an article in *Economica* (of which Phillips was a co-editor) on 'Inflation and Long-Run Growth', thanked Phillips for 'comments and suggestions'. Black (1959, 147–150) apologised for being 'unable to think of any other name' (other than aggregate supply curve) for his function relating the 'behaviour of prices over time which will result from any given level of employment'. Black's 'Phillips curve' was a rectangular hyperbola with full employment as one asymptote and a deflationary floor as the other. The location of Black's 'Phillips curve' was dependent on three parameters: first, A, the size of the rectangle linking the curve to the asymptotes, which was determined by (among other factors) the 'strength or weakness of general fears of inflation'; second, I, an investment function; and third, P,

> the price expectations function, which relates vertical shifts in the aggregate supply curve to the price changes experienced by price and wage setters in recent periods... the position of the supply curve can be made to shift vertically in a way determined by the rate of change of the price level over some past period. This implies that as both buyers and sellers get attuned to regarding a given rate of increase of prices as normal, and come to expect it to continue, the whole supply curve shifts upwards... The position of the aggregate supply schedule in any period, however, will itself reflect the effects of earlier price changes on price expectations... the adverse effect on the level of output at any time via the upward shift in the schedule due to price increases in earlier periods.

The possibilities for growth depended on the empirical size of the lags, including 'the lags in the effects of current price changes on price expectations'.

Phillips was also aware of Bent Hansen's *A Study in the Theory of Inflation* and recommended the text to Lipsey: 'Bill first put me on to this source and I came to accept this view of the Phillips curve as being a Hansen-type reaction curve for the labour market' (correspondence from Lipsey to one of the authors, 19 February 1993). Hansen (1951, 139, 249) offered the 'explicit inclusion of disequilibrium in the labour market in the analysis' and also discussed the relationship between inflation and the supply side: 'during inflation quite drastic changes in productivity'. He also analysed expectations. In 'Final Remarks', Hansen (1951, 246–248) concluded that

> ...price expectations do disturb the analysis in so far as they can render the price-reaction equations unusable... it is clear that in practical forecasting, price expectations and their changes are a difficulty of the first order, and that a policy which aims to maintain monetary equilibrium is forced to accord a great deal of weight to holding expectations in check.

Thus, orthodoxy continued to allow an important role for expectations. For example, in their seminal extension of Phillips' analysis, Samuelson and Solow (1960, 189, 193) entertained the possibility that a switch in policy regime might alter the shape of the Phillips Curve. They also allowed for a vague and loosely defined role for expectations: policies producing 'low pressure of demand could so act upon wages and other expectations so as to shift the curve downwards in the long run'. Alternatively, this might increase structural unemployment, shifting the menu of choice upwards. The expectation of a continuation of full employment, they believed, might have been responsible for an upward shift in their Phillips Curve in the 1940s and 1950s. Samuelson and Solow were not ignorant of inflationary expectations; neither did they believe it was policy invariant. For example, in December 1965, Samuelson acknowledged that targeting a point on a Phillips Curve could shift the curve itself: 'One ought to admit that the overausterity of the Eisenhower Administration may have done something to give America a better Phillips curve' (cited by Haberler, 1966, 130).

Inflationary expectations played an important role in Phillips' dynamic stabilisation exercise; the archival evidence reinforces this conclusion. The narrow inflation–unemployment trade-off that implicitly underlies current inflation-targeting regimes corresponds to the narrow compromise trade-off section of his curve in *'which we are interested'* [emphasis added] (CW 2000 [1961], 201). Targeting low inflation (typically between 1 and 3 per cent) is a 'better Phillips curve' than those curves which alluded to the possibility of outcomes outside this low inflation zone of 'interest'. The lack of interest in the dynamics of knowledge creation and destruction has allowed economists to be led by the nose into believing an expectational story of mythical proportions.

Acknowledgements

We are grateful to the late Milton Friedman for allowing his correspondence to be cited, and to the literary executors for permission to cite from correspondence between Dennis Robertson and A. W. H. Phillips.

Bibliography

Ackerlof, G. 1982. A Personal Tribute and a Few Recollections. In Feiwel Ed., Samuelson and Neoclassical Economics. Boston: Kluwer.

Arrow, K. J. and Nerlove, M. 1958. A Note on Expectations and Stability. *Econometrica* 26: 297–305.

Barr, N. 2000. The History of the Phillips Machine. In Leeson Ed.

Black, J. 1959. Inflation and Long Run Growth. *Economica* May, 26: 145–153.

Boulding, K. 1948. *Economic Analysis.* New York: Harper Brothers.

Bradley, P. D. Ed. 1959. *The Public Stake in Union Power.* Richmond: University of Virginia Press.

Cagan, P. 1956. The Monetary Dynamics of Hyperinflation. In Friedman Ed.

—— 2000. Phillips' Adaptive Expectations Formula. In Leeson Ed.

Committee for Economic Development. 1958. *Problems of United States Economic Development.* New York: CED.

Court, R. 2000. The Lucas Critique. Did Phillips Make a Comparable Contribution? In Leeson Ed.

Croome, D. R. and Johnson, H. G. Eds. 1970. *Money in Britain 1959–1969.* London: Oxford University Press.

Cross, R. Ed. 1988. *Unemployment, Hysteresis and the Natural Rate Hypothesis.* Oxford: Blackwell.

Cross, R. and Allan, A. 1988. On the History of Hysteresis. In Cross Ed.

Dorrance, G. 2000. Early Reactions to Mark 1 and 11. In Leeson Ed.

Feiwel, G. R. Ed. 1982. *Samuelson and Neoclassical Economics.* Boston: Kluwer.

Fellner, W. 1959. Demand Inflation, Cost Inflation and Collective Bargaining. In Bradley Ed.

Fellner, W., Machlup, F. and Triffin, R. Eds. 1966. *Maintaining and Restoring Balance in International Payments.* Princeton: Princeton University Press.

Friedman, M. 1950. Wesley C. Mitchell as an Economic Theorist. *Journal of Political Economy* December LVII (6): 465–493.

—— 1953. *Essays in Positive Economics.* Chicago: University of Chicago Press.

—— Ed. 1956. *Studies in the Quantity Theory of Money*. Chicago: University of Chicago Press.

——1957. *A Theory of the Consumption Function*. Princeton: Princeton UP.

——1958. The Supply of Money and Changes in Prices and Output. In Lehman, Ed.

——1962. *Price Theory: A Provisional Text*. Chicago: Aldine.

——1966. What Price Guideposts? In Schultz and Aliber Eds.

——1968a. The Role of Monetary Policy. *American Economic Review* May, 58: 1–17.

——1968b. Factors Affecting the Level of Interest Rates. In Jacob and Pratt Eds.

——1976. *Price Theory*. Chicago: Aldine.

——1977. Inflation and Unemployment: Nobel Lecture. *Journal of Political Economy* 85(3): 451–472.

Haberler, G. 1958. Creeping Inflation Resulting from Wage Increases in Excess of Productivity. In Committee for Economic Development.

Haberler, G. 1961. *Inflation: Its Causes and Cures*. Washington: American Enterprise Association.

—— 1966. Adjustment, Employment and Growth. In Fellner, Machlup and Triffin Eds.

Hansen, A. H. 1964. *Business Cycles and National Income*. Norton: New York.

Hansen, B. 1951. *A Study in the Theory of Inflation*. London: George Allen and Unwin.

Hayek, F. 1958. Inflation Resulting from Downward Inflexibility of Wages. In Committee For Economic Development.

——1972. A Tiger by the Tail. London: IEA.

Holt, C. C. 2000. Interactions with a Fellow Engineer-Economist. In Leeson Ed.

Holt, C. C., Modigliani, F., Muth, J. F. and Simon, H. 1960. *Planning Production, Inventories and Work Force*. Englewood Cliffs: Prentice-Hall.

Holt, C. C., MacRae, D., Schweitzer, S. and Smith, R. 1971. *The Inflation-Unemployment Dilemma: A Manpower Solution*. New York: Urban Institute.

Hood, W. C. and Koopmans, T. G. Eds. 1953. *Studies in Econometric Method*. Cowles Commission monograph 14. New York: Wiley.

Jacob, D. P. and Pratt, R. T. Eds. 1968. *Savings and Residential Financing*. US Savings and Loan League: Chicago.

Johnson, H. G. 1970. Recent Developments in Monetary Theory – A Commentary. In Croome and Johnson Eds.

Kalecki, M. 1954. *Theory of Economic Dynamics*. London: George Allen and Unwin.

Kendal, M. Ed. 1968. *Mathematical Model Building in Economics and Industry*. London: Charles Griffin.

Klamer, A. Ed. 1984. *Conversations with Economists*. New Jersey: Rowman and Allanheld.

Knight, F. 1921. *Risk, Uncertainty and Profit*. Boston: Houghton-Mifflin.

Leeson, R. 2000. A Remarkable Life. In Leeson Ed.

Leeson, R. Ed. 2000. *A. W. H. Phillips: Collected Works in Contemporary Perspective*. Cambridge: Cambridge University Press.

—— forthcoming. *The Political Economy of the Inflation Unemployment Trade-Off*. Cambridge: Cambridge University Press.

Lehman, J. Ed. 1958. *The Relationship of Prices to Economic Stability and Growth*. Papers Submitted before the Joint Economic Committee. Washington: USGPO.

Lipsey, R. G. 1960. The Relation Between Unemployment and the Rate of Change of Money Wage Rates in the United Kingdom 1862–1957: A Further Analysis. *Economica* February, 27: 456–487.

—— 1981. The Understanding of Control of Inflation: Is There a Crisis in Macro-Economics? *Canadian Journal of Economics* November, XIV (4): 545–576.

Lucas, R. E. 1973. Some International Evidence on Output-Inflation Trade-Offs. *American Economic Review* June, 63 (3): 326–334.

——1976. Econometric Policy Evaluation: A Critique. In Brunner and Meltzer Eds, *The Phillips Curve and Labor Market*. Amsterdam: North-Holland.

——1980. The Death of Keynesian Economics. *Issues and Ideas* Winter: 18–19.

——1981. Tobin and Monetarism: A Review Article. *Journal of Economic Literature* June, XIX: 558–567.

——1984. Robert E. Lucas, Jr. In Klamer Ed.

Lucas, R. E. and Sargent, T. 1978. After Keynesian Macroeconomics, and Response to Friedman. In *After the Phillips Curve: Persistence of High Inflation and High Unemployment*. Boston: Federal Reserve Bank of Boston.

Lucas, R. E and Rapping, L. A. 1969. Real Wages, Employment and Inflation. *Journal of Political Economy* October, 77 (5): 721–754.

Marschak, J. 1953. Economic Measurements for Policy and Prediction. In Hood and Koopmans Eds.

Meade, J. E. 2000. The Versatile Genius. In Leeson Ed.

Metzler, L. A. 1941. The Nature and Stability of Inventory Cycles. *Review of Economic Statistics* 23: 113–129.

Muth, J. 1961. Rational Expectations and the Theory of Price Movements. *Econometrica* 29: 315–335.

Nerlove, M. 1958. Adaptive Expectations and the Cobweb Phenomena. *Quarterly Journal of Economics* 72: 227–240.

Nerlove, M., Grether, D. M. and Caravalho, J. L. 1979. *Analysis of Economic Time Series: A Synthesis*. New York: Academic Press.

Phelps Brown, E. H. and Weber, B. 1953. Accumulation, Productivity and Distribution in the British Economy 1870–1938. *Economic Journal* June, 63: 263–288.

Phelps, E. S. 1967. Phillips Curves, Expectations of Inflation and Optimal Unemployment Over Time. *Economica* August, 34: 254–281.

——1968. Money Wage Dynamics and Labor Market Equilibrium. *Journal of Political Economy* July–August, 76: 678–711.

——Ed. 1970. *Microeconomic Foundations of Employment and Inflation Theory*. London: Norton.

Phillips, P. 2000. The Bill Phillips Legacy of Continuous Time Modelling and Econometric Model Design. In Leeson Ed.

Rees, A. 1970. The Phillips Curve as a Menu of Policy Choice. *Economica* August, 37: 223–238.

Rousseas, S. W. Ed. 1968. *Inflation: Its Causes, Consequences and Control*. Calvin K. Kazanjian Economics Foundation: Wilton, Connecticut.

Samuelson, P. A. and Solow, R. 1960. Analytical Aspects of Anti Inflation Policy. *American Economic Review* May, 50: 177–204.

Sargent, T. 1996. Expectations and the nonneutrality of Lucas. *Journal of Monetary Economics* 37: 553–548.

Saulnier, R. J. 1963. *The Strategy of Economic Policy*. New York: Fordham UP.

Schultz, G. P. and Aliber, R. Z. Eds. 1966. *Guidelines: Informal Controls and the Market Place*. Chicago: University of Chicago Press.

Solow, R. 1968. Recent Controversy on the Theory of Inflation: An Eclectic View. In Rousseas Ed.

—— 1978. Summary and Evaluation. In *After the Phillips Curve: Persistence of High Inflation and High Unemployment*. Boston: Federal Reserve Bank of Boston.

Stone, J. R. N. 1968. Economic and Social Modelling. In Kendal Ed.

Stigler, G. 1941. Review of Hart's *Anticipations, Uncertainty and Dynamic Planning*. *American Economic Review* June, 31: 358–359.

Swade, D. 2000. The Phillips Machine and the History of Computing. In Leeson Ed.

Tinbergen, J. 1956. *Economic Policy: Principles and Design*. Amsterdam: North Holland.

Tobin, J. 1968. Discussion. In Rousseas Ed.

Tobin, J. 1972. Inflation and Unemployment. *American Economic Review* March, 62 (1): 1–18.

Vines, D. 2000. The Phillips Machine as a Progressive Model. In Leeson Ed.

von Mises 1974. *Planning for Freedom*. Illinois: Libertarian Press.

Wold, H. O. and Jureen, L. 1953. *Demand Analysis*. John Wiley: New York.

Wold, H. O. 1968. Model Building and Scientific Method: A Graphical Introduction. In Kendal Ed.

Yamey, B. 2000. The Famous Phillips Curve Article: A Note on its Publication. In Leeson Ed.

8
From Fixed to Floating Rates: The British Experience, 1960–1972

Michael J. Oliver

Introduction

The Bretton Woods pegged exchange-rate regime, generally dated 1946–1971/1972, has often been seen as the standard with which to judge all other monetary systems. The system is revered largely because it is thought to have brought stability to the international monetary system after the interwar problems of confidence, liquidity and adjustment. One of the central tenets of Bretton Woods, and one which its many supporters would single out as the sine qua non, was the system of fixed but adjustable exchange rates, administered by the International Monetary Fund (IMF).

The exchange-rate system was enshrined in Article IV of the Articles of Agreement of the IMF. Every member country of the IMF was expected to establish a par value for its currency and to maintain it within a 1 per cent margin on either side of the declared par value. Although currencies were treated equally in the articles, Article IV defined the linchpin of the system as either gold or the US dollar (the fixed price of gold was $35 per ounce). As the United States was the only country that pegged its currency in terms of gold, all other countries would fix their parities in terms of dollars and would intervene to monitor their exchange rates within 1 per cent of parity with the dollar.

The IMF frowned upon floating exchange rates and the majority of countries favoured fixed rates to floating. This stemmed from their experience on the international economy during the interwar years, which in turn had been fuelled by a League of Nations report written by Nurkse (League of Nations, 1944). In essence, this was based on the perception that 'departures from the gold standard occurred in the face of serious speculative attacks, that devaluations were almost always accompanied

113

by capital flight, and the French experience with floating as a free-fall' (Bordo and James, 2002, p. 172). Whether or not the Nurkse report on the evils of floating exchange rates is true (and as others have argued quite persuasively, it probably is not), it did cause a fear of floating in European policy-making circles, which still persists today (Endres and Fleming, 2002; Haberler, 1985; James, 2001, pp. 167–96).

Over the past 15 years, work by economists and economic historians has begun to question the assumptions which have underpinned the Bretton Woods system, but the full story of how each country managed its exchange-rate policy under Bretton Woods has yet to be told through the use of archival documents (Bordo and Eichengreen, 1993; Toniolo, 2005). In the case of sterling, one of the key currencies in Bretton Woods, there have been a number of works that have used primary sources to look at the inconvertible period of the 1940s and 1950s but the period between convertibility and the float of sterling has had far less attention based on archival sources (Burnham, 2003; Cairncross, 1985; Cairncross and Watts, 1989). Burnham (2003, p. 181) briefly summarises what we have known about the 1960s until recently: 'the decade began with rumours about the adoption of floating rates and ended, of course, with devaluation and bizarre contingency measures known as Operation Brutus'.[1] The insights from the archives provide a lot more information, and the focus of this chapter is on how the monetary authorities – the Treasury and the Bank of England (the Bank) – moved from a fixed to a floating exchange rate between 1960 and 1972.

To examine this period, the chapter is divided into two. The first part examines the period leading up to the devaluation of sterling in November 1967, when the $2.80 sterling parity, which had been set in 1949, was abandoned. During the pre-devaluation period, the Treasury and the Bank were firmly committed to fixed rates and hostile to floating rates. The first section of the chapter examines the arguments about the pros and cons of floating in the contingency planning undertaken for devaluation and considers why the policy makers and the politicians did not wish to float the pound. The second section of the chapter examines the gradual change in the attitude of the authorities to currency management after devaluation, which was prompted by the growing tensions in the international monetary system. As Harold James noted, between 1971 and 1974 the entire international community was pushed towards floating 'not so much because this was an agreed solution, but because it emerged out of a failure to produce an agreed solution' (James, 1996, p. 213). As this chapter shows, this was never more true than in the case of the United Kingdom.

Pre-1967

The position of the Bank towards floating rates at the start of the 1960s is nicely captured in a Treasury note, which is part of a sequence discussing the IMF's intention to persuade member countries to eliminate quantitative restrictions and multiple currency practices in the move to Article VIII status. In 1960, the IMF Staff proposed that a number of countries should adopt a fluctuating rate as a halfway house as they moved towards freedom from restrictions and a fixed rate of exchange. The Bank was not happy about this suggestion. As Symons from the Treasury observed, the Bank feared that 'the floating rate is becoming a too familiar system and that the strictness of Article IV may become permanently weakened'.[2] Symons expressed some misgivings about the Bank or the Treasury adopting too rigid a stance, recognising that only a few years had passed when both institutions were at one in agreeing that if pressure were brought to bear on sterling, the pound would have to float. In short, he asked, 'is it inconceivable that such circumstances should recur, and if they did should we not regret an over-zealous initiative now?'[3] There seemed to be some agreement with Symons' assessment in the Treasury.[4] However, a year later, when the Bank submitted a paper on floating rates to the Treasury another official commented on the Bank's 'rather over-dogmatic style' towards floating, and the paper was redrafted.[5]

If it appeared that some mild disagreement had emerged since a joint Bank/Treasury paper on floating exchange rates in 1958 (Fforde, 1992, p. 589), by April 1964 the Bank seemed to be in general agreement with the Treasury's position on devaluation and floating which had been written in a 1963 paper. Maurice Parsons from the Bank remarked that 'the conclusions reached...are pretty much in accordance with our views', although he added that some of the argument 'is a little lame'.[6] What particularly concerned the Bank was any concession by the Treasury to the possibility of devaluation. If such a policy was considered as a necessity it should be regarded as a 'confession of ineptitude and irresponsibility' and the Treasury also needed to rethink the 'strange concept' that the impact of a world recession on the UK balance of payments could be corrected by a devaluation of sterling.[7]

During the summer of 1964 the Bank and Treasury worked with the Board of Trade under the chairmanship of the Permanent Secretary of the Treasury, Sir William Armstrong, to consider the longer-term trend of the balance of payments. There was little in the final report about devaluation but Sir Alec Cairncross, Director of the Economic Section, had written a paper on devaluation to accompany the final report in case ministers asked more detailed questions. The initial draft of the paper in June caused the Bank some problems and the Deputy Governor noted that it was 'not a happy effort', but by the time it was revised in August he conceded that it was probably as 'satisfactory as we could reasonably expect'.[8] The Governors were urged to accept the Cairncross paper by W M Allen, one of the Bank's advisers, and the Governor, Lord Cromer, noted how there had been a 'meeting of minds' between the two institutions.[9]

The Cairncross paper was later inserted into the briefing papers prepared for the incoming Labour administration along with a paper on floating exchange rates and a number of different options to reign in the expected £800 million balance of payments deficit.[10] The paper on devaluation began by recognising that devaluation was a drastic measure with far-reaching consequences, before listing the arguments against this 'act of desperation'.[11] These included the following: severely straining Britain's relations with other countries, particularly the sterling area, where the main holders of sterling would begin to withdraw their balances from London; threatening the stability of the international monetary system by throwing into question the practice of reserve currencies; and finally, provoking retaliatory measures in Western Europe and a 'scramble for gold' as the future of the dollar would be put into question. The paper went on to argue that even if the pound was not a key currency, and the United Kingdom's external liabilities were not as grim, there were grounds on which devaluation could be considered inappropriate and difficult to justify. In the final analysis, would devaluation fix Britain's competitive position in the long term?

The Treasury dismissed the case for floating exchange rates in six pages. The paper's criticisms were fourfold: the value of the pound was more likely to sink than float, and released from the fixed constraint, the authorities would be less willing to take action; fluctuating rates would create difficulties in trade and investment; the exchange rate would be determined by 'speculative views' which would be destabilising; and floating would break up the sterling area.[12]

The die had been cast and the two institutions charged with defending the parity had reaffirmed their commitment to defend the pound. On the political side, of the three ministers who took the decision not to devalue after taking office, the Prime Minister (Harold Wilson) and the Chancellor (James Callaghan) also shared the objections raised by the Bank and the Treasury, whilst George Brown, the First Secretary of State, had changed his mind by July 1965.[13] However, what is not as well known is the extent to which Harold Wilson vacillated over whether to float the pound during intense periods of downward pressure on sterling.

One of the interesting questions this raises is as to whether Wilson was serious about floating in this period or whether he was merely employing scare tactics to shock the Americans, the IMF and the wider international community into extending their credit lines to the United Kingdom. There is some evidence to suggest that the contingency planning which the Treasury and the Bank undertook in case of a devaluation, which did include papers on floating the pound, was viewed by Wilson and Callaghan merely as a technical exercise.[14] They were largely indifferent to many of the papers which were produced and did not share these with other members of the Cabinet or even the Ministerial Steering Committee on Economic Policy (SEP). It would also be accurate to say that there was no serious attempt made by the Labour Government to rethink the external strategy between 1964 and 1967 although there was some discussion on international liquidity.

What led to the political outbursts (albeit behind closed doors in Downing Street) with the attendant calls for floating and, occasionally, devaluation were the weaknesses of sterling over the period. The seeds for the first speculative attack on sterling were sown after the government publicised the £800 million deficit when it announced its balance of payments programme. This was followed by a neutral budget on 11 November which did not impress the city, precipitating a run on the pound.

Additional losses totalling £75 million on 24 November prompted Wilson to tell the Governor that he was 'coming to the conclusion' that an acceptable alternative to devaluation was to allow the pound to float.[15] The following day, the pressure on the reserves was more intense, and on this occasion Armstrong asked Robert Neild, one of the Treasury's economic advisers, to draft a paper on floating rates and devaluation.[16] Before any of the papers were discussed, Cromer managed to secure credits of $3 billion from other central banks, and at that point, devaluation became 'unmentionable' and the papers were destroyed (Cairncross, 1996, p. 105). Although calm was temporarily restored to the exchange market, big reserve losses from the 3rd December led Cairncross, Neild and MacDougall to write top-secret papers on the suggestion of William Armstrong. Only David Walker (Armstrong's Private Secretary) and Armstrong were to see the finished results.[17] The three advisers were asked to form preliminary views on the amount of any adjustment in the rate, the merits of fixed or floating rates, the question of compensation for overseas sterling holders and of possible guarantees against future exchange risks, and how changes could be made to the international monetary system if a change in parity occurred. Although the advisers discussed the papers between themselves, Armstrong did not discuss them nor did he suggest that further work should be undertaken. However, the areas the papers examined were later subjected to intense discussion through the committee which planned the devaluation.

The committee, known as the 'FU' Committee, was set up in March 1965, as Armstrong realised that ministers needed an alternative to re-fixing the parity if they were forced to devalue. There were a range of issues which the committee examined including the accompanying measures to devaluation, choosing the rate and guarantees for overseas holders of sterling, but what concerns us here is the discussions between the Treasury and the Bank on whether to re-fix or float the pound. The majority of the discussion on this issue occurred during 1965 although it was examined briefly in 1966 and 1967.

The Economic Section of the Treasury drafted a paper on the choice of a new fixed rate on 2 April (it suggested that the choice was between 10 and 15 per cent)[18] and Cairncross submitted a paper on floating rates the same day. Neither paper seems to have been discussed at the third meeting; instead, Robert Neild's paper on the merits of fixed and floating rates was considered. Neild was one of the most pro-floating of the economic advisers but he was asked by Armstrong to provide a paper that was impartial to either regime. In his first draft, 'Fixed or Flexible Rates', Neild's preference in the event of a devaluation was for a floating rate. If the rate fell below $2.40, support should be given 'but without any firm commitment to holding the rate at this or any other level'.[19] *Per contra*, Cairncross's antipathy towards floating is clear from his paper and he suggested that the arguments against floating were stronger than when he had drafted the General Briefing paper for the incoming government in October 1964.[20]

The tenor of the meeting seemed to be that to float from a position of weakness was a 'gamble which it was hard to contemplate taking'.[21] This position was adopted in the next draft of the paper, discussed at the fourth meeting on 13 April. Although the conclusion of the paper was acceptable to those present at the meeting, there was general agreement that the paper gave inadequate weight to the objections to a flexible rate.[22] Neild produced a revised draft on 26 April,[23] but it was not until the sixth meeting on 19 May that the conclusions were 'completely in accord with the views of the Group'.[24] The only remaining problem was that the underlying premise of the paper favoured flexible rates and it was felt necessary to add an 'official and impersonal' document, the drafting of which was handed to the Bank.

The minutes can once again give us a flavour of how the group received the first draft of the Bank's paper, 'Fixed and Flexible Rates'.[25] The group suggested that the paper needed more work to stress the case against flexible rates, the main argument being that it was impossible to have a floating rate and retain sterling's role as a reserve currency. Section 6 of the paper suggested that there could be a floor of \$2.40 and a ceiling of \$2.60 to the pound for an interim period although in the Bank's opinion even a temporary recourse to a floating exchange rate was not an attractive option. The Bank was concerned that flexibility with pre-announced limits would engender doubts as to whether the margins could be honoured and suggested that the economy would function more smoothly under fixed rates than it would under continuous movements in the exchange rate.[26]

The alternative to a pre-announced range was discussed, namely allowing the pound to float freely, which could be coupled to an announcement by the authorities to restore a fixed parity within a specified period.[27] One strong reason for unannounced target ranges was that it avoided the difficulty of selecting the right rates; wide margins suggested little confidence in sterling and with narrow margins the advantages of flexibility would disappear. This debate within the group was a very interesting development and marked a return to some of the ideas formed at the time of ROBOT (Burnham, 2003, Chapters 3 and 4). Armstrong ended the seventh meeting with a call for more discussion on free floating, and Jenkyns was instructed to prepare a further note on the consultations with the United States and IMF in respect of the London Gold Market if the United Kingdom were to adopt flexible rates.

In a subsequent discussion of the Bank's paper, Neild again returned to press the case for floating rates and argued for a temporary period of flexibility, without declared limits, but he did accept, however, that the option of a permanent system of flexible rates should not be put to ministers.[28] The group seems not to have been swayed by Neild's arguments. Specific objections were raised to his assertion that following a devaluation to \$2.50 or \$2.40 the pound would not fall below this level because speculators would begin to buy sterling on a considerable scale. This was considered 'an uncertain proposition' as it was more likely that speculators would only start buying sterling once the rate had fallen by an 'unacceptable large amount'. Holders of sterling were also more likely to withdraw funds from London under a floating regime and this would outweigh any inflow of funds on private account.[29] However, what really made the Bank's interim solution unviable was that it was extremely unlikely that there would be any international acceptance for a floating rate even if it was a temporary measure and 'there would be no point in canvassing in advance for support for it'.[30] In the light of this discussion, the general view of the meeting was that the paper needed to be redrafted so that ministers would not be given the option of flexible rates. Floating should be considered as a workable choice only if the reserves were at the point of exhaustion and then as a temporary measure, probably without prescribed limits.

Both the Bank's final paper and Neild's earlier paper (retained as a statement of his personal position) were inserted in a ministerial dossier and it seemed that the 'fix or float' issue had been settled. It was not to be. On 22 July 1965, another sterling crisis blew up that again opened the door for the floaters. At a meeting on 29 July, Armstrong informed the group that in the event of a devaluation the Prime Minister had a 'firm preference' for floating, the Chancellor 'veered towards it' but was not 'completely committed' and the First Secretary probably favoured a fixed rate, though the strength of his attachment was 'very uncertain'.[31] To this end, Neild had drafted another paper on fixed or floating rates on 22 July. Neild's paper is a far more feisty appeal to floating than his earlier revised paper of 26 April. He suggested that there was a powerful economic case for flexible rates that could be justified on the immediate needs of the United Kingdom and on long-term grounds 'that the world needs to break away from the present regime and dogma of rigid exchange rates'.[32] He asked whether ministers were ready to face and follow through this tough course of action, and if so, the United Kingdom would probably have to take an 'independent, defiant posture in the world, similar to that of de Gaulle'. His preference for a flexible rate would require 'skilful day-to-day manipulation' with a 'command structure'. This allowed Neild to take a swipe at the existing system of economic decision-making, the Troika, which was 'ill-suited' for a flexible rate. One minister should have responsibility for managing the exchange rate and 'that minister is bound to be the Chancellor [who] should make this a firm condition of adopting a flexible rate'. Neild's rallying cry for floating was joined from outside the group by Nicholas Kaldor, who submitted a 20-page paper to William Armstrong on the same day.[33] Kaldor argued that Britain would experience a very big improvement in her export performance following the floating rate and noted that the sterling area thrived after the pound floated in 1931.

The Governor's response to both papers bordered on contempt. He suggested that if Neild's proposals were accepted 'no banker would advise any client to hold one penny of sterling' and that insofar as Kaldor's paper was concerned he was 'ashamed and sad to read such a paper on HM Treasury stationery'.[34] Despite this assault, the Bank appears to have been concerned that the floaters were beginning to carry the argument and the Deputy Governor wanted the Governor and the Bank to have 'ample opportunity' to present their case to ministers.[35] Although the FU Committee did not discuss the Neild or Kaldor papers at length, there were some objections raised to the latter's paper made at the tenth meeting of the group in 1965.[36]

How likely was it that the Prime Minister and Chancellor would decide to float in the event of a parity change? The Committee had known in July 1965 that Wilson was in favour of floating rather than re-fixing the rate if an adjustment to the exchange rate had to be made.[37] Although Wilson consistently opposed devaluation, he always believed that floating was not devaluation and so he would frequently advocate it at times of crisis but he was just as likely to reverse his mind.[38]

For example, in January 1967, Wilson reminded the First Secretary and the Chancellor that at the time of the July 1966 sterling crisis he had thought that there 'might be circumstances in which it was reasonable for the pound to float'; since then, however, he admitted that he had changed his mind and it was 'manifestly wrong' to float and added that he was also against devaluation to a fixed rate.[39] On 5 November 1967, Wilson confirmed to Callaghan that despite the warnings he supported floating the pound, if only for three to four months, as some of the earlier FU papers had suggested.[40] At the SEP meeting on 8 November 1967 he claimed his mind was open to floating (Crossman, 1979, p. 357).

Callaghan's anti-devaluation stance has always appeared consistent between 1964 and 1967 but the official papers show that it was not. Just after the November 1964 sterling crisis, the Deputy Governor reported that the Chancellor was 'losing confidence in the ability of the Government to avoid devaluation', and that he was prepared to float for a few months.[41] At the January 1967 meeting, Callaghan admitted he had 'some doubts' in the summer of 1966 but these worries were 'primarily based on the unwillingness of [my] colleagues to take the drastic and painful steps which were needed to deal with the economic situation'. The more he considered the possibility of floating, 'the more undesirable he thought this course of action'.[42] He echoed the anti-floaters in the FU Committee when he stated that he did not believe that the United Kingdom had reached a position of strength to float. However, Callaghan's arguments to justify his stance against floating do not seem particularly well developed and suggest that it is not clear whether he understood how floating worked or whether he had in mind a temporary float. For instance, Callaghan claimed that if the pound were to increase in value, some countries would conclude that sterling would float downwards and would immediately seek to diversify their holdings; this would then create a chain reaction and the 'inevitable reaction' would be that the pound would have to be pegged at a lower level than at present.

Apart from Neild and Kaldor, however, there were few proponents of floating in the Treasury. On rare occasions a Treasury paper might make a favourable reference to floating; for example, Bill Ryrie had argued in 1966 that if the pound was in a position of strength, the arguments for floating were forceful.[43] Given that the Bank was ever jittery of any pro-floating argument in case it gathered support amongst ministers, it would quickly move to stifle the debate. In response to Ryrie's argument, for example, McMahon expressed concern that the paper should come down more strongly against a floating rate and he continued to express concerns: in a letter to the Governor in September 1967, he offered to redraft the paper.[44] McMahon was clearly unhappy that if the pound was forced off its parity the Prime Minister could be 'hot' for floating and might harness the support of others for a regime change.[45] Ironically, one of the more radical plans (known as 'Plan X'), which the Federal Reserve had considered in 1966, was to use a sterling devaluation to abandon fixed exchange rates and dollar–gold convertibility (Gavin, 2004, pp. 169–171). If the UK authorities had known of the existence of such plans it is highly probable that the supporters of floating rates would have been in a more powerful position to press their case. At the time of the November 1967 devaluation, however, the Johnson administration did not implement any far-reaching response.

1967–72

The British had expressed dissatisfaction with the workings of the international monetary system long before the 1967 devaluation of sterling, but their focus prior to 1968 tended to be on improving international liquidity. Arguably, if the British had pressed for greater flexibility within the system this would have prompted the international community to suggest that this stemmed from the government's difficulties in maintaining sterling's parity. There were few public calls amongst the practitioners (i.e. policy makers) for the adjustment mechanism to be altered, and the IMF hardened its stance on exchange-rate adjustment; indeed, from the end of 1965 the Board did not even discuss the general role of exchange rates in the adjustment process.[46] To be sure, there were advocates of floating exchange rates before the 1967 devaluation and although they were largely confined to the academic community, they gradually became more vocal in their calls for greater flexibility.[47]

The economists who were initially more influential on the policy debate, however, did not advocate floating but instead suggested that the adjustment mechanism could be improved in two ways: either through widening the band or through the introduction of a crawling peg.[48] Yet each of the international economists who submitted evidence to the US Congress Joint Economic Committee's Subcommittee on International Exchange and Payments (chaired by Henry Reuss) in 1968 expressed caution on the way forward (United States, 1968). Edward Bernstein and Robert Triffin favoured a high-level study on exchange-rate flexibility, and Robert Mundell favoured a widening of the band for some currencies (specifically the deutschmark and the franc). Fritz Machlup favoured a 10 per cent band and a 3 per cent per annum crawling. Although the Reuss report did recommend a widening of the band, John Williamson in the Treasury noted that at this stage, 'the reasons for desiring a little more exchange-rate flexibility are strong, but the proposition that the wider band is a particularly suitable form was not discussed'.[49]

There was support for change within the Treasury at this stage. Cairncross was in favour of a crawling peg but doubted whether it could be implemented during 1969 because of transition and credibility problems.[50] Michael Posner, a part-time adviser in the Treasury, argued that both the crawling peg and the wider bands would make the pegged exchange-rate system more akin to 'adjustable peg' system rather than the 'immovable peg' which had followed the disastrous G-10 Bonn meeting in November 1968.[51] Indeed, in September Posner had even gone as far as suggesting a radical rethink:

> The Ministry of Power is accustomed to contemplate a future without coal mines. The Ministry of Technology is often urged to think of a future without a British Aircraft industry. The Ministry of Housing and Local Government should be planning of a future in which rent control might disappear. As part of an exercise in long-term planning of this sort – looking ahead to the mid-1970s – we should, I suggest, in all leisure be looking forward to an international monetary regime in which the present fixed exchange-rate rules were abandoned.

This was quickly followed by two sentences which still clung to the status quo:

> This would have nothing to do with ourfears about the immediate future, although it would presumably have some effect on some of our medium term planning. Willingness to contemplate such a future would not of course commit anyone to a judgment that the abolition of the Bretton Woods system would be a good thing.[52]

While the discussions about wider margins and the crawling peg were important considerations for policy makers in the United Kingdom, at times of crisis after 1968, they were frequently forced to consider something which had previously been more distasteful to them than devaluation, namely floating the pound. Floating was not seen as a pre-ferred solution to the problems facing the international monetary system in its own right, but as the only immediate and effective response if pres-sure on the reserves grew to such an extent that a forced change in parity was necessary. Indeed, even before the ink was dry on the agreement with the IMF following the 1967 devaluation, Kit McMahon from the Bank of England was already considering the possibility of being pushed off the parity, in which case, he noted sadly, 'there would be no alterna-tive to floating' which everyone would agree would be an 'unqualified disaster'.[53] McMahon's sense of gloom if this were to happen was not shared by everyone, but at a joint Treasury and Bank meeting in early February 1968, it was felt that everything possible should be done to avoid this scenario.[54]

In essence, there were a limited number of options open to policy makers in the short run but a number of formidable threats to sterling before the full extent of the devaluation could be realised. Officials were prompted into further discussions on parity changes, or even a float, as they feared reserve diversification by sterling area countries, a further outflow by non-sterling area (NSA) private holders, or from an overall loss of confidence by UK resident owners of capital, which would result in leading, lagging and speculation by moving funds into sterling area countries (many of which did not devalue with the United Kingdom in November 1967).[55] By the time of the gold crisis in March 1968, a number of options had considered in the event of being forced off the parity. For the Treasury, the 'least evil' course of action was blocking the sterling balances.[56] However, the Bank of England vehemently opposed blocking as it felt that it would be defaulting on its clients' balances and it would undermine the position of the City of London. Far better, argued the Bank, to float the pound.[57]

Neither blocking nor floating was introduced in March 1968 as the United States and the G-10 extended a facility of $4050 million to protect the pound.[58] While the Treasury continued to hone the plan to block the sterling balances (known as 'Operation Brutus'), the Bank initiated a series of discussions with other European central banks and the Bank for International Settlements which was to culminate in the 1968 Basle Agreements (Oliver and Hamilton, 2007, pp. 7–9). The outcome was swap facilities to offset most of any reduction in their reserves caused by fluctuations in sterling held both publicly and privately overseas.

The Treasury recognised, however, that the agreements did not preclude the possibility that the United Kingdom might be forced to float the pound and needed to be prepared in case the pound came under another sustained attack or if there was confusion on the foreign exchange markets as other countries adjusted parities. Officials devised two plans concurrently and either could be implemented depending on the circumstances. The first was code-named 'Operation Hecuba' and the second 'Operation Priam'.

Operation Hecuba was concerned with contingencies resulting in the floating of sterling in an emergency, essentially in case the Bank's resources were exhausted as a result of severe pressure on sterling in foreign exchange markets. Officials would be forced to consider whether or not to add to their already 'enormous short-term debts' by further borrowing.[59] The general objective of the operation was to achieve an effective and permanent depreciation in the exchange rate, which would provide a stimulus to exports (it was recognised that a short-term depreciation would only cut imports).

The floating mechanism was very straightforward. Once it was decided to float, the Bank would simply cease intervening in the Exchange Equalization Account. Steps would be made to warn the IMF, the United States and the rest of the G-10 about the change in policy, and a full explanation would be provided in the Parliament and broadcast through the media. It was also decided to cease to publish monthly reserves figures as it would be very costly to 'window dress' and because it was hoped that floating would be such a major policy change that the market might not attach much significance to the publication of reserve figures.[60]

Hecuba would first and foremost be a 'confession that the $2.40 rate was not sufficient to return [the UK] to a balance of payments surplus'.[61] Ministers would seek to stimulate exports while at the same time maintaining confidence in the pound sterling 'even at the expense of overkill in [accompanying] policy'.[62] There were three main sources from which a lack of confidence could lead to a deterioration of the sterling rate, forcing the Treasury to unleash Hecuba: (i) foreigners could doubt Britain's intention to maintain price stability; (ii) liquid asset holders might fear that the price level would get so out of control that it would lead to a flight out of money and into goods; and (iii) a lack of confidence in the stability of sterling which would lead to wage demands.[63]

A good deal of time was spent deciding how to prevent a speculative rush caused by the loss of confidence following the announcement to float. Floating would signal to sterling holders that the Bank had effectively no liquid resources for market intervention and that short-term debts were larger than they had until then believed. Holders might anticipate a general loss of confidence – causing a chain-reaction in speculation. First, the sterling rate would be pushed way down. Second, once the rate began to rise, the increase would be constantly interrupted and reversed as speculators unloaded sterling.

Ironically, the Treasury's preferred blocking scheme had envisaged that the development of these consequences would make sterling holders fear their assets would be blocked and would lead to a flight from sterling.[64] So the blocking operation was created to use when sterling holders acted on their fear of having the convertibility of their assets blocked. From the Government's standpoint, the blocking operation would mitigate reserve losses immediately following the move to float. By June 1968 the Cabinet had agreed to endorse Operation Brutus and was a contingency to be used as a last resort, 'only if it became impossible, for whatever reason, to resist renewed pressure on our reserves as the result of a further crisis of confidence in the international monetary system'.[65]

It was also important to design a series of measures to accompany floating which would make sure that resources were available to increase exports, prevent successive and cumulative falls and/or fluctuations in the exchange rate, and prevent inflation.[66] A powerful committee set up by the Cabinet (known as MISC 205) considered most of the accompanying measures during 1968 and 1969. These actions would place controls on prices, cut public expenditure, increase direct and indirect taxation, enable credit controls, and increase the interest rate. Over time, the accompanying measures became more detailed.

Price stability, as per the Keynesian doctrine which permeated the Treasury at the time, was to be pursued through wage constraint. It would be important to gain some price stability while floating; otherwise 'any residual competitiveness [would] be whittled away' by wage rises.[67] If real income was not kept in check, the added competitiveness might encourage employers to grant wage increases increasing domestic costs, which would increase the price of exports.[68] A wage ceiling of 3 per cent was agreed upon by 1970, with no loopholes or exceptions being implemented.[69] This ceiling would reflect the expectations that wages would eat away at some of the gains of competitiveness. Therefore, prices would be merely influenced and not directly controlled, and floating would not lead to a rapid fall in the purchasing power of the domestic currency.[70] Overseas expenditures would also be cut, such as travel vouchers, in an attempt to ensure that the exchange rate remained competitive by showing the public the government's ambition to be effective and genuine.[71]

It was decided that Bank Rate would be raised in order to tighten credit by 1–2 per cent in order to control credit.[72] As it was perceived, other countries (particularly the United States) might object to a rise in interest rates for domestic reasons, and it was hoped that countries would be more forthcoming in providing facilities for market intervention, which would help ensure that Bank Rate never reached double digits.[73]

The second operation, code-named 'Operation Priam', was a plan to float the pound in response to uncertainty in the foreign exchange market following changes in the parities for the French franc and German deutschemark. It differed from Hecuba in two ways. First, the introduction of import controls was considered inappropriate and inconsistent with the presentation of the operation. Second, the duration of the float was not predicted to last quite as long as under Hecuba because it could have been possible to reopen markets in a matter of days, following satisfactory agreements with Germany, Italy, Switzerland and France.[74] This would depend on the ability of the Germans and the Americans to pressure the rest of the world to realign, facilitating a realistic adjustment of the dollar/Deutschmark rate.[75]

The key to Priam was the portrayal of Britain as a victim of external circumstance. Hecuba would be a confession of chronic British trade imbalances, while Priam would be in response to a sudden external event, provoking a widespread expectation of an imminent realignment of exchange-rate parities and consequent pressure on sterling – specifically a French devaluation and/or a German revaluation. British officials preferred Priam to Hecuba for four reasons: first, there would be more sympathy abroad for the plight of sterling; second, there would be less pressure from the sterling area countries to get out of sterling; third, the domestic position would be less 'hopeless' than under Hecuba; and finally, the monetary conference that would likely follow in the Priam contingency was likely to produce a general settlement of exchange rates that would provide an opportunity to quickly return to a fixed parity.[76]

After the November 1968 Bonn conference, planning for Priam ceased and the Chancellor Roy Jenkins publicly ruled out a new Bretton Woods conference in January 1969, despite the growing criticism of current exchange-rate arrangements.[77] However, the Treasury noted that the Chancellor was 'anxious that we proceed with all speed' on international liquidity and reform of the international monetary arrangements and set up secret talk with the Federal Reserve and the US Treasury to exchange ideas about how it would be possible to instigate a more flexible system.[78]

General discussions about greater flexibility at the international level intensified after 1969, as can be seen from the published proceedings arising from the Claremont Graduate Conference, Bellagio Group and Bürgenstock Group among others (Halm, 1970; Hinshaw, 1971; Marris, 1970). However, in his concluding remarks to the Arden House meeting of the Bürgenstock group in January 1970, Harry Johnson noted that whilst calls for greater flexibility appeared to have grown amongst the academics, they had receded amongst policy makers. Johnson 'sensed that an air of hostility to increasing flexibility still emanated from official quarters' and ended gloomily that 'euphoria about the status quo may again be setting in as even the problems caused by the recent realignments [the French devalued in August 1969 and the Germans revalued in October 1969] begin receding in our minds'.[79]

Johnson had, perhaps unwittingly, summarised the attitude of the British who were still opposed to any substantial widening of the margins – although they would accept a slight widening of the margins to 2 per cent – and who were opposed to a crawling peg system in which sterling would crawl downwards (the British were open to discussion about a system where all currencies crawled upwards). From a wider perspective, although international monetary reform had been given a boost with the election of President in 1968 and his assuming office in 1969, who surrounded himself with proponents of floating exchange rates on his Council of Economic Advisers,[80] the frustrations with the pace of reform were beginning to show. In June 1969, President Nixon considered how his administration could push the pace of international monetary reform with the Europeans and one of the suggestions included closing the gold-window to force the Europeans to consider (Gavin, 2004, pp. 191–192).

Nixon's announcement of this very policy in August 1971 essentially pulled the rug from under the British Treasury, and as the former Governor of the Bank noted, 'the deterioration of the American monetary situation in the global setting has been part of the World scene so long that it has perhaps blunted our sense against the eventual inevitable showdown which has now come upon us'.[81] The Treasury now had every incentive to plan for floating with a newfound sense of urgency, whilst the Cabinet's primary objective was to restore currency stability as a basis for international trade and economic growth. This implied currency realignment through international agreement but the Treasury acknowledged that floating was more likely, although they feared that once the appreciation (at that point in time, perhaps optimistically, to float meant to appreciate) had taken place, it would lead to a less competitive trade position and unfavourable effects on the UK balance of payments.[82]

The Treasury had contemplated a range of alternatives to Bretton Woods after 1968 which included generalised floating, a development of a European bloc floating against the dollar; intervening with one national currency without reunifying the gold markets; a European bloc with a central bank issuing and intervening with a new European currency and possibly backed by some form of gold pool and an adoption of a dual-rate system for capital and current account transactions, allowing the rate in the capital market to float. It had also contemplated another devaluation.[83] It was only after Nixon's announcement – which fatally damaged the Bretton Woods system of fixed exchange rates – that the British monetary authorities finally agreed a 'half float' for four months until the Smithsonian Agreement of December 1971.[84] After the haemorrhaging of the reserve between 15 June and 21 June 1972 – over $1 billion was lost – policy makers were finally forced to accept a floating rate.

Conclusions

This chapter has shed new light on how the United Kingdom's monetary authorities struggled with adjustment problems under Bretton Woods between 1960 and 1972. It has shown that prior to the 1967 devaluation, both the Treasury and the Bank were set firmly against floating but by the time of the gold crisis in March 1968, the Bank wanted to float the pound and was opposed to the Treasury's suggestion that the sterling balances should be blocked. The Bank's response was to initiate discussions with other central banks and the Bank for International Settlement which culminated in the provision of swap facilities to offset most of the reduction in the United Kingdom's reserves caused by fluctuations in sterling held both publicly and privately overseas. The Treasury continued to hone the blocking exercise and, when it realised that the Basle Agreements might not work, began to plan for floating with the Bank.

This chapter has shown that the inexorable move to floating rates in the British case owed less to the intellectual work of academic economists and more to the sheer practical necessity of having to adopt the only available alternative in the event of being forced off the $2.40 parity. The plans to redesign the adjustment mechanism of Bretton Woods preceded slowly, much to the chagrin of the Americans. To be sure, Treasury officials such as Sir Frank Figgures and Anthony Rawlinson did become more involved in the discussions of the Bellagio and Bürgenstock groups, rather than merely commenting on the papers produced for the conferences ex-post. However, it is probably fair to say that the majority of senior Treasury officials were not intellectually committed to changing the international monetary system. Concomitantly, throughout the period, the condition of sterling never deteriorated to an extent that demanded immediate action; instead pressure on sterling simply sustained itself, and worked slowly to undermine the stability of the pound, and thereby the stability of the international monetary system.

This chapter has considered, albeit briefly, the political support for fixed and floating rates during this period. Although Harold Wilson did allow a wider group of ministers to discuss sterling and the international monetary system through the MISC 205 committee, the Prime Minister was still nervous about allowing a frank and full discussion on exchange rates. In November 1968, Wilson instructed the Chancellor to provide an oral statement to MISC 205 and not circulate a paper on floating, perhaps fearing that the floaters on the committee (Barbara Castle and Richard Crossman) would press for unilateral action in the wake of the disastrous G-10 Bonn conference.[85] Unease about discussing floating was not confined to the leader of the Labour Party. After Labour lost the 1970 election to the Conservative Party – who were elected on a free market platform – the Prime Minister, Edward Heath, ignored the pleas from Milton Friedman in a face-to-face meeting that he should float the pound.[86]

Roger Middleton (2002) has suggested that the UK authorities attempted to 'struggle with the impossible' under fixed exchange rates between 1949 and 1972. They also continued to struggle to manage sterling even after being released from the external constraint in 1972. This was largely because their Keynesian instruments could not control inflation, especially in a world without any internationally agreed monetary rules. Economic historians have yet to explain why UK policy makers were still wedded to the practices of a fixed exchange rate some four years after the float. By 1976, floating was no longer a temporary expedient and the authorities should have accumulated experience of managing the currency in the new environment. Significant policy differences then opened up between the Bank and the Treasury over issues of intervention, the level of the foreign exchange reserves and the efficacy of depreciation before another sterling crisis hit the British economy. However, this is part of a bigger story in the move away from Keynesian economics.

Acknowledgements

The author would like to thank Forrest Capie and John Williamson for their helpful comments.

Notes

1. O'Hara (2003) provides a confused account of Brutus.
2. The National Archives, Kew, London (hereafter TNA), T312/2023, Symons to Pitblado, 8 July 1960.
3. Ibid.
4. TNA T312/2023, Pitblado to Rickett, 26 July 1960, handwritten note by Sir Denis Rickett.
5. TNA T312/2023, Allen to Mitchell, 16 January 1961, handwritten note by Anson.
6. Bank of England archives (hereafter BE), BE OV44/132, Parsons to The Governors and Allen, 24 April 1964.
7. Ibid.
8. BE OV44/132, Cairncross to Allen, 15 June 1964, handwritten note; O'Brien to Parsons and Allen, 17 August 1964.
9. BE OV44/132, Allen to Governors, 28 August 1964, handwritten note by Cromer.
10. At the time of the 1967 devaluation, Harold Wilson claimed that the former Chancellor Reginald Maudling had ordered the preparation of these three papers but this was denied by Maudling and all the evidence suggests this was undertaken at Armstrong's initiative. See TNA PREM 13/1668, Maulding to Wilson, 23 November 1967; 'Note for the Record', 27 November 1967; and Christ Church College Archives, Nigel Lawson Papers, 'Conversation with William Armstrong', 20 November 1967.
11. TNA T171/758, 'Devaluation', GB (64) 61, 15 October 1964.
12. TNA T171/758, 'Floating Exchange Rates', GB (64) 62 (second circulation), 15 October 1964.
13. TNA PREM 13/255, Brown to Wilson, 23 July 1965. Sir Donald MacDougall, Director-General of the Department of Economic Affairs, had successfully convinced George Brown that the objectives of the National Plan could not be achieved without devaluation. See MacDougall (1987, p. 157).
14. Callaghan correspondence with Oliver, 2 September 2003, and interview with Sir Gerald Kauffman, 9 February 2006.
15. PREM 13/261, 'Record of a Meeting', 24 November 1964.

16. Sir Donald MacDougall and Tommy Balogh, economic adviser to the Cabinet, also contributed to Neild's paper.
17. TNA T312/1635, 'Contingency Planning', Memorandum by Walker, 5 May 1966.
18. TNA T312/1398, 'Choice of a New Fixed Rate', FU (65) 12, 2 April 1965.
19. TNA T312/1401, FU (65) 3rd Meeting, 5 April 1965.
20. TNA T312/1398, 'Floating Rates', FU (65) 17, 2 April 1965.
21. TNA T312/1401, FU (65) 3rd Meeting, 5 April 1965.
22. TNA T312/1401, FU (65) 4th Meeting, 13 April 1965.
23. TNA T312/1398, 'Fixed or Flexible Rates', FU (65) 21 (Revise), 26 April 1965. Neild wanted to take responsibility for a revised version fearing an agreed document by the group, 'with a mass of pros and cons', would obfuscate Ministers. See BE OV44/132, 'Contingency Planning', 22 April 1965.
24. TNA T312/1401, FU (65) 6th Meeting, 19 May 1965.
25. TNA T312/1401, FU (65) 7th Meeting, 16 June 1965.
26. TNA T312/1401, FU (65) 8th Meeting, 24 June 1965.
27. TNA T312/1401, FU (65) 7th Meeting, 16 June 1965. Bridge, apparently commenting on the paper, had expressed his desire that at the outset the paper needed to recognise Britain's responsibility to the international community. See BE OV44/133, 'Mr Fforde's Three Papers', Bridge to Governor, 8 June 1965.
28. TNA T312/1401, FU (65) 8th Meeting, 24 June 1965.
29. After the discussion on fixed or floating rates, the group considered the Bank's paper on 'Guarantees and Compensation', FU (65) 11 (Revise), where a further objection to floating was that a package of guarantees or compensation would have to be given to official holders of sterling in London.
30. It was suggested in the meeting that Ministers needed to be advised that the international community would probably place floating rates on par with a temporary import surcharge. The 15 per cent surcharge introduced in 1964 had not been well received by EFTA, GATT or the OECD; see Cairncross (1996, p. 94).
31. TNA T312/1401, FU (65) 10th Meeting, 29 July 1965.
32. TNA T312/1399, 'Fixed or Flexible Rate', FU (65) 47, 22 July 1965; TNA T312/1399, 'Fixed or Floating Rate', FU (65) 48, 22 July 1965.
33. TNA T312/1399, 'Fixed or Floating Rate', FU (65) 48, 22 July 1965.
34. BE OV44/133, handwritten note by Cromer, 26 July 1965, on the covering page of 'Fixed or Flexible Rate', FU (65) 47 and FU (65) 48.
35. TNA T312/1401, FU (65) 10th Meeting, 29 July 1965. In the immediate aftermath of the Neild and Kaldor papers there were a couple of memos in the Bank which were very critical of the arguments deployed. See BE OV44/134, 'Fixed or Flexible Rates', undated and 'Fixed or Flexible', Bridge to Rootham, 3 August 1965. A more measured critique by Allen appears in BE OV44/134, 'Comments on Mr. Kaldor's paper FU (65) 48', 24 August 1965.
36. TNA T312/1401, FU (65) 10th Meeting, 29 July 1965. Cairncross was despatched by Armstrong to counter some of the claims made by Kaldor in a paper. See TNA T312/1399, 'Fixed or Floating', FU (65) 54, 28 July 1965.
37. TNA T312/1401, FU (65) 10th Meeting, 29 July 1965.
38. Interview with Sir Fred Atkinson, 25 May 2003.
39. TNA PREM 13/1439, 'Note of a Meeting', 11 January 1967.

40. Wilson to Callaghan, 5 November 1967, TNA PREM 13/1447. Wilson referred to a 'Bank document of July 1966' – this appears to have been Kit McMahon's paper, 'Interim Flexibility or Immediate New Parity', 18 July 1966, BE OV44/136.

41. BE OV44/123, O'Brien to Cromer, 4 December 1964.

42. TNA PREM 13/1439, 'Note of a Meeting', 11 January 1967.

43. TNA T312/1636, 'Fixed or Flexible Rates', FU (66) 10, 22 September 1966. Ryrie's paper did not go unchallenged by Robert Neild, who expressed a preference for seeing his position stated differently.

44. BE OV44/135, FU (66) 10, 30 September 1966. There was also a concern that the paper did not distinguish clearly between a proposal for a permanent float and that for limited floating, see TNA T312/1637, FU (66) 1st Meeting, 11 November 1966.

45. BE OV44/137, McMahon to Governor, 14 September 1967. McMahon suggested Douglas Allen might 'throw his weight' towards floating, and in a letter to Parsons on 22 September he also suggested Posner was a possible convert to floating. A paper by Posner a month later confirmed McMahon's suspicions; see BE OV44/138, 'Fixed and Floating Rates', 25 October 1967.

46. See de Vries and Horsefield (1969, p. 116). No doubt the suggestion by Sherman J. Maisel from the Federal Reserve of San Francisco in 1965 for a widening of the bands through lowering the purchase price of gold would have caused the US Treasury a great deal of consternation at the time. See 'Reserve Member asks a Study on Currency Exchange Rates', *New York Times*, 12 November 1965.

47. Prior to 1967, see for example, Meade (1949, 1955) and Friedman (1953). After 1967, and in particular, relating to the British case, see Johnson, 'Case for Flexible Exchange Rates' and 'The Safety Valve in a Floating Exchange Rate', *The Times*, 9 December 1968, p. 23, col. C; 'Exchange Cooperation', *The Times*, 17 September 1970, p. 24, col. F. For political support see 'A Floating Exchange Rate', *The Times*, 10 June 1969, p. 11, col. C; 'Powell on Maudling and Floating Exchange Rates', *The Times*, 30 October 1969, p. 25, col. D; Johnson (1969). For an alternative view, see Sir Maurice Parsons' contribution 'A Floating Exchange Rate not the Answer', *The Times*, 15 September 1970, p. 22, col. E; Sir Eric Roll, 'Floating Above the Ground', *The Times*, 3 September 1970, p. 21, col. R. Leeson (2003) has a discussion about how intellectual discussions on floating rates became imbued in the policy process during this period.

48. Wider margins had been mooted by Halm (1965) and Meade (1965), and John Williamson (1966) had proposed the crawling peg.

49. TNA T312/2023, Williamson to Hubback, 15 November 1968. Williamson's work on crawling pegs has been subjected to internal Treasury comment since the mid-1960s but from the autumn of 1968 he was employed as an economic consultant to the Treasury. It was felt that his appointment would give the Treasury an authoritative expertise on international monetary affairs.

50. TNA T312/2023, 'International Monetary Arrangements', Cairncross to Figures, 2 December 1968.

51. TNA T312/2023, 'Proposals on International Monetary Arrangements', Posner to Figures, 28 November 1968. Cf. Johnson (1969).

52. TNA T312/2023, 'The Future of Exchange Rates', Posner to Goldman, 18 September 1968.

53. TNA T312/2549, 'The Question for Planning for Floating', 20 December 1967.
54. TNA T312/2549, 'Note of a Meeting', 7 February 1968.
55. TNA T312/2549, 'Contingency Planning – in What Circumstance might it be Necessary to Float?', 20 February 1968.
56. TNA T295/489, 'Contingency Planning', Hubback to Goldman, 15 March 1968.
57. BE OV53/38, Morse to the Governors, 14 March 1968; BE OV53/38, 'Note for the Record', 18 March 1968; Hamilton (2008).
58. TNA CAB 130/497, 'Minutes of Misc. 205 (68) Second Meeting', 17 March 1968.
59. TNA CAB 130/497, 'The Hecuba Plan', undated.
60. TNA T312/2131, 'The Hecuba Plan (Annex – Subsidiary Matters)', 9 December 1968.
61. TNA T312/2137, 'Economic Accompanying Measures', 10 October 1968.
62. TNA T312/2131, 'Domestic Economic Policy', 4 September 1968.
63. TNA T312/2137, 'Economic Accompanying Measures', 10 October 1968.
64. Ibid.
65. TNA CAB 130/498, 'Minutes of Meeting', MISC 209, 14 June 1968.
66. TNA T312/2131, 'Discussion on Hecuba on 13 November', 13 November 1968.
67. TNA T312/2137, 'Priam: Accompanying Measures', 1 November 1968.
68. TNA T312/2906, 'Considerations Relating to a Change in the Present Sterling Parity', 26 November 1970.
69. Ibid.
70. TNA T312/2131, 'Measures Accompanying a Floating Rate', Atkinson to Cairncross, 21 November 1968.
71. TNA T312/2137, 'Priam: Accompanying Measures', 1 November 1968.
72. TNA T295/607, 'Hecuba', 14 January 1969.
73. TNA T312/2137, 'Contingency Planning: Hecuba', 13 December 1968.
74. TNA T295/607, Note of meeting on 'Contingency Planning: Priam and Hecuba', 15 October 1968.
75. TNA T295/607, Main paper 'Hecuba', 14 January 1969.
76. Ibid.
77. 'Jenkins against New Bretton Woods', *The Times*, 14 January 1969, p. 15, col. D; 'Time to Start Orderly Exchange Variations', *Financial Times*, 21 November 1968; 'Maudling Urges More Flexible Exchange Rates', *Financial Times*, 5 June 1969. For a discussion on the Bonn conference, see James (1996, pp. 177–8, 193–5) and Gray (2006).
78. T312/2023, Figgures to Hubback, 27 November 1968; TNA T312/2334, 'Discussion with Americans about Monetary Reform', Rawlinson to Ryrie, 7 March 1969. The discussions with the Americans are discussed in Oliver and Hamilton (2007).
79. T312/3290, 'Arden House Monetary Conference', 30 January 1970.
80. Each of the three – Paul W. McCracken, Hendrik S. Houthakker and Hebert Stein – had expressed pro-floating views prior their appointments. See 'Nixon to Discuss Monetary Reform', *The Times*, 15 February 1969, p. 11, col. E.
81. TNA PREM 15/309, 'International Monetary Situation', 23 August 1971.
82. TNA T312/3215, 'Floating', Gilmore to Rawlinson, 17 August 1971.
83. TNA T312/3215, 'Baytown', undated.

84. TNA PREM 15/309, 'Note of meeting', 24 August 1971.
85. TNA T312/2135, 'Note for the Record', 27 November 1968. The speaking note which was drafted for the Chancellor is very cautious. See 'Contingency Planning for Floating' in the same file dated 28 November 1968.
86. TNA PREM 15/722, 'Note for the Record', 18 September 1970, and conversation with Brian Reading (Heath's economic adviser) on 12 April 2005. It is doubtful whether Heath was a committed floater. He had told Samuel Brittan, economics editor of the *Financial Times*, who had argued the case for floating, at an open Conservative Economic Conference in July 1967 that 'If you must talk bollocks, talk bollocks in private' (Brittan, 1988, p. 53).

References

Bordo, M. D. and Eichengreen, B. (eds) (1993), *A Retrospective on the Bretton Woods System: Lessons for International Monetary Reform*, Chicago, Ill: The University of Chicago Press.

Bordo, M. D. and James, H. (2002), 'The Adam Klug Memorial Lecture: Haberler Versus Nurkse: The Case for Floating Exchange Rates as an Alternative to Bretton Woods?', in A. Arnon and W. Young (eds), *The Open Economy Macromodel: Past, Present and Future*, Boston, MA: Kluwer Academic Publishers, pp. 161–182.

Brittan, S. (1988), 'Symposium, 1967 Devaluation', *Contemporary Record*, Vol. 1, pp. 44–53.

Burnham, P. (2003), *Remaking the Postwar World Economy: Robot and British Policy in the 1950s,* Basingstoke: Palgrave Macmillan.

Cairncross, A. K. (1985), *Years of Recovery: British Economic Policy 1945–51*, London: Methuen.

Cairncross, A. K. (1996), *Managing the British Economy in the 1960s: A Treasury Perspective*, London: Macmillan.

Cairncross, A. and Watts, N. (1989), *The Economic Section 1939–1961: A Study in Economic Advising*, London: Routledge.

Crossman, R. H. S. (1979), *The Crossman Diaries: Selections from the Diaries of a Cabinet Minister, 1964–1970*, London: Cape.

de Vries, M. and Horsefield, J. K. (1969) *The International Monetary Fund, 1945–1965: Twenty Years of International Monetary Cooperation*, Volume II: Analysis, Washington, DC: IMF.

Endres, A. M. and Fleming, G. A. (2002), *International Organizations and The Analysis of Economic Policy, 1919–1950*, Cambridge: Cambridge University Press.

Fforde, J. S. (1992), *The Bank of England and Public Policy, 1941–1958*, Cambridge: Cambridge University Press.

Friedman, M. (1953), 'The Case for Flexible Exchange Rates', in M. Friedman (ed.), *Essays in Positive Economics*, Chicago, IL: University of Chicago Press.

Gavin, F. J. (2004), *Gold, Dollars, and Power: The Politics of International Monetary Relations, 1958–1971*, Chapel Hill, NC: University of North Carolina Press.

Gray, W. G. (2006), ' "Number One in Europe": The Startling Emergence of the Deutsche Mark, 1968–1969', *Central European History*, Vol. 39, pp. 56–78.

Haberler, G. (1985), 'The World Economy, Money and the Great Depression', in A. Y. C. Koo (ed.), *Selected Essays of Gottfried Haberler*, Cambridge, MA: MIT Press.

Halm, G. N. (1965), *The Band Proposal: The Limits of Exchange Rate Variations*, Special Papers in International Economics, No. 6, Princeton, NJ: Princeton University Press.

Halm, G. (ed.) (1970), *Approaches to Greater Flexibility of Exchange Rates: The Burgenstock Papers*, Princeton, NJ: Princeton University Press.

Hamilton, A. (2008), 'Beyond the Sterling Devaluation: The Gold Crisis of March 1968', *Contemporary European History*, Vol. 17, pp. 73–95.

Hinshaw, R. (ed.) (1971), *The Economics of International Adjustment*, Baltimore, MD: The Johns Hopkins Press.

James, H. (1996), *International Monetary Cooperation since Bretton Woods*, Oxford: Oxford University Press.

James, H. (2001), *The End of Globalization: Lessons from the Great Depression*, Cambridge, MA: Harvard University Press.

Johnson, H. G. (1969), 'The Case for Flexible Exchange Rates, 1969', in H. G. Johnson and J. E. Nash (eds), *UK and Floating Exchange Rates*, Hobart Papers, No. 46, pp. 9–37.

League of Nations (1944), *International Currency Experience: Lessons of the Inter-War Period*, Geneva: League of Nations.

Leeson, R. (2003), Ideology and the International Economy: The Decline and Fall of Bretton Woods, London: Palgrave Macmillan.

MacDougall, D. (1987), *Don and Mandarin: Memoirs of an Economist*, London: Murray.

Marris, S. (1970), *The Bürgenstock Communiqué: A Critical Examination of the Case for Limited Flexibility of Exchange Rates*, Essays in international finance, No. 80, Princeton, NJ: Princeton University.

Meade, J. E. (1949), *Planning and the Price Mechanism: The Liberal Socialist Solution*, London: Macmillan.

Meade, J. (1955), 'The Case for Variable Exchange Rates', *Three Banks Review*, No. 27, pp. 3–27.

Meade, J. (1965), 'Exchange-Rate Flexibility', *Three Banks Review*, No. 70, pp. 3–27.

Middleton, R. (2002), 'Struggling with the Impossible: Sterling, the Balance of Payments and British Economic Policy, 1949–72', in A. Arnon and W. Young (eds), *The Open Economy Macromodel: Past, Present and Future*, Boston, MA: Kluwer Academic Publishers, pp. 103–54.

O'Hara, G. (2003), 'The Limits of US Power: Transatlantic Financial Diplomacy under the Johnson and Wilson Administrations, October 1964–November 1968', *Contemporary European History*, Vol. 12, pp. 257–78.

Oliver, M. J. and Hamilton, A. (2007), 'Downhill from Devaluation: The Battle for Sterling, 1968–72', *Economic History Review*, Vol. 60, pp. 486–512.

Toniolo, G. (2005), *Central Bank Cooperation at the Bank for International Settlements, 1930–1973*, Cambridge: Cambridge University Press.

United States (1968), *Next Steps in International Monetary Reform; Report*, Washington, DC: U.S. Govt. Print. Off.

Williamson, J. H. (1966), *The Crawling Peg, Essays in International Finance*, No. 50, Princeton, NJ: Princeton University Press.

9
The Evolution of the Kydland–Prescott Research Program: Transformation, Recollections, and New Documents

Warren Young

Introduction

There are a number of retrospective narratives regarding the development of the path-breaking works of Kydland and Prescott (1977a, 1982) for which they received the Nobel Prize in economics. These include the personal recollections of Prescott (1998, 2004, 2006e), Kydland (2005, autobiography), and Lucas (2001, 2005), and the survey of the Royal Swedish Academy (2004). While important in their own right, the history of the Kydland–Prescott research program is even more intriguing than that recounted in these narratives, especially when the development of their ideas is dealt with in detail by *combining* the recollections and documents that characterize their *evolution*.

The approach taken here both complements and supplements these narratives. The published accounts of Prescott, Kydland, and Lucas mentioned above are supplemented via additional recollections collected – by means of correspondence and in-depth background interviews – from them and others who influenced and were influenced by the Kydland–Prescott research program, while detailed textual analysis of drafts of papers involved in its evolution complements the narrative recollections. Moreover, as Hicks put it, since 'memory is treacherous' (1973, 2), utilization of these drafts can clear up minor anomalies in the narratives themselves.

Some examples should suffice to illustrate the efficacy of the approach taken here. In his insightful Nobel Lecture, Prescott mentioned that he and Kydland 'had read the Lucas critique,' and searched for the 'best rule to follow' – from the context of the paragraph where the account appears – as early as 1973 (2004, 374, 2006e). But in the references, only the 1976 version of the Lucas Critique is cited (1976a), although in additional recollections both Prescott and Kydland recalled reading and being influenced by the 1973 *drafts* of Lucas.

Indeed, just how and to what extent they were influenced will be recounted below. According to Prescott, a 'key' element in the evolution of the Kydland–Prescott approach was the development by Lucas and Prescott of 'recursive competitive equilibrium theory' in their seminal 1971 paper 'Investment under uncertainty' and in Lucas (1972), and its further development 'in Prescott and Mehra (1980)' (2004, 392, 2006e). But while the difference between the published and the draft version of Lucas and Prescott *is* mentioned by Prescott in a note (2004, 392, note 15, 2006e), the December 1977 draft of Prescott and Mehra is not, leaving the impression of a long gap in the evolution of the theory. Moreover, the *cardinal* role of the 1971 Lucas–Prescott paper (written in 1969) and how it changed Prescott's approach to macroeconomics will be shown by using the information he provided in correspondence, while other key episodes in the evolution of the Kydland–Prescott approach will also be enriched by utilizing correspondence and interview material as supplementary narrative. Finally, in his retrospective 'recollections' (2005) Lucas posed the crucial albeit up to now unanswered question regarding the 1982 Kydland–Prescott paper: 'How did they ever think to put all these pieces together in just this way?' (2005, 777).

The object of this study is to show how Kydland and Prescott put all the 'pieces' together; that is to say, how their *overall approach*, which, as will be shown, encompasses *both* their 1977 and 1982 papers, evolved and brought about what Prescott, in his Nobel lecture, called 'a transformation' in modern economic analysis. This is done by

 (i) surveying their early work on optimal policy rules and stabilization, and dynamic equilibrium models of the business cycle;
 (ii) analyzing the impact of those 'pieces' which catalyzed their approach, such as the early drafts of the Lucas Critique (1973a, 1973b) and Hodrick–Prescott (1978);
(iii) integrating this with the evolution of their approach based upon the variorum drafts of their 1977 'Rules,' and 1982 'Time to build' papers and the relationship between these papers;
(iv) unifying the accounts and narratives, by means of in-depth questioning as to the intellectual process involved in their path-breaking work.

In his Prize lecture, Prescott wrote (2004, 370, 2006e), 'all stories about transformation have three essential parts: the time prior to the key change, the transformative era, and the new period that has been impacted by the change.' But what is the 'transformation' that Kydland and Prescott brought about? It is *not* simply the synthetic combination of the work of Frisch, Solow, Lucas, and others. It *is a totally new* approach, one that extends the work of these giants, in conjunction with a *new economic weltanschuung and empirical methodology* that has brought about a sea change in macroeconomic research and policy analysis.

The 'essential sections' in the context of this chapter are, then, as follows. In the first section of the chapter, the 'pre dynamic general equilibrium' phase of the early work of Prescott and Kydland, over the period 1967–1973, is surveyed. The second section of the chapter deals with the 'transitional' phase in the Kydland–Prescott approach, encompassing dynamic equilibrium models, their 'search' for rules, and their work on stabilization policy, over the period 1973–1978. The third section of the chapter examines in detail the evolution of their work on business cycles, including the 'empirical investigation' of Hodrick–Prescott and 'Time to build' and their aftermath, covering the period from 1978 to 1982 onwards.

Before the transformation: The pre dynamic general equilibrium tradition and the Lucas Critique

Prescott's early contributions

In his Nobel lecture, Prescott described the nature of macroeconomic models and policy discussion prior to what he called the 'transformation,' saying that he had 'worked in this tradition' and went on to outline the approach to policy selection taken in his dissertation (2004, 372–73). Prescott's early published contributions (1971, 1972), along with his collaboration with others (Lovell and Prescott, 1968, 1970; Lucas and Prescott, 1971), are important for understanding of how his thought evolved. Prescott's 1967 Carnegie Tech dissertation was entitled 'Adaptive decision rules for macroeconomic planning' and was supervised by Lovell. It dealt with the optimization problem with special emphasis on the issue of how uncertain parameters affect decisions. Prescott considers that his dissertation 'was in the old tradition' (2005a). According to Lovell (Personal Communication, 8 November 2005a), the thesis

> was concerned with a problem of optimal learning while doing. Theil was using macroeconometric models he had estimated in a control

theory framework to determine optimal fiscal policy for the next period. As each new observation became available with the passage of time Theil would re-estimate the model, and then work out the optimal policy under the assumption that the policy parameters had been estimated with precision. Among other results, Ed showed that one could do better than successive one-period optimizations, in terms of minimizing loss, if one sacrificed a little of next-period optimization of the control problem in order to design a better experiment which would yield more precise parameter estimates that would more accurately guide future policy decisions.

There are two important points in Lovell's description of Prescott's 1967 thesis, that of control theory and experimentation respectively; for these aspects are key issues in the work that emanated from his thesis, and collaborative work between them during the period. The first of these was a joint paper with Lovell published in *Southern Economic Journal* *(SEJ)* (1968), originally presented at the December 1964 meeting of the Econometric Society (1968, 60).

Almost four decades later, Lovell and Prescott provided recollections of the central message of their 1968 paper. According to Prescott (2005a, 7 November), in the paper, they 'broke from treating the equations governing the evolution of the national account statistics as data tradition whom...we had rational expectations with regard to "desired capital stock" and examine the mapping from policy rules to statistical properties of the time series.' In his retrospective assessment of the paper, Lovell wrote (2005a, 8 November),

I would put a rather different spin on it. Our paper challenged the assertion that the Fed's actions were necessarily destabilizing if it allowed the money supply to move procyclically. To show this in as simple a framework as possible we introduced money into the multiplier–accelerator model of the business cycle. We made the money supply endogenous, the Fed adjusting the money supply in response to movements in GNP. The interest rate was influenced by M, and investment depended in part on the rate of interest. We then showed that one could not say without knowing the parameters of the system what value of the policy parameter would best smooth the cycle (i.e., yield the smallest characteristic root). We then added stochastic shocks to the system and found that the value of the policy parameter minimizing the variance of output could not be specified *a priori*. Obviously, this is not RBC Prescott. He had not yet liberated himself from my influence.

To this, Prescott added (2005b, 16 November),

> I am in basic agreement with Mike on the *SEJ* paper. But there the idea of evaluating a policy rule by looking at operating characteristics of the model (the model was not an economy so I do not say model economy) was a different way to think about things. Also in the investment equation, there was a future value of a variable. This means that expectations as to this variable had to be formed. One expectation scheme we considered was rational expectations. Except for this the model was in the pre dynamic general equilibrium tradition.

In his recollections, Lovell also described the impact of his 1970 paper with Prescott on his own view of econometric results (2005a, 8 November):

> Ed and I wrote a second paper, 'Multiple Regressions with Inequality Constraints: Pretesting Bias, Hypothesis Testing and Efficiency' (JASA, 1970). We found that dropping variables with incorrect sign from a multiple regression would lead to biased estimates of the parameters of the variables remaining in the model; although the estimates would be efficient *if the* stochastic disturbance was normally distributed. Worse, the *t* statistics could be grossly exaggerated. Partly as a result of this paper, I became more and more disillusioned about the validity of econometric results.

It is not surprising, then, that Prescott would also turn away from empirical econometrics, when this outcome was combined with the early impact of the Lucas Critique (1973) on him, as will be seen below.

At this point, a caveat is necessary. Due to its importance as the turning point in the evolution of his thought – on his own account, as will be seen below – Prescott's 1971 paper with Lucas, 'Investment under uncertainty,' will be dealt with after the papers emanating directly from his 1967 dissertation.

Prescott published a paper with the same title as his thesis in the December 1971 issue of *Western Economic Journal*. This paper cites both the unpublished thesis and his forthcoming paper 'The multi-period control problem under uncertainty.' Both papers indicate that Prescott was starting to think about alternative methods of analysis, albeit still in 'the old tradition.' In his 1971 paper, Prescott introduced the 'concept of experimentation' as an 'additional element' (1971, 369–70) and 'backward inductions and numerical methods' for two-period analysis (1971, 370–372). He noted that 'a more complete analysis of the multi-period control problem' could be found in his forthcoming *Econometrica* paper (1971, 372, note 9; 1972). In the final part of his 1971 paper, Prescott utilized, as a baseline, the small-scale Keynesian econometric model formulated by Chow (1967) to simulate the US economy and assess the outcome of linear as against adaptive – and both against perfect information – decision rules. He found that the outcome of the testing procedure he used clearly demonstrated that the adaptive approach gave superior results in the context of the economies simulated. Prescott concluded that additional research was required, including 'how best to approximate policy makers' preference ordering using a quadratic function' (1971, 374–78). The importance of this will be seen below.

Prescott's paper 'The multi-period control problem under uncertainty' appeared in the November 1972 issue of *Econometrica*. It was also presented in May 1972 at the first Optimal Control Conference (Chow, Personal Communication, 26 October 2005). The manuscript was received in December 1970 and its revision in June 1971 (1972, 1057). This paper constitutes perhaps the earliest application of multi-period control theory to economics (Kendrick, 2005a, 18; Prescott, 1972, 1043, note 2). In this paper, he analyzed the control problem by applying numerical methods and showed, among other points, that 'the more periods remaining in the planning horizon, the more important is experimentation' (1972, 1056). Indeed, as Kendrick recently wrote in correspondence (2005b, 26 October), 'Prescott's 1972 paper was one of his most important contributions and one that has not received the attention it deserves.'

Lucas and Prescott published their paper 'Investment under uncertainty' in the September 1971 issue of *Econometrica*, although the work had been completed in 1969. This paper, according to Prescott, was also in the pre-transformation tradition. In his words (2004, 373, 2006e), 'the macroeconometric models organized the field. Success in macroeconomics was to have your equation incorporated into the macroeconometric models. Indeed, Lucas and I were searching for a better investment equation when in 1969 we wrote our paper...' But more is involved here than simply the search for a 'better investment equation.' And indeed, in subsequent correspondence, Prescott stated just how his paper with Lucas changed the direction of his thought. As he wrote (2005d, 20 November),

> Investment under Uncertainty was the paper that led me to work on dynamic equilibrium models of business cycles. After writing that paper in 1969 (it appeared in 1971 after a very long delay subsequent to acceptance), I stopped teaching macro. Another approach was needed. Finn and I developed the needed approach.

The Lucas Critique and its impact on Prescott and Kydland

At this point, the role of the Lucas Critique has to be taken into account. However, before assessing its impact on Prescott and Kydland, the evolution of this watershed paper itself must be dealt with. In his Nobel lecture, Prescott indicates that he and Kydland had read the Lucas Critique paper as early as 1973 (2004, 373–74, 2006e). There are, in fact, two drafts of 'Econometric policy evaluation: A critique.' The first is dated April 1973, and was prepared for the Phillips Curve conference, University of Rochester, 20–21 April; the second is the May 1973 revision of the April 1973 paper, which was the version eventually published in 1976. There are differences between the April and May drafts of the Critique, such as changes in the model in the section entitled 'Taxation and investment demand,' inclusion of responses to discussion at the Rochester Conference, and a specific point made by Prescott. In the April 1973 draft, the section on taxation and investment contains an approach based upon a 'standard accelerator model of investment behavior with a cash flow expression incorporating the tax structure, following Jorgenson [1963],' and aggregated from the firm to industry level (Lucas 1973a, 17). The May 1973 revision, which was eventually published in 1976, also has a section entitled 'Taxation and investment demand,' but the approach is that of a standard accelerator model of investment behavior, based, in part, on Hall and Jorgenson (1967). In recent correspondence, Lucas recalled (2006, 13 August) that 'the later model is an improvement... the problem here was exposition: How to explain what the point was simply.' In the acknowledgements on the title page of the May draft, Lucas thanked Prescott, among others, for 'helpful reactions to an earlier draft of his paper.' Lucas recalled (2006) that 'It is hard to isolate Ed's influence. He and I had working out the theory of investment together long before this, so all my thinking on investment was influenced by him. Note 16 in the May version is certainly a response to Ed: He had kidded me about being careless about time units earlier: "If you want a big effect, why not measure time in seconds?"'

Moreover, as Lucas also recalled (2006), the concluding paragraphs in the section on Phillips Curves in the May draft were 'probably added on in response' to the Rochester discussions. In the April 1973 draft, Lucas concluded this section by writing that 'Evidently, the *actual* [his emphasis] consequences of an increase in p (that is an increase in the average inflation rate . . .) will have no relation to the long-run prediction based on [equation] (22)' (1973a, 25). In the May 1973 revision, Lucas added two paragraphs to the end of this section. In these he stated the central message of his Critique regarding empirical Phillips Curves: first, that the 'long run . . . relationship as calculated or simulated in the conventional way has *no* bearing on the actual consequences of pursuing a policy of inflation'; second, that 'empirical Phillips curves will appear subject to "parameter drift" . . . unpredictable for all but the very near future' (1973b, 29).

Interestingly enough, the importance of detailed textural analysis can also be seen in the January 1976 *Econometrica* paper of Cooley and Prescott, 'Estimation in the presence of stochastic parameter variation.' A close inspection of this paper shows that the manuscript was originally received in August 1972, *before* the presentation of the April 1973 draft of the Lucas Critique. The 'last revision' was received in November 1974 (1976, 180). This explains the inclusion in the text of the *central message* of the Lucas Critique (1976a, 167). The reference, however, is *not* to the *published* version of the Lucas Critique, but to a 'Carnegie–Mellon working paper, 1973' (1976a, 183).

The Lucas Critique impacted on Prescott, for one, *even before the April 1973 draft, on Prescott's own account*, for, as he recalled (2006a, 8 August), 'When Bob discussed with me the theme of Econometric Policy Evaluation (which was when he was orchestrating the theme in his paper), the importance of his insight did not hit me. That was in 1972. As soon as I saw the paper, it hit me and hit me hard.' In further correspondence, he wrote (2006c, 15 August),

> When in 1972 he pointed out to me that the equations of the macro econometric models were not policy invariant, I did not realize the importance of the point. After hearing the Critique presented and reading one of the versions, I realized the importance of the point. We had to do something different to evaluate policy. I did see how to evaluate policy rules in theory at least after hearing the Critique. I did not consider the details of the examples important. The Critique

led me to conclude that econometrically, something had to change. Eventually I came to the conclusion that we had to organize our empirical knowledge around preferences and technology, that is people's willingness and ability to substitute and not around equations. Given the policy rule and preferences and technology, economists should compute the equilibrium law of motion for that policy rule.

Moreover, in his Nobel lecture, he wrote (2004, 373, 2006e),

A key assumption in the system-of-equations approach is that the equations are policy invariant. As Lucas points out in his critique...this assumption is inconsistent with dynamic economic theory. His insight made it clear that there was no hope for the neo-classical synthesis – that is, the development of neo-classical under-pinnings of the system-of-equations macro models. Fortunately, with advances in dynamic economic theory an alternative set of tractable macro models was developed for drawing scientific inference. The key development was recursive competitive equilibrium theory in Lucas and Prescott (1971), and Lucas (1972). Equilibrium being represented as a set of stochastic processes with stationary transition probabilities was crucial to the revolution in macroeconomics.

The evolutionary story of the overall Kydland–Prescott approach, however, does not end with Lucas and Prescott (1971) and the Lucas Critique (1973); rather, it starts there. In correspondence, Prescott recalled (2001, 29 December),

Kydland in his dissertation (1973)...extends recursive methods to...class symmetric dynamic games. This formulation is exploited in Kydland and my paper 'Rules rather than discretion: the time inconsistency of optimum plans' (1977a), written in 1975 while I was visiting the Norwegian School of Business and Economics, and in my and Rajnish Mehra's paper 'Recursive competitive equilibrium' (1980).

Kydland, for his part, described his 1973 Carnegie–Mellon thesis entitled 'Decentralized macroeconomic planning,' which was supervised jointly by Ed Prescott and Sten Thore, as placing emphasis on Stackelberg dynamic games, the time inconsistency issue, and player dominance, with the fiscal policy maker dominant and the monetary policy maker the follower (Kydland, interview, 10 October 2005).

However, in order to fully comprehend the evolution of the Kydland–Prescott approach, we must now turn to the phase of transition and transformation, that is, from 1973 to 1978, which encompasses their 'search' for dynamic models and rules in order to evaluate policy. For, as Prescott said in correspondence (2005d, 20 November), 'Lucas's Critique did influence Finn and me to search for optimal policy rules. This is discussed in my Nobel address.' And indeed, in it he wrote (2004, 374, 2006e),

> Finn and I had read the Lucas critique and knew that for dynamic equilibrium models, only policy rules could be evaluated. This led us to search for a best rule to follow, where a rule specifies policy actions as a function of the state or position of the economy. We had worked on this problem before Finn left Carnegie–Mellon to join the faculty of the Norwegian School of Business and Economics in 1973. In academic year 1974–1975 I visited the Norwegian School of Business and Economics, and in the spring of 1975 Finn and I returned to this problem. This is when we wrote our paper 'Rules rather than discretion: the inconsistency of optimal plans...'. Kydland and Prescott, then, *had read Lucas Critique in 1973*, and by 1975 had written a first draft of their 'Rules vs. Discretion' paper. But before this, they had to throw off what they considered to be the intellectual blinder of 'optimal control.'

The transitional phase: Dynamic equilibrium models, rules, and stabilization policy

As Prescott wrote in his Nobel lecture (2004, 373), 'before the transformation, optimal policy selection was a matter of solving...a control problem...the optimal policy is time-consistent, and dynamic programming techniques can be used to find the optimal policy. This is true even if there is uncertainty in the model economy.' And, in a series of papers, Kydland and Prescott individually, and jointly – Prescott with Cooley, as noted above, and then Mehra – made the transition from the pre-dynamic general equilibrium 'systems of equations' approach to the post-transformation approach as manifest in their 1977 and 1982 papers.

Control vs. game theoretic approaches to stabilization

The first of the joint Kydland–Prescott papers influenced by the April 1973 Lucas Critique was their 1973 paper 'Optimal stabilization.' The first draft of the paper was presented in June 1973 at the NBER-NSF

Chicago conference on stochastic control and economic systems with the subtitle 'a new formulation.' As Kydland recalls (2005a, 24 October),

> Ed and I ... [were] influenced by a paper by Lucas in writing our paper for the June 1973 conference in Chicago at which we presented the first draft of the paper, which we started to work on in April 1973 (I remember mainly because we started just before I defended my dissertation)....

As Chow recalls (2005, 26 October),

> There were a number of papers presented in that conference by (at least by now) well-known economists, including Ed Burmeister, J Philip Cooper, Richard Cyert, Richard Day, Morris DeGroot, Ray Fair, Stan Fischer, David Kendrick, Robert Holbrook, Michael Intrilligator, Morton Kamien, Robert Pindyck, Gordon Rausser, Steve Ross, Michael Rothschild, Nancy Schwartz, Chris Sims, and John Taylor, among others. The paper by Kydland and Prescott did not seem to stand out among some of these other good papers.

In the 1973 paper, as Kydland later wrote (1975, 334), 'the problem of finding optimal stabilization policies for a competitive economy was formulated as a dominant player stochastic game. The policy maker is the dominant player, taking into account the reaction functions of economic agents. The results were found to have important implications for econometric policy evaluation.' A second version of the paper, with the subtitle 'a new approach,' was presented at a conference on modeling and simulation in May 1974, and what would seem to be an abridged version was published in the conference proceedings (1974). Besides the *methodological* impact described by Prescott, Kydland also recalled the *expositional* impact of Lucas's April 1973 draft, stating (2005a), 'that paper by Bob already included an investment-tax-credit example, and Ed's and my key example, in both our 1973 paper and later in the rules vs. discretion paper, involved investment tax credit.'

As will be seen below, Kydland's recollection is confirmed by reference to Prescott's unpublished April 1974 paper 'Money, expectations and the business cycle.' This paper, 'written for discussion only' (Prescott, 1974), was presented by Prescott 'in the fall of 1974' at the Norwegian School of Business and Economics, which, as noted above, he visited in 1974–75 (2005e, 20 November). On the title page, Prescott said that the paper represented 'work in progress.' In the introduction, he outlined the *'operational* framework' (his emphasis) he wanted to develop. This involved the utilization of 'a dynamic general equilibrium framework, in its true sense' (1974, 1). Prescott went on, in a note, to refer to both the 1973 version of Lucas's Critique and also his 1973 paper with Kydland, cited above (1974, 2). As he wrote, 'Kydland and Prescott [1973] used this approach [i.e. the analysis and evaluation of "policy *rules*" (his emphasis) which specify, as he put it "a vector of policy variables ... as a function of state variables (and possibly lagged variables)] to evaluate investment tax credit policies..."' (1974, 2).

But again, more is involved here than simply the confirmation of rec-ollections. For Prescott's April 1974 paper can be said to have set out a *dual-purpose research agenda*. This is seen in his statement of 'goals' and again in his summary and conclusions. As he put it, these goals were '(1) to develop a theory of the business cycle which is a competitive equilib-rium ... and (2) to develop operational procedures to evaluate alternative stabilization policy rules' (1974, 19). He also talked about the relation-ship between the 'business cycle application' and a 'full employment path, which can be determined using optimal growth theory' (1974, 18) and the need for 'methods ... to compute the competitive equilibrium' (1974, 19). He then presented as an example of the proposed approach, a model including a production function with a technology shift param-eter, capital stock equations, a utility function for preferences, policy functions, and an objective function; the model also included state and decision variables (1974, 20–21). He went on to say that 'there is a need for developments which permit the direct calculation of the competitive equilibrium for structures of reasonable complexity' (1974, 24). Finally, Prescott concluded (1974, 25), 'In summary, this is but a first step towards the development of a theory of the business cycle and an operational framework for correctly evaluating stabilization policy. Much research remains to be done.' But this task would only be made easier by resolu-tion of the issue of how, and whether, 'control theory' could be applied to the problem of economic stabilization.

Kydland's early contributions

In a series of conference presentations and published papers based upon his own 1973 dissertation 'Decentralized macroeconomic planning,' over the period 1974–1977, Kydland dealt with, among other issues, the question of whether 'decentralized policy-making' could be consid-ered 'as a dynamic game'; for example, in his June 1975 *IER* paper (1975, 334) (received March 1974, revised August 1974).

The same year, 1975, according to his own recollections, Kydland submitted his 'assignment problem paper ["Decentralized stabilization policies: optimization and the assignment problem"] to a stochastic control conference to take place in Boston in May' (Kydland, Nobel auto-biography, 2005). According to the conference program as reported in the Spring 1976 issue *Annals of Social and Economic Measurement*, this was the paper that was listed in the May 1975 conference program (Chow, Personal Communication, 26 October 2005). And indeed the 'assign-ment problem' paper was published in 1976 in the *Annals*. However, as Kydland recalled,

> At some point early in the conference, Gregory Chow announced a session for work in progress. I signed up to talk about Ed's and my paper, and was told I could go first. All hell broke loose. Everyone was trying to locate the error [time inconsistency]. Admittedly, we had chosen a rather provocative title for our first draft: 'On the inapplica-bility of optimal control for policymaking'. I was certain nothing was wrong. With all my experience in dynamic dominant-player games, I knew time inconsistency had to be an issue. I suppose at that point, after what happened at that presentation, I realized our findings could generate considerable attention. Moreover, as a consequence of the difficulty people had in understanding the time inconsistency, we decided to add, for expository reasons, a Phillips-curve example to our investment-tax-credit example before we submitted our revised version of the paper to the *Journal of Political Economy*. As I recall, it was motivated by a model in a recent paper by Phelps and Taylor. Of course, that example has turned out to be used a lot by subsequent writers (Kydland, Nobel Autobiography, 2005).

Prescott, for his part, said, 'Finn and I have different recollections as to how the Phillips Curve example was added. I remember the paper being submitted to the *JPE* and the editor Jacob Frenkel saying a simple example was needed. We made this addition and resubmitted the paper' (2008).

Kendrick, for his part (2005a, 15), recalled that Kydland's 'talk at the meeting was well attended and listened to carefully.' According to Kendrick, this talk, in conjunction with the Lucas Critique, brought about a situation in which 'work on control theory models in general and stochastic control models in particular went into rapid decline and remained that way for a substantial time.' In his view, this was 'a ter-rible case' of 'throwing the baby out with the bath water,' as 'work on uncertainty (other than additive noise terms) in macroeconomic policy mostly stopped and then slowly was replaced with methods of solving models with rational expectations and with game theory approaches' (2005a, 15). Kendrick qualified this (2005a, 15, note 6), however, by referring to exceptions in papers by Turnovsky and Brock (1980, 1981).

In March 1975, while at the Norwegian School of Economics and Business Administration, Kydland circulated a discussion paper entitled 'Equilibrium solutions in dynamic dominant-player models,' which was eventually published in *JET* in August 1977. Kydland referred to this paper in his 1976 paper 'Decentralized stabilization policies: optimization and the assignment problem,' published in *Annals of Social and Economic Measurement*, as noted above, and this discussion paper was also referred to by Kydland and Prescott in their June 1977 *JPE* paper 'Rules vs. Discretion.'

Rules vs. discretion, time-to-build, stabilization, control, recursive competitive equilibrium, and the business cycle

The 'key example' in their seminal 1977 paper, as Kydland put it, was the 'investment–tax–credit example.' *What is important to realize is that this example encompasses a 'two-period time to build approach'* reflecting 'the fact that time is required to expand capacity, and investment expenditures occur over the entire time interval' (1977, 482), as recognized by both Kydland (2005, interview, 10 October) and Prescott (2006d, 17 August). *This is a crucial point in the evolution of the Kydland–Prescott approach, for it illustrates the inherent linkage between their 1977 and 1982 papers.*

In recent correspondence (2006d, 17 August), Prescott has also stressed the dynamic general equilibrium nature of the 'Rules vs. discretion' paper. After acknowledging that the investment–tax–credit example did 'exploit the rental price of capital theory of Jorgenson and of Jorgenson and Hall,' he continued on to say,

> but what is important is that it exploits the theory developed in 'Investment under uncertainty' to derive the equilibrium process given the policy rule. Unlike Bob's [Lucas] 'Neutrality' paper, there is capital accumulation so it was truly dynamic. Lucas comes up with the mapping from an investment tax policy rule to the equilibrium process of the economy...Finn and my analysis introduces maximizing households, so we have a dynamic general equilibrium analysis.

In 1977, Prescott also published a paper entitled 'Should control theory be used for economic stabilization?' in the Carnegie–Rochester series. In this paper, Prescott concluded that not only should control theory not be utilized for stabilization, but 'until a tested theory of the business cycle is available, it is best that active stabilization not be attempted' (1977, 33). Modigliani and Taylor, among others, commented on the paper. Modigliani was critical of what he called 'Prescott's provocative paper,' but still said that it had 'sensitized "him" to a potentially important problem' (1977, 98). Taylor, for his part, made the point that in his paper Prescott had distinguished between 'optimal control theory' which 'is inappropriate for stabilization problems' and 'optimal design theory,' which, according to Taylor, on Prescott's view, 'should be used to find policy rules which generate the best operating characteristics for the economy.' Taylor's conclusion was 'not that optimal control theory is inappropriate for stabilization problems but simply that its incorrect use is inappropriate' (1977, 94). In a rejoinder, while disagreeing with a number of issues raised by Modigliani in his critique, Prescott reiterated what he took to be 'the major point' of his own paper, which he said is that 'if dynamic economic behavior (e.g. fluctuation in economic activity) is viewed as an equilibrium phenomenon, with agents forecasting efficiently conditional on their information sets, then optimal control is inappropriate' (1977, 101).

In December 1977, Prescott and Mehra circulated a draft paper entitled 'Recursive competitive equilibria and capital asset pricing' (Prescott and Mehra, 1977). In 1978, this paper was revised and given the title 'Recursive competitive equilibrium: the case of homogenous households,' and circulated as a Columbia University Graduate School of Business working paper. The paper was eventually published in the September 1980 issue of *Econometrica*. The 1978 draft of the paper was received in December 1978, and the final corrected version in December 1979 (1980a, 1378). In their 1977 draft, Prescott and Mehra further developed the recursive competitive equilibrium framework originally presented in Lucas and Prescott (1971). Moreover, they extended it to the analysis of the cases of 'many consumers' and 'small fluctuations in aggregate output.' In the former case, their analysis was of 'an economy with many consumer classes, where each class has different preferences, but the same discount factor' (1977, 21). The latter was an analysis of the case where 'fluctuations in aggregate output are but a few per cent' (1977, 22). They concluded (1977, 23), 'These difficult and important extensions and applications will be the subject of future inquiry within our recursive competitive equilibrium framework.'

The former case is an important one, since – based upon the 1977 draft, as cited above – if all agents have the same discount rate, and if conditions satisfy that a competitive equilibrium Pareto Optimum is ensured, then, as Prescott and Mehra later wrote (1980a, 1365), 'equilibrium processes for economic aggregates and prices [for some heterogeneous consumer economy] will be observationally equivalent to those for some homogeneous consumer economy.' Moreover, that fluctuations in aggregate output are mentioned in their 1977 draft is also significant, although there is no mention of this in the 1980 version. The importance of the 1977 and 1978 drafts of Prescott and Mehra lies not only in them being the linkage between Lucas and Prescott (1971) and their 1980 paper, but also in their impact, it would seem, on Long and Plosser's 1983 paper, that is to say, on the *1980 draft* of Long and Plosser, as will be shown below.

In their 1983 *JPE* paper, Long and Plosser wrote (1983, 43, note 4),

> The model we employ is quite similar to the model described in Prescott and Mehra (1980). Their remarks (p. 1365) about the identical consumers assumption (i.e. it is not quite as restrictive as it may appear) and their treatment of the optimality of competitive equilibrium are particularly relevant. They do not, however, explicitly consider the business-cycle implications of their models.

Moreover, in correspondence with Mehra (2005a, 6 September; 2005b and 6 September 2005c), he acknowledged that Long had seen the 1977 version of Prescott–Mehra at a Rochester 'job seminar' that took place in 'late 1977 or early 1978.' The Prescott–Mehra paper was published in September 1980. Now, the earliest citation of what was to become the Long–Plosser paper this author has found dates to 1980, as cited in the August 1980 draft of the now classic 'Two Charlie's paper' (Nelson and Plosser, 1980). This implies that unless either Long or Plosser, or both, were referees of the 1980 Prescott–Mehra paper – which is doubtful – it can be surmised that Long and Plosser most probably extended the 1977 and 1978 Prescott and Mehra approach.

Enigmas and variorum drafts: The Kydland–Prescott NBER conference paper

The transitional phase in the evolution of the Kydland–Prescott approach reached its ultimate stage with the presentation of a paper by Kydland and Prescott at the 1978 NBER conference on rational expectations and economic policy. The story surrounding this watershed paper is *enigmatic,* to say the least. This is because those who attended the conference, and commented on the Kydland–Prescott paper, did not realize its significance, as will be seen below, although this is not unique, as the same phenomenon occurred when Muth's original Rational Expectations paper was presented at an Econometric Society meeting in December 1959 (see Young and Darity, 2001). Moreover, the evolution of the 1978 conference paper itself, from its *initial* form, through *the draft presented at the conference,* to its *final published version* in the 1980 NBER conference volume, is a key element in the 'Time to build' story.

In order to understand the importance of this paper in the *ongoing* intellectual process that culminated in the 1982 'Time to build' paper, however, we must first turn to how Lucas – and Kydland—perceived what occurred at the conference where the Kydland–Prescott paper on 'Stabilization Policy' was given. There are two versions of Lucas's recollections regarding the NBER conference held at the Bald Peak Colony Club, New Hampshire, October 1978 (Fischer, 1980). In his 'Professional Memoir,' Lucas wrote (2001, 28),

> At that conference, Ed Prescott presented a model of his and Finn Kydland's that was a kind of mixture of Brock and Mirman's model of growth [Brock and Mirman, 1972] subject to stochastic technology shocks and my model of monetary shocks. When Ed presented his results, everyone could see they were important but the paper was so novel and complicated that no one could see exactly what they were. Later on, as they gained more experience through numerical simulations of their Bald Peak model, Kydland and Prescott found that monetary shocks were just not pulling their weight: By removing all monetary aspects of the theory, they obtained a far simpler and more comprehensible structure that fit postwar US time series just as well as the original version. Besides introducing an important substantive refocusing of business cycle research, Kydland and Prescott introduced a new style of comparing theory to evidence that has had an enormous, beneficial effect on empirical work in the field.

Lucas published 'Present at the creation: reflections on the 2004 Nobel Prize to Finn Kydland and Edward Prescott' in the *Review of Economic Dynamics* (2005). Lucas wrote (2005, 777),

> The first public presentation of 'Time to build...' occurred at an Oct. 1978 conference sponsored by the Federal Reserve Bank of Boston. You might picture the scene as something like the New York

appearance of King Kong, when the theater curtain is drawn and the 40-foot ape is revealed, struggling with his chains. But it was nothing like that. The paper . . . was too hard to be read in advance, and Ed's presentation was technical and confusing.

He continued (2005, 778),

I should say that this paper was not the version that was published in *Econometrica* in 1982. The 1978 version had a kind of nominal wage stickiness, related to my 1972 information-based model (Lucas, 1972). This feature is now interesting mainly as evidence that Ed and Finn did not start out by attempting to show that business cycles were real in origin or that monetary influences were unimportant. Their substantive aims at the time were pretty standard. But their methods were brand new, and it was only after much experimentation with the model that they were led to the *discovery* [his emphasis] that the real, technology shocks were doing all the work, and the sticky wage part was contributing nothing.

In his Nobel autobiography, Kydland also recalled events surrounding the 1978 NBER conference paper. As he put it (2005, autobiography),

For an NBER conference in 1978, we wrote a paper that was somewhat schizophrenic. It contained a business cycle model, but also evaluated stabilization policy. The main idea behind the latter was that changes in taxes were costly as a way to balance the government budget over the cycle. Instead the 'slack' should be picked up by fluctuations in government debt. In the end, we were asked to reduce the length of the paper for the resulting conference volume published by the NBER in 1980, and we had to leave out much of that material.

Detailed comments on the Kydland–Prescott conference paper were made by Feldstein (1980), Hall, (1980) and Taylor (1980), 187–194. The general discussion appearing in the volume also cited comments by Blinder and Nelson, among others. Recollections of some of those who attended the conference, and also of those who commented on the paper, are now presented so as to gauge the reactions to the paper then, and now.

Blanchard, who attended the conference, recalled (2002, 21 August) that he did not think that the Kydland–Prescott paper 'made much of a splash . . . we were still much more in the standard IS-LM AS with expectations frame, to listen to that paper in the right way.' Parkin also attended, and recalled (2002, 21 August) that

> The 1978 NBER conference presentation of 'A competitive theory of fluctuations and the feasibility and desirability of stabilization policy' made virtually no impact. Everyone to whom I spoke about the paper thought it was an interesting exercise that had no implications for either policy or future research. We were still wrestling with short-run non neutrality. The idea that *real* disturbances could generate fluctuations and that money might be neutral after all was just too far off the radar screen for (almost) everyone. The same can be said about both the 1982 paper and the L–P [Long–Plosser] paper. People just were not thinking the way that Finn and Ed (or John and Charlie) were.

Howitt, for his part, recalled (2005, 5 September),

> Yes, I was at the NBER conference, but I have no memory at all of the Kydland–Prescott paper. Nor do I recall ever seeing it referred to subsequently. My attention at the time was all on the issue of how monetary policy matters, and I probably saw this paper as being too far off topic to take seriously.

When asked about his recollections, Blinder (2005, 30 August) – as Howitt – said that while he was at the 1978 conference 'given what has happened since, I am a bit embarrassed to confess that I have no recollection at all of the Kydland–Prescott paper,' adding that as regards the impact of the NBER conference paper, there was 'not much at the time ... Hardly anyone appreciated where this might lead until after the 1982 Kydland–Prescott paper.' Hall, who commented on the Kydland–Prescott paper at the conference recalled (2002, 2 July), 'My comments refer to the "equilibrium model" which was the way I thought about those models the time.'

Nelson, for his part, had perhaps the clearest recollections of the NBER conference, while also making significant comments on the Kydland–Prescott paper. As he recalled (2002, 3 October),

> It was a great conference and I remember the general scene vividly (including noticing that Paul Samuelson was reading the St. Louis Fed weekly newsletter on money supply, and it had his name as addressee

on it!). I can't really say that I recall the Kydland–Prescott paper making a splash, but we all had our personal reaction. Mine was that sources of lags they mention, particular time to build, did not seem sufficient to account for the very great persistence of business cycle fluctuations as implied by their AR equation on page 171 [of the conference volume]. My comment is directed to the fact that the sum of coefficients is quite close to unity, so in light of the Dickey–Fuller problem of downward bias (which I was working on at the time in connection with the Nelson–Plosser paper), it is not clear that the sum is significantly below unity. The Nelson–Plosser view was that if it is unity than the cycle is not just long-lived but possibly not stationary. Of course, what we argued in our paper was that the unit root – sum equal to one – could not be rejected, so detrending may be entirely artifactual and the trend process may account for variation that the Kydland–Prescott's simple linear detrending attributes to the cycle. Indeed we argued that perhaps all the variance in output is attributable to trend, leaving no transitory 'cycle' to explain.

Above, the term *enigmatic* was used to describe the story of the 1978 Kydland–Prescott paper. Close inspection of the comment by Taylor on the paper published in the conference volume reveals the following anomaly. In his comment, Taylor wrote (1980, 193), 'Kydland and Prescott build their equilibrium business cycle model upon the assumption of utility maximization. That is, they posit a representative household utility function which depends on consumption, leisure, and *government expenditures*, and they assume that households maximize this utility function subject to budget constraints' [my emphasis]. However, in the utility function in the version of the paper as published in the conference volume, *government expenditures do not appear* (1980a, 174, 177). When asked about this, Kydland replied (2006, 30 August),

We wrote a paper for the NBER conference containing a business cycle model (not unlike, as I recall, that in the paper I had written up in preparation for my 'job talk' – that is, converting my one-year visiting position to permanent – at CMU that same spring) along with an application to public finance. That application would have shown that fluctuation in the desired provision of public goods, combined with cyclical fluctuations otherwise, implied that the fluctuation ought to be picked up primarily by changing government debt and not by changing tax 'rates.' In other words, the paper had somewhat of a dual-focus (often not a good idea), as reflected also in its title. After the conference, the editor (Stan Fischer, as I recall) told us the paper was too long for the volume and had to be cut. So we more or less omitted the portion emphasizing cyclical public finance (with a heavy heart, because we thought the message was really interesting and innovative). Of course, with that emphasis removed, there was no longer any point in keeping government purchases in the utility function.

But more is involved than simply the elision of material from the version of the conference paper as presented by Prescott, and commented uponby Taylor, among others. There are, in fact, *five versions* of the 1978 Kydland–Prescott conference paper, four drafts (1978a, b, c, d), and the published version (1980a). Finn Kydland has kindly provided the author with some of these drafts. Kydland has also explained – in an extensive interview (2005, interview, 10 October) – their significance and relation to the published version of the conference paper, and the relationship of the conference paper to *other work* in the context of what can be called the 'time to build research program,' all within the framework of the *overarching* Kydland–Prescott research program.

According to Kydland (2005, interview, 10 October), the 'first draft' of the October 1978 NBER paper, that is to say 'Time to build,' as Lucas put it (2005), was a draft paper by Kydland and Prescott entitled 'Persistence of unemployment in equilibrium,' dated 19 April 1978 (1978a). This draft was the basis for the 'time to build' research program, in Kydland's view (2005, interview, 10 October), *as it was the first modern real business cycle paper, in that it was quantitative and encompassed models of people and businesses* (1978a, 5). The catalyst for this paper was that both Kydland and Prescott were 'bothered by "persistence" based upon rigidities and adaptive expectations' (Kydland, 2005, interview, 10 October). The draft included an explicit time to build feature in 'the basic model' (1978a, 5–6) and a quadratic utility function, in addition to the possibility of monetary shocks (1978a, 9).

Significantly, the earliest version of the Hodrick–Prescott paper (1978) is cited; the importance of this paper to the story overall will be dealt with below. As Kydland and Prescott wrote (1978a, 2),

It has generally been the belief that prices and output move procyclically (See Lucas (1977) and Sargent (1978)). Recent empirical results by Hodrick and Prescott (1978) for the period 1947–77 indicate, however, that deviations from trends in the two series are negatively correlated. This is true even when the years after 1973 are excluded.

This observation would hardly be consistent with monetary shocks being the major cause of fluctuations. In view of this, it appears appropriate to look to real shocks, such as technology shocks, as an explanation of this perhaps surprising phenomenon.

According to Kydland (2005, interview, 10 October), the April 1978 draft is linked to both the 1978 Kydland–Prescott NBER paper and to the paper by Kydland entitled 'Analysis and policy in competitive models of economic fluctuations' (1980). A notable feature of the April draft was that according to the title page it was 'preliminary and incomplete' and comprised 'Background material for GSIA Seminar, April 19th, 1978.' According to Kydland (2005, interview, 10 October), he gave this seminar, as he was being considered at the time for a tenure track position. Interestingly enough, according to Kydland (2005, interview, 10 October), Black read the paper and mailed a list of questions to him.

Most importantly, however, is the fact that the model presented in this April 1978 draft was the basis for the model that appeared in the *published* version of the 1978 Kydland–Prescott paper, as will be shown below. There is no government expenditure in the utility function in the April 1978 draft, and 'the driving terms of the model are productivity and possibly tastes' (1978a, 11). The model is in a 'dynamic competitive equilibrium' (dynamic general equilibrium) framework (1978a, 11–13). The 'draft' entitled 'On the possibility and desirability of stabilization policy' actually had *two draft* versions: the first, a *preliminary* version (1978b), dated September 1978; *and* the second, *an amended version of the same title actually presented at the NBER conference, also dated September 1978* (1978c). According to the title pages, *both* were 'Prepared for the NBER conference on rational expectations and economic policy, October 13–14, 1978.' The *major* differences between the preliminary version (1978b) and that submitted to and presented at the NBER conference by Prescott (1978c) were the inclusion, in the latter, of a number of important illustrative examples, and the addition of two figures. The final version was dated 'October 1978, revised December 1978' (1978d). According to the title page, the title was changed to 'A competitive theory of fluctuations and the feasibility and desirability of stabilization policy.' This was also the title of the paper *as published* in the conference volume.

Interestingly enough, an additional joint Kydland–Prescott paper that impacted somewhat on their NBER paper was a paper originally dated 'November 1977, revised May 1978,' entitled 'Rational Expectations,

Dynamic Optimal Taxation, and the Inapplicability of Optimal Control' (1977b). This paper later appeared, with a slightly different title and in revised form, in *Journal of Economic Dynamics and Control* (1980), but it was cited by them with its *earlier* title in the October (December) 1978 'revised' version of 'A Competitive Theory,' with the last paragraph of the initial 'Dynamic Optimal Taxation' paper actually becoming the basis for a 'footnote' in the 'Competitive Theory' paper.

There are a number of differences between the amended September 1978 version (1978c), which, on the basis of Taylor's comment and Kydland's recollection as cited above, *was that presented at the conference*, and the October–December 1978 revision (1978d) – both formal and substantive. Moreover, there is one very minor – albeit significant – difference between the October–December 1978 revision and the version published in 1980 (1980a), in the form of an additional reference in a note in the text, as will be seen below.

Moreover, the October–December 1978 revision contained an abstract, absent from the September 1978 amended version, which read as follows:

A competitive theory combining elements of Lucas' (1972, 1975) monetary shock theory with a model of equilibrium capital accumulation, under uncertainty is developed. The model assumes that multiple periods are required to build new capital goods. The resulting equilibrium process displays both the observed co-movements of economic aggregates and observed serial correlation of real output from trend. A conclusion is that the tax rates should be constant over the cycle. This does not minimize fluctuations but does minimize the burden of financing government expenditures.

The difference between the references in the September 1978 amended version, October–December 1978 revision, and the 1980 published version include citation, in the *latter versions*, of published papers by Debreu (1954) and Friedman (1948), working papers by Brock (1978) and Prescott and Mehra (1978), and two 1978 Carnegie–Mellon working papers by Kydland and Prescott, including their paper 'Persistence of unemployment in equilibrium.' Moreover, to the note (1978d, 10, 5; 1980a, 175, note 5) referring to the passage 'Ours is a competitive theory which combines the Lucas (1972) monetary shock model with a model of capital accumulation in an environment with shocks to technology,' the following was added in the 1980 published version: 'Black (1978b) has argued that real factors can explain aggregate fluctuations.'

But the crucial difference between the September 1978 amended version (1978c), the October–December 1978 revision (1978d) and the 1980 published version (1980a) can be seen in the *model* in the latter versions; a model which emanates from the Kydland–Prescott 'Persistence' paper of April 1978 vintage (1978a), that is, in Kydland's view, as cited above, the *first modern real business cycle paper*. Indeed, as Prescott recalled (2008, 13 February), 'I remember the summer of 1978 when Finn and I figured out how to use the neoclassical growth model and the growth facts to restrict the parameters of the linear-quadratic economies. That changed everything.'

The post-transitional phase: Fluctuations, empirical investigation, time to build, and aftermath

In his paper 'Business cycle research: methods and problems' (1998), Prescott included a section entitled 'History and overview of business cycle theory.' In it he said (1998, 5–6) that 'Lucas defined business cycles to be recurrent fluctuations of output and employment about trend. He wrote that the key business facts were the co-movements of economic time series.' Prescott continued, 'Hodrick and I (1980) developed a statistical definition of the business cycle component of an economic time series... Exploiting Arrow–Debreu language, recursive methods, and computational methods, Kydland and I (1982) derived the implications of growth theory of business cycle fluctuations.'

In correspondence, Prescott later provided retrospective assessments of the history and the impact of the 1978 and 1982 'Time to build' *papers*. Because of their significance, they are cited at length here. He wrote (2001, 29 December; 2002, 24 July),

> the 1978 paper did not have much of an impact. In fact Finn and my 1982 paper did not have much of an impact. At the time... the only person who thought it was important was Bob Lucas. The big break in Finn and my thinking... came [in 1978] when [we] decided to begin with the growth model with the leisure decision endogenous... [and] to use the growth model to study fluctuations. The beauty of growth theory is the connection between it and the system of national accounts. Restricting our linear-quadratic economy so that it behaved in the same way as the growth model when not to distant from the steady state seems little in retrospect, but was a major [breakthrough]... At the time we... were convinced that monetary shocks were the cause of business cycle fluctuations... Finn and my paper forced to change my mind. Prior to writing the

paper, and finding that the productivity shocks were of the right magnitude and persistence, I was certain that monetary shocks were the factor giving rise to business cycle fluctuations and the problem was to find the propagation mechanism for these shocks. We were searching for a propagation mechanism for monetary shocks along lines suggested by... Frisch many years before. At the time... Black and... Plosser... [were] the only people I know who would argue that real shocks are all important... Finn and I (1982) were surprised when we found that persistent changes in the factors that affect the steady state of the deterministic growth model gave rise to business cycle fluctuations. Finn and I in this paper broke a taboo against general equilibrium in macro.

In order to fully appreciate Prescott's recollections as cited above, the evolution of the 1982 Kydland–Prescott paper, in its variorum drafts, has to be dealt with. Moreover, as he is specifically mentioned in the recollections of Kydland and Prescott, and cited in the 'Time to build' papers, the role of Fisher Black in the story also has to be dealt with (that of Plosser and the development of the Long–Plosser approach will be considered in a separate paper). But before doing this, we have to consider the development of the *1978 versions* of the Hodrick–Prescott paper and its impact on the Kydland–Prescott approach to aggregate fluctuations.

Variorum drafts of Hodrick–Prescott

The importance of the Hodrick–Prescott paper in the evolution of the Kydland–Prescott approach cannot be overstressed. Indeed, as shown above, it was cited as early as the April 1978 draft of the NBER 'Time to build' conference paper, and also in the 1980 published version of this paper. The first draft of Hodrick–Prescott paper was originally entitled 'Money and business cycles in dynamic competitive equilibrium.' This was the title that appeared in the published program of the Fall 1978 Econometric Society meeting (1979, 245). The first version of the Hodrick–Prescott paper was presented on a Wednesday afternoon, 30 August 1978. The chairman of the session 'Macroeconomic implications of rational expectations' was McCallum; the discussant was Kmenta. Other papers in the session were by Evans and Sargent. But the title of the paper *actually* presented at the session was 'Postwar US business cycles: a descriptive empirical investigation' (Hodrick–Prescott, 1978). As the Hodrick–Prescott paper is a central component of the 'time to build' approach, its origin and development is an important element in the Kydland–Prescott research program overall. In recent correspondence, Hodrick provided his detailed recollections. He wrote (2005a, 24 December; 2005b, 25 Decenber),

> The genesis of the Hodrick–Prescott paper occurred when [Ed] asked me what were the stylized facts regarding the velocity of circulation of money over the business cycle. We started thinking about this issue and submitted a preliminary idea for a paper to the Econometric Society meetings. What we realized when we started working on the project was that the only way people had to describe the cyclical properties of any data series was the NBER's specific cycle and reference cycle terminology, which was not amenable to time series analysis. We needed to develop something new.
>
> We decided that we needed a way to decompose any time series into a trend and cyclical component, and we wanted the trend component to be able to change over time, but not too much. All that we were able to accomplish by the time of the Econometric Society meetings was the HP filter and some descriptive statistics...The 'Money and Business Cycles title was what we hoped to deliver, and the "Post-War..." was a descriptive title of what we actually delivered.'
>
> I presented the paper, and Jan Kmenta was the discussant. I remember him being not particularly positive about the paper, and I was at a loss for how to respond. Tom Sargent came to my defense with an eloquent speech about the importance of this type of work.
>
> There is another interesting story about the paper. We first submitted the paper to the AER, and it was rejected because the referee wanted us to use formal Bayesian smoothness priors. Around the time of the rejection, Ed was talking at the Carnegie–Rochester Conference to Bill DeWald, who was the editor of the Journal of Money, Credit and Banking. Bill said that he would like to have the paper reviewed for the JMCB, and promised to get a good referee. We submitted the paper and received a rejection because DeWald's referee didn't like the paper, at all.
>
> The referee was Milton Friedman! He indicated this in his report stating 'I have no reason the authors should not know my opinion of their paper.' He didn't like the idea that we were doing 'measurement without theory.' He thought that this issue had been settled by the Cowles Commission in the 1950s–1960s. I wish I had that report, but I don't think I do. It always seemed ironic to me that Friedman had made part of his reputation on the Monetary History of the US, and later developed theory to support the measurements done in that book.

By this time, Ed had left CMU for Minnesota, and I was on my way to Kellogg's finance department at Northwestern. We planned to revise the paper and resubmit it, and I spent a week one summer at Minnesota in the mid-1980s doing some revisions. But, we never resubmitted it.

Hodrick continued (2005b),

In early 1996, I got a call from Steve Cecchetti, who was editing the JMCB. He asked if he could publish the HP filter paper, and after talking with Ed, we said yes. We agreed that Ed and I would update the descriptive statistics, but we would not modify the paper with lots of references to the intervening literature. Steve did not know the history of the paper and was shocked by the Friedman story.

Now, this is not the place for the detailed discussion of the differences between the August 1978 version of Hodrick–Prescott and the November 1980 revision. However, it should be noted that the title itself was changed by the elision of the word 'descriptive.' In the 1978 version, the April 1978 Kydland–Prescott 'Persistence' paper is cited, while mention of this paper is elided in the November 1980 version of Hodrick–Prescott. In the introduction to the 1978 version, both stochastic monetary and real shocks are mentioned, and 'correlation between deviations from trend rate of inflation and deviations from trend real output' are analyzed (1978, 2–3). A 'two-shock theory of the business cycle is also presented' (1978, 3; also see 1978, Section 4). According to the 1978 version (1978, 3), 'it appears reasonable to conclude that an econometric analysis using dynamic equilibrium theory which is structured around real supply side and monetary or inflation shocks will one day explain a large part of the aggregate economic fluctuations including the persistence of deviations from trend experience by the US. 'In the 1980 version, emphasis is focused on the interaction of growth and cycle in investigating 'aggregate economic fluctuations.' According to this introduction (1980, 2), 'At a substantive level our primary objective...is to examine the magnitudes and stability of covariances between various economic time series and real output and the autocovariances of real output.' The 1980 version concludes by saying (1980, 23) that 'In this article no explanation of the cyclical regularities is offered. We think such an explanation can be provided only within the context of a well specified economic model. We do think it appropriate, however, to study the observations prior to theorizing.'

In June 1980, Nelson wrote Hodrick regarding the Hodrick–Prescott paper, referring to the August 1978 version, and asked for information as to its revision or publication status, so as to be able to cite the paper in the 'Two Charlie's paper' he was then putting together with Plosser. In November 1980, Prescott sent Nelson a copy of the November 1980 revision, and in a covering letter wrote,

> Enclosed is the revised version ... subsequent to our telephone conversation I learned that our method has a long history of use. We do agree that the method of decomposing high and low frequency variation matters. The question is whether first differencing is a good procedure for studying cyclical fluctuations or Bob's and my procedure or some other procedure. My view is that there are many ways to look at the data and theory is needed in the selection of the way.
>
> (Prescott, 1980b)

And it is to the application of that theory in the form of the 1982 Kydland–Prescott paper that we now turn.

'Time to build' and competitive models of economic fluctuation

The manuscript of the 1982 Kydland–Prescott paper was received by *Econometrica* in January 1981, and the revision was received a year later, in January 1982 (1982, 1369). Publication of the paper was announced in the list of accepted manuscripts that appeared in the July 1982 issue of *Econometrica* (1982, 1085), and the paper eventually appeared in the November 1982 issue. Much has been written about the impact of this paper in the form of the subsequent Kydland–Prescott Real Business Cycle research program that emanated from it. However, the evolution of the 1982 paper itself – in terms of its variorum drafts from 1977 onwards – has not been dealt with. Moreover, the 'sting in the tail' of the paper – that is, according to Kydland and Prescott, the need for 'methods ... to analyze policy rules in competitive environments' (1982, 1369; citing Kydland, 1980) – has not been noted, or discussed, and it is to these aspects of the 1982 paper that we now turn.

As in the case of their 1978 NBER 'Time to build' paper and its final version as published in 1980 (1980a), the evolution of the 1982 Kydland–Prescott 'Time to build' paper is characterized by a number of draft versions and the final version, as published in 1982. Now, the link between the April 1978 Kydland–Prescott paper 'Persistence of unemployment in equilibrium' and the 1982 'Time to build' paper can be seen in what Kydland considers(2005) to be the *first* 'formal draft' of the

1982 paper, that is, the October 1979 revised draft version entitled 'Time to build and equilibrium persistence of unemployment.' According to Kydland, this draft was just circulated for comment, 'probably to Lucas.' The term 'equilibrium persistence of unemployment' remained in the title in the October 1979, September 1980, and December 1980 versions, and was changed to 'aggregate fluctuations' *only in the December 1981 revision* sent for publication.

What is also important about the October 1979 revised version is that it contains handwritten amendments and additions attesting to the inter-action between Prescott, who was then at Minnesota and Northwestern, and Kydland at Carnegie Mellon. For example, Prescott changed the orig-inal term 'the relative demand shift "to" productivity shock' (1979, 3); added 'adjustment costs' (1979, 7; 1982, 1348) and a footnote regarding 'beginning of period stocks' (1979, 9; 1982, 1349). But more important was the utilization in this version of an *exponential* 'constant relative risk aversion utility function' (1979, 12), which is made *quadratic* in the September 1980 version (1980b, 12). According to Kydland (2005, inter-view, 10 October), the September 1980 version should be regarded as the first *complete* version; it was issued as a GSIA working paper (No. 28-80-81) and sent to Cornell for a seminar given by Kydland (2005, Nobel autobiography). Moreover, in Kydland's opinion (2005, interview, 10 October), the September 1980 version *also contained the central mes-sage* of the 1982 Kydland–Prescott paper in the form of the sentence '*Our approach integrates growth and business cycle theory*' (1980b, 2; 1982, 1345); this, according to Kydland (2005, interview, 10 October) and Prescott (2004, 376, note 1), follows from the 1978 and 1980 versions of the Hodrick–Prescott paper. Interestingly enough, the December 1980 revi-sion of 'Time to build' was submitted to *Econometrica* under the title 'Time to build and the persistence of unemployment.' The change in title in the December 1981 revision sent to *Econometrica* was to make it, in Kydland's words (2005, interview, 10 October), 'more general.'

Finally, as regards the influence of Black, while Prescott wrote in cor-respondence (2002) that he 'did not influence my thinking on business cycles,' Black's November 1979 MIT working paper entitled 'General equilibrium and business cycles' *is* cited in both the December 1980 and December 1981 revisions of the Kydland–Prescott 'Time to build' paper, and in the 1982 published version. Moreover, an earlier 1978 version of Black's working paper was cited in the drafts and published version of the Kydland–Prescott NBER conference paper.

There are five versions of Black's paper. The original version appeared in April 1978 as an MIT–Sloan School working paper (1978a), which was first revised in September 1978 (1978b) and later revised in November 1979. A 1978 version of Black's paper was not cited in the Kydland–Prescott NBER conference paper draft dated September 1978, but *was* cited in the Kydland–Prescott draft dated October 1978 and revised December 1978, and also appears in the Kydland–Prescott paper as published in the NBER conference volume (1980a, 196). Interestingly enough, the third version, that is, the November 1979 revision of Black's 1978 paper, was cited by Kydland–Prescott as early as in the September and December 1980 revisions of 'Time to build,' and also in the published version of the 'Time to build' paper (1982, 1369). The fourth version of Black's paper appeared in August 1982 as an NBER working paper. The fifth and final version was published in Black's 1987 book.

'Loose Ends': 'competitive models of economic fluctuation,' 'The role of money in a business cycle model,' and interim summary

In the section of his Nobel autobiography entitled 'Loose Ends,' Kydland recalled that in 1980 he 'wrote a first draft of a paper in which I focused on the role of money for the business cycle'; a paper which, although revised a number of times and submitted to various journals, 'remains unpublished.' Kydland did not cite the title of this paper in his Nobel piece, but acknowledged (2005, interview, 10 October) that he was referring to his May 1980 draft of 'Analysis and policy in competitive models of economic fluctuations,' which was cited at the very end of the 1982 Kydland–Prescott paper. Moreover, Kydland asserted (2005, interview, 10 October) that his 1980 paper had a 'double focus' problem, which was rectified only by its revision and transformation into his December 1987 paper 'The role of money in a business cycle model.' In this December 1987 revision, parts of the April 1981 draft of his 'Analysis and policy in competitive models of business fluctuations' (e.g. 1981, 21–30) formed the basis for an analysis of the role of money in a 'real model of aggregate fluctuations' (1987, 3–10). The final version of Kydland's May 1980 paper was issued as a Minneapolis Fed discussion paper in December 1989.

Three additional points that have to be dealt with are (i) the role of Solow's 1956 and 1957 papers; (ii) the influence of Lucas's 1972 paper 'Expectations and the neutrality of money'; and (iii) the impact of Lucas's 1977 paper 'Understanding business cycles' on the Kydland–Prescott program. With regard to Solow's papers, it is interesting to note that from the October 1979 draft of 'Time to build' to the 1982 published version of the paper, neither of Solow's papers is cited. According to Kydland (interview, 10 October 2005), while they are not mentioned because they were not directly utilized, the influence of the Solow papers was 'at the back of their minds.' This is clearly evident in Prescott's Nobel lecture (2004, 379). With regard to Lucas (1972), while it is cited in both the October 1979 and the December 1980 versions of 'Time to build,' it is not cited in the 1982 published version. Despite this, Kydland asserted (interview, 10 October 2005) that it was very influential on his thinking, and that he had originally been introduced to it in Lucas's Spring 1970 class on 'Economic fluctuations,' where an early version was taught. Kydland's explanation (interview, 10 October 2006) of why it was not cited in the published version of 'Time to build' is that this version put 'monetary shocks' to one side, and concentrated on 'real shocks,' whereas the October 1979 version included a shock that 'mimics the effect of a Lucas (1972) monetary shock' (1979, 2), and the reference was brought over into the December 1980 version, but such a shock did not appear in the published version, where the reference to Lucas (1972) was elided.

More important, however, is the role of Lucas's 'Understanding business cycles.' The paper was originally presented at the June 1976 Kiel Conference on Growth without Inflation (1976b) and, according to the introductory note in its published version, was revised in August 1976 (1977, 7). While there are a number of textural differences between the original and the revised versions, the *central message of the Lucas paper, as seen by Kydland, already appeared in the June 1976 version*. Interestingly enough, while the June 1976 version *is not mentioned*, the 1977 published version of the paper *is* cited a number of times in the Kydland–Prescott *April 1978* draft 'Persistence of unemployment in equilibrium,' which is the *first draft* of the later 'Bald Peak' paper (Lucas's 'Time to build' paper), or as Kydland put it, the *first draft* of 'Time to build' (interview, 10 October 2005). Moreover, as Kydland said (interview, 10 October 2005), they had made Lucas (1977) *operational*, and thus brought about a change from the methodological approach they took in their April 1978 'Persistence' draft to that in their 'Time to build' draft of October 1979, which, in Kydland's view, *forms one research program*. In the October 1979 version of 'Time to build,' according to Kydland (interview, 10 October 2005), Lucas's 1977 statement that 'one exhibits understanding of business cycles by constructing a <u>model</u> (Lucas's emphasis) in the most literal sense: a fully articulated artificial economy which behaves through time so as to imitate closely the time series behavior of actual economies' (1977, 11) became one of the methodological precepts for the 1982 'time to build' approach.

There are still elements in this story that remain to be told, including the influence of the Brock-Mirman papers (1972, 1973), and the ostensible impact of work of Shoven and Whalley (1972) [according to Heckman and Hansen (1996)]; and the relationship between the Kydland–Prescott story and the Long–Plosser story.

This chapter, therefore, only reflects *work in progress*, since there is more material regarding the evolution of the Kydland–Prescott research program still extant. These include unpublished correspondence and comments on papers by Kydland and Prescott, correspondence regarding the relationship between the Kydland– Prescott approach and that of Long and Plosser, and referees' reports on 'Time to Build.' This material has only recently been collected by the, and remains to be collated and integrated with what has been presented above. Moreover, recollections and documents provided by Brock, Radner, Shoven, Whalley, and Plosser, among others, remain to be assessed and integrated into the story. There is, in fact, *much more work* to be done so as to tell the *complete* story of the evolution of the Kydland–Prescott research program.

Acknowledgments

This research is sponsored by Royal Economic Society Grants. I am responsible for any errors and omissions. I wish to thank Finn Kydland, Ed Prescott, Bob Lucas, Charlie Nelson, and Bob Hodrick for providing unpublished manuscripts and their comments, and all those who allowed their unpublished papers and correspondence to be cited here.

References

Black, F. (1978a), 'General Equilibrium and Business Cycles', MIT Industrial Liason Program, Sloan School Working Paper 5-44-78, April 1978.
—— (1978b), 'General Equilibrium and Business Cycles', Sloan School Working Paper 5-44-78, revised September 1978.
—— (1979), 'General Equilibrium and Business Cycles', Sloan School Working Paper, revised November 1979.
—— (1982), 'General Equilibrium and Business Cycles', NBER Working paper No. 950, August 1982.
—— (1987), 'General Equilibrium and Business Cycles', Chapter 13 in F. Black, *Business Cycles and Equilibrium*, Blackwell: Oxford and New York.
Brock, W. (1978), 'Asset Prices in a Production Economy', Report of Center for Mathematical Studies in Business and Economics, University of Chicago: Chicago.
Brock, W. and Mirman, L. (1972), 'Optimal Economic Growth and Uncertainty: The Discounted Case', *Journal of Economic Theory* 4: 479–513.

—— (1973), 'Optimal Economic Growth and Uncertainty: The No Discounting Case', *International Economic Review* 14: 560–573.

Chow, G. (1967), 'Multiplier, Accelerator, and Liquidity Preference in the Determination of National Income in the United States', *Review of Economic Statistics* 49: 1–15.

Cooley, T. and Prescott, E. (1976), 'Estimation in the Presence of Stochastic Parameter Variation', *Econometrica* 44: 167–184.

Debreu, G. (1954), 'Valuation Equilibrium and Pareto Optimality', *Proceedings of the National Academy of Science* 40: 588–592.

Feldstein, M. (1980), Comment on Kydland and Prescott, in S. Fischer, S., ed., *Rational Expectations and Economic Policy*, NBER and University of Chicago Press: Chicago, 187–189.

Fischer, S. (ed.) (1980), *Rational Expectations and Economic Policy*, NBER and University of Chicago Press: Chicago.

Friedman, M. (1948), 'A Monetary and Fiscal Framework for Economic Stability', *American Economic Review* 38: 245–264.

Hall, R. (1980), Comment on Kydland and Prescott, in S. Fischer, S., ed., *Rational Expectations and Economic Policy*, NBER and University of Chicago Press: Chicago, 191–92.

Hall, R. and Jorgenson, D. (1967), 'Tax Policy and Investment Behavior', *American Economic Review* 57: 391–414.

Hansen, L. and Heckman, J. (1996), 'The Empirical Foundations of Calibration', *Journal of Economic Perspectives* 10: 87–104.

Hicks, J. (1973), 'Recollections and Documents', *Economica* (n.s.) 40: 2–11.

Hodrick, R. and Prescott, E. (1978), 'Post-War U.S. Business Cycles: A Descriptive Empirical Investigation', Carnegie-Mellon Working Paper 4-78-79, August 1978.

—— (1980), 'Post-War U.S. Business Cycles: An Empirical Investigation', Discussion paper No. 451, revised November 1980.

Kendrick, D. (2005a), 'Stochastic Control for Economic Models: Past, Present and The Paths Ahead', *Journal of Economic Dynamics and Control* 29: 3–30.

—— (2005b), Personal Communication, 26 October.

Kydland, F. (1973), *Decentralized Macroeconomic planning*, unpublished Ph.D. thesis, Carnegie-Mellon University.

—— (1975), 'Noncooperative and Dominant Player Solutions in Discrete Dynamic Games', *International Economic Review* 16: 321–335.

—— (1976), 'Decentralized Stabilization Policies: Optimization and The Assignment Problem', *Annals of Economic and Social Measurement* 5: 249–261.

—— (1977), 'Equilibrium Solutions in Dynamic Dominant-Player Models', *Journal of Economic Theory* 15: 307–324.

—— (1980), 'Analysis and Policy in Competitive Models of Economic Fluctuation', unpublished manuscript, Carnegie-Mellon University, May 1980.

—— (1981), 'Analysis and Policy in Competitive Models of Business Fluctuation', Carnegie-Mellon Working Paper No. 74-79-90, revised April 1981.

—— (1987), 'The Role of Money in a Business Cycle Model', Carnegie-Mellon University, revised December 1987.

—— (1989), 'The Role of Money in a Business Cycle Model', Discussion paper No. 23, Institute for empirical macroeconomics, Federal Reserve Bank of Minneapolis and University of Minnesota, December 1989.

—— (2005, Nobel autobiography), from *Les Prix Nobel, The Nobel Prizes 2004*, ed., Tore Frangsmyr, Nobel Foundation, Stockholm.

Kydland, F. and Prescott, E. (1973), 'Optimal Stabilization Policy: A New Formulation', presented at the NBER-NSF conference on stochastic control and
economic systems, Chicago, June 1973.

—— (1974), 'Optimal Stabilization: A New Approach', in W. Vogt and M. Mickle,
eds, *Modeling and Simulation*, vol. 5, Proceedings of 5th annual conference on
modeling and simulation, Pittsburgh, May 1974, 217–222.

—— (1977a), 'Rules Rather Than Discretion: The Inconsistency of Optimal Plans',
Journal of Political Economy 85: 473–492.

—— (1977b), 'Rational Expectations, Dynamic Optimal Taxation, and the
Inapplicability of Optimal Control', November 1977, revised May 1978.

—— (1978a), 'Persistence of Unemployment in Equilibrium', unpublished,
background material for GSIA seminar, 19 April 1978.

—— (1978b), 'On the Possibility and Desirability of Stabilization Policy', September 1978; Preliminary version, prepared for NBER conference, 13–14 October
1978.

—— (1978c), 'On the Possibility and Desirability of Stabilization Policy',
September 1978; prepared for NBER conference, 13–14 October 1978.

—— (1978d), 'A Competitive Theory of Fluctuations and the Feasibility and
Desirability of Stabilization Policy', NBER conference paper, October 1978;
revised, December 1978.

—— (1979), 'Time to Build and Equilibrium Persistence of Unemployment',
unpublished draft manuscript, revised October 1979.

—— (1980a), 'A Competitive Theory of Fluctuations and the Feasibility and
Desirability of Stabilization Policy', in S. Fischer (1980), ed., *Rational Expectations
and Economic Policy*, NBER and University of Chicago Press: Chicago; 169–187.

—— (1980b), 'Time to Build and the Persistence of Unemployment', Carnegie-
Mellon working paper No. 28-80-81, September 1980.

—— (1980c), 'Time to Build and The Persistence of Unemployment', Carnegie-
Mellon working paper No. 28-80-81, December 1980.

—— (1980d), 'Dynamic Optimal Taxation, Rational Expectations and Optimal
Control', *Journal of Economic Dynamics and Control* 2: 79–81.

—— (1981), 'Time to Build and Aggregate Fluctuations', Carnegie-Mellon
working paper No. 28-80-81, Revised December 1981.

—— (1982), 'Time to Build and Aggregate Fluctuations', *Econometrica* 50:
1345–1370.

Long, J. and Plosser, C. (1983), 'Real Business Cycles', *Journal of Political Economy*
91: 36–69.

—— (2005b), Personal Communication, 17 November.

Lovell, M. and Prescott, E. (1968), 'Money, Multiplier Accelerator Interaction, and
the Business Cycle', *Southern Economic Journal* 35: 60–72.

—— (1970), 'Multiple Regression with Inequality Constraints: Pretesting Bias,
Hypothesis Testing and Efficiency', *Journal of the American Statistical Association*
65: 913–925.

Lucas, R. (1972), 'Expectations and the Neutrality of Money', *Journal of Economic
Theory* 4: 103–23.

—— (1973a), 'Econometric Policy Evaluation: A Critique', draft prepared for
the Phillips curve conference, University of Rochester, 20–21 April, 1973; April
1973.

—— (1973b), 'Econometric Policy Evaluation: A Critique', Revised May, 1973.

—— (1975), 'An Equilibrium Model of the Business Cycle', *Journal of Political Economy* 83: 1113–1144.

—— (1976a), 'Econometric Policy Evaluation: A Critique', *Carnegie-Rochester Conference Series on Public Policy* 1: 19–46.

—— (1976b), 'Understanding Business Cycles', paper prepared for the Kiel Conference on Growth without Inflation, June 22–23.

—— (1977), 'Understanding Business Cycles', *Carnegie-Rochester Conference Series on Public Policy* 5: 7–29.

—— (2001), 'Professional Memoir', 5 April 2001.

—— (2005), 'Present at the Creation: Reflections on the 2004 Nobel Prize to Finn Kydland and Edward Prescott', *Review of Economic Dynamics* 8: 777–779.

Lucas, R. and Prescott, E. (1971), 'Investment Under Uncertainty', *Econometrica* 39: 659–681

Nelson, C. (1980), Letter to Robert Hodrick, 10 June 1980.

Nelson, C. and Plosser, C. (1980), 'Trends and Random Walks in Macroeconomic Time Series', University of Washington Discussion paper 80–13, August 1980.

Prescott, E. (1967), *Adaptive decision rules for macroeconomic planning*, unpublished Ph.D. thesis, Carnegie Institute of Technology, 1967.

—— (1971), 'Adaptive Decision Rules for Macroeconomic Planning', *Western Economic Journal* 9: 369–378.

—— (1972), 'The Multi-Period Control Problem Under Uncertainty', *Econometrica* 40: 1043–1058.

—— (1974), 'Money, Expectations and the Business Cycle', Discussion paper, 4 April 1974.

—— (1977), 'Should Control Theory be used for Economic Stabilization', *Carnegie-Rochester Conference Series on Public Policy* 7: 13–38.

—— (1980a), 'Comments on the Current State of the Theory of Aggregate Investment Behavior', *Carnegie-Rochester Conference Series on Public Policy* 12: 93–101.

—— (1980b), Prescott to Nelson, letter dated 5 November 1980.

—— (1998), 'Business Cycle Research: Methods and Problems', Federal Reserve Bank of Minneapolis, Working Paper 590, revised October 1998.

—— (2004), 'The Transformation of Macroeconomic Policy and Research', Nobel Prize lecture, 8 December, 2004 (on Nobel website).

—— (2005b), Personal Communication, 16 November.

—— (2005e), Additional Personal Communication, 20 November.

—— (2006e), 'The Transformation of Macroeconomic Policy and Research', *Journal of Political Economy* 114: 203–235.

Prescott, E. and Mehra, R. (1977), 'Recursive Competitive Equilibria and Capital Asset Pricing', Discussion paper, December 1977.

—— (1978), 'Recursive Competitive Equilibria: The Case of Homogenous Households', Columbia University Graduate School of Business Working Paper, 1978.

—— (1980), 'Recursive Competitive Equilibria: The Case of Homogenous Households', *Econometrica* 48: 1365–1379.

Program of Econometric Society Fall 1978 North America Meeting (1979), *Econometrica* 47: 235–251.

Royal Swedish Academy of Sciences (2004), 'Finn Kydland and Edward Prescott's Contribution to Dynamic Macroeconomics: The Time Consistency of Economic

Policy and the Driving Forces Behind Business Cycles', Advanced information on the Bank of Sweden Prize in Economic Science in Memory of Alfred Nobel, 11 October 2004.

Sargent, T. (1978), 'Estimation of Dynamic Labor Demand Schedules Under Rational Expectations', *Journal of Political Economy* 86: 1009–1044.

Shoven, J. and Whalley, J. (1972), 'A General Equilibrium Calculation of the Effects of Differential Taxation of Income from Capital in the U.S.', *Journal of Public Economics*, 1: 281–322.

Solow, R. (1956), 'A Contribution to the Theory of Economic Growth', *Quarterly Journal of Economics* 70: 65–94.

—— (1957), 'Technical Change and the Aggregate Production Function', *Review of Economics and Statistics*, 39: 312–320.

Taylor, J. (1980), 'Comment on Kydland and Prescott', in S. Fischer, S., ed., *Rational Expectations and Economic Policy*, NBER and University of Chicago Press: Chicago, 191–194.

Turnovsky, S. and Brock, W. (1980), 'Time Consistency and Optimal Government Policies in Perfect Foresight Equilibrium', *Journal of Public Economics* 13: 183–212.

—— (1981), 'The Analysis of Macroeconomic Policies in Perfect Foresight Equilibrium', *International Economic Review* 22: 179–209.

Young, W. and Darity, W. (2001), 'The Early History of Rational and Implicit Expectations', *History of Political Economy* 33: 773–813.

10
Vilfredo Pareto's Correspondence as a Significant Source for the Knowledge of his Economic Thought

Fiorenzo Mornati

Introduction

No archives of Vilfredo Pareto exist, to the best of our knowledge, besides the small collections kept at the Cantonal University Library of Lausanne and at the National Library of Florence, which mostly consists of already published writings.[1] So, in the current research, by 'archives' I mean Pareto's letters that have so far been published in the collection of his *Œuvres Complètes*.[2]

The elements of theoretical or applied analysis that can be found in the correspondence of an economist of the past are not necessarily negligible. They can consist of, for example, introductive discussions to the theories (which can assist in determining how the author's intellectual work actually took shape); first drafts of the theories (from which it is possible to gauge the elaboration the theories underwent before reaching publication); and free comments on the reactions triggered by the theories. In Pareto's case, I am integrating these elements with the analytical elements that are present in his volumes and articles, as well as with the relevant part of the vast secondary bibliography and with the history of the events and ideas of his time. These elements have been detailed in the Paretian intellectual biography that I have been preparing for some years.

Thus, the question needed to be asked is, how should one present the analysis of Pareto's correspondence, which includes nearly 5000 letters, in a sufficiently interesting way for those who are not scholars of his work? As a solution, I have chosen to divide the results according to three themes: Pareto's conceptions of science, economic theory, and economic policy. I have also tried to indicate the connections among these themes and to develop them in chronological order – unless this approach was threatening to obscure their logical reconstruction, in which case I have followed the latter criterion.

Elements of Pareto's conception of science

As is known, the studies on Pareto's epistemology are still in their infancy. This is probably because today's epistemological schemes are ill suited to the quite different and temporally remote epistemological conceptions – that also have to be reconstructed – on which Pareto was drawing. In addition, the elements that Pareto himself provides about his epistemology are scattered in his chaotic and monumental scientific production, although they can be found in his correspondence too.

Delimitation of scientific activity

Traces of Pareto's critical reflection on the characteristics of scientific activity can already be found in his earlier letters, where his thought is inspired by the study, for example, of John Stuart Mill's *System of Logic* (that in 1874 he read in its 1866 French translation);[3] of Buckle's *History of English Civilization* (probably read in its 1865 French translation);[4] and of *The principles of psychology* by Spencer (probably read in its 1874 French translation).[5]

Pareto believes that all that can be known are the phenomena, which he sees as 'facts and relationships of facts'.[6] With regard to these phenomena, he believes that by following the crucial example given by the natural sciences, one can determine only '*how* they happen, and not *why*'.[7] All this leads Pareto to proclaim himself 'the most positivist of positivists'.[8] It should thus be noted that he will always regard as *self-evident* the notion of 'facts'. Therefore, he will never see the distinction between the agent that studies and the reality that is studied as problematic. Nor does he see as problematic the distinctions between the study of subjective phenomena, which he understands as those 'that take place in the minds' of people, and the study of objective phenomena – that is those 'that take place outside' human minds.[9]

One should also take into account that there exist two categories of phenomenal relationships. If fact A acts on fact B and fact B does not act on fact A, 'one can, if one wishes, call A the cause and B the effect'. If fact A acts on fact B and fact B reacts on fact A, instead of a relationship of cause and effect there is a relationship of interdependence, as can very frequently be observed in the economic and sociological phenomena of a continuous kind.[10] Interdependence (a concept that Pareto borrows from Spencer[11]) can only be dealt with through mathematical logic.[12]

Pareto also thinks that phenomenal (*alias* experimental, *alias* scientific) knowledge is only relative,[13] in the sense that every proposition it arrives at (including pure logic propositions) is valid only 'within the space and time limits that are known to us'.[14] His research programme, partly realized through his *Trattato di sociologia*, therefore also presented to the social sciences the concept of relativity that was gradually introduced in the natural sciences by Galileo and Copernicus, and later followed by Newton, Poincaré, and finally Einstein.[15]

According to Pareto, since the human mind is 'always the same', the knowledge of the history of natural sciences is extremely useful for the purpose of scientific studies. This is because by showing us the ways (at all times inevitably similar) in which the sciences have developed in the past, it lets us know how the new sciences will develop[16] – though generally through an increasingly minute (and inevitably arbitrary) subdivision of their topics.[17] Furthermore, such a history also shows that observation and theory alternate at the forefront of scientific development, as is necessary because 'observation without theory is empiricism', whereas 'theory without observation runs the risk of being mere imagination'.[18]

Finally, with regard to science, Pareto opposes metaphysics, which he always criticizes in disparaging terms,[19] and which he envisages as going from the name to the thing that the name designates. Moreover, in metaphysical arguments, a thing consists of a 'nebula of sentiments' – such as 'good, evil, the beautiful, right, wrong' – which have never been able to be defined, and consequently, the discussions on such confusing topics have no resolving criteria and are therefore fatally inconsistent.[20]

Modalities for carrying out scientific activity

As just mentioned, it is language that allows an explanation of the phenomena investigated. Thus, only those expressions that correspond 'in a rigorous and precise way to some real objects' can be used.[21] This refrains from the belief that words are 'the things themselves' and not merely some signs of them[22] – insignificant in themselves.[23] Natural sciences are the 'only sciences worthy of such a name' precisely because they are the only sciences that have been able to connect facts, whereas the moral sciences only connect ideas.[24] In the absence of such a correspondence between facts and ideas, one can only admit postulates, but with the condition that the consequences that are inferred from them be verified by experience, as is the case with Euclid's postulate.[25]

Scientific investigation can be carried out in two ways. Through mathematics, formal errors of reasoning are avoided. The other, the experimental method, is the method of the natural sciences, which is different from the empirical method because it studies all the known elements of the phenomena and is not satisfied with investigating them all together.[26] This allows the grounding of the scientific propositions in those 'positive and real' premises, without which they would end up meandering in the realm of metaphysics.[27] More precisely, while mathematics is a type of logic drawn from experience, which makes it possible 'to undertake lines of reasoning that are too long and complex'[28] to be developed verbally, the experimental method is the method that goes from things to names.[29] In actual terms, this method, which is even more powerful than self-observation,[30] consists in directly observing 'the facts'[31] – that is, the real entities, people and things – that have an infinite number of properties that science cannot but study separately[32] and through successive approximations.[33] On the one hand, this implies that it will not be possible to have the complete theory of any phenomenon but only the causes that give its 'main part'.[34] On the other hand, for the purpose of the application of scientific results to reality, it will be necessary to take them all into consideration – that is, it will be necessary to make a synthesis of them.[35]

Pareto will never accept any approach that sees the recourse to mathematics as an alternative to the experimental method. Moreover, if the case arose, he would not hesitate to abandon mathematics altogether 'because in all physical sciences the experimental method is sovereign'.[36]

Scientific work arrives at identifying natural laws, which Pareto ended up thinking of as simple uniformities, of the kind phenomenon A accompanies phenomenon B, and, as such, devoid of any aspect of necessity,[37] which at first Pareto also had assigned to them.[38] Therefore, in order to explain a fact one needs to show that it accompanies other facts.[39] In this sense, the experimental method makes it not only possible to explain the past, but also, and above all, to foresee the future.[40]

Finally, the scientific propositions into which scientific laws are formally expressed are of two kinds: descriptive ('oxygen is a gaseous body') and hypothetical ('if oxygen is combined with hydrogen, water is produced').[41]

Scientific truth

Since his youth, Pareto believed that the truth of a doctrine depends only on its intrinsic characteristics and never on the number of its supporters, since it has been amply demonstrated that no error has ever existed that has not found a majority of supporters.[42]

Later, he places the term 'truth' among those that are obscure to him. He manages to define it – obviously only within experimental knowledge – as the coincidence between the two only existing 'orders of phenomena': the interior (i.e. psychological) order and the exterior order.[43] More precisely, truth is only 'an agreement between experience and thought'.[44]

At first, Pareto deems an interesting test of the truth of a doctrine to be the number of critical arguments that the doctrine has suc-ceeded in rebutting.[45] However, he later realizes that such a method is erroneous because it is possible to oppose refutable arguments to a theory that, contrary to our impressions, is false.[46] This observation will lead him to be generally satisfied with considering a scientific doctrine 'as good, until someone proves it false through reasoning or through facts'.[47]

Pareto's conception of economic theory: Methodology, contents, and limitations

It is in Pareto's conception of science – of which I have reconstructed the elements that are present in his correspondence – that his approach to economic theory must be placed.

The first important reference Pareto makes to economic theory is dated at the end of 1888. He regrets not having yet carried out his project to write a treatise on '*rational* political economy', which, following the example of rational mechanics treatises, he envisages as the clearest and most concise possible exposition, feasible only through mathematics,[48] of the 'general principles of economic science in their most general aspects'.[49] The first book he quotes as coming close to such a treatise is *Les lois naturelles de l'économie politique* by the French–Belgian *économiste* Gustave de Molinari.[50]

However, on the eve of Pareto's professional approach to political economy two years later, it seems to him that the elements that he considers to be the fundamental variables of an economic system (pop-ulation, taxes, public debt, foreign trade, etc.) can be correctly evaluated only in relation to the trend of the system's wealth, even though the available statistical data are still very imperfect.[51] He consequently deems Pantaleoni's book *Dell'ammontare probabile della ricchezza in Italia* 'the best study of political economy that has been published in Italy in many years'. Moreover, he bases the investigations he is thinking of doing on the Italian economy on this work.[52] He also greatly appreciates Pantaleoni's article 'Indice della variazione dei prezzi di importazione e di esportazione in Italia dal 1878 al 1889' (*Giornale degli Economisti*, May 1891) because he believes that 'by following this path that it will be possible to make political and economic progress'. Furthermore, the growing wealth of economic knowledge of an empirical kind makes one hope that it will be possible to emulate Kepler, who availed himself of very precise observations and was finally able to calculate the orbit of Mars.[53] On the other hand, in the current state of affairs, he believes that pure political economy falls within the realm of metaphysics.[54] As Auspitz and Lieben's demonstration shows, a country obtains profits through protectionism, whilst 'protection is a folly and a fraud . . . an anti-economic regime' whose evils are unquestionable.[55]

The theory of exchange

The starting point of Pareto's economic theory studies is his reading (that took place in the summer of 1891) of Pantaleoni's *Principi di economia pura*.[56] In line with his aforementioned experimental conception of science, it seems to Pareto that its main topic – that is, the theory of exchange – should set off from the 'naked' fact that, for a quantity of good, everyone is prepared to pay what they reckon is its market price. Furthermore, they believe they have got a good deal if they pay a lower price, and a bad deal if they pay a higher price. They react to a possible increase by necessarily saving on other goods even though they choose them at random and not because of their lower degree of utility.[57]

Continuing in his analysis of hedonistic political economy, Pareto believes that the explanation it gives through the *homo economicus* hypothesis inevitably captures only one part of the reality (as the case of the infinite number of reasons for exchange indicates) because such a hypothesis implies that the trader is not only an egocentric, but also someone who acts on the basis of reasoning alone or, above all, on the basis of habit, as demonstrated by experience. On the other hand, even if *homo economicus* were 'very close to real man', this would not guarantee that hedonistic economics would achieve results 'very close to the real ones' because a small difference in the causes can produce a very great difference in the effects.[58]

Pareto's first critical conclusion with regard to economic theory is therefore that hedonistic economics must proceed cautiously, always starting from experience and always being open to theoretical extensions, as was the case for theoretical mechanics.[59]

Pareto quickly realizes that the final degrees of utility of goods (not their total utilities, of which an individual is never aware) actually govern exchanges.[60] However, he is left with the crucial doubt of not knowing how to measure them: a doubt which had originally led him to think of starting his study of exchange from the better-known curves of supply and demand.[61] More specifically, Pareto cannot accept the hypothesis of continuity of consumption, since it is disproved by the common experience of consumers.[62] Nor can he accept the hypothesis of the coincidence of the final degree with the last quantity consumed, since it is disproved by the case of short-term speculators, who do not consume but whose activity is decisive in the formation of the prices.[63] The generality of the hypothesis of the decreasing of the final degree of utility is also unacceptable, since it is disproved by various empirical counter-examples.[64] Furthermore, maximum pleasure, which is another fundamental concept of hedonistic economics, is a situation that traders do actually achieve, but without being able to predetermine it. The consequence is such that the exchanges are likely to oscillate around the point of maximum pleasure. He believes that this is a trend that must be demonstrated anyway, thus necessarily paving the way to a new, dynamic branch of hedonistic economics.[65]

Pareto takes all these cautions into account and critically analyses the two available conceptions of the final degree of utility. According to the first and very general conception, the final degree of utility depends on all the circumstances affecting it, which, by leaving the final degrees of utility 'entirely undetermined', renders 'the fundamental theorem' of the proportionality of the prices to the degrees heuristically sterile.[66] If one accepts instead Wicksteed's conception, according to which the final degree is defined, once a consumer and a good are given, the aforementioned theorem increases our knowledge: that is even though one is not able to measure the final degrees, and even though, as it happens on the stock exchange, for example, share prices depend also on their variation in time.[67]

Thus, Pareto ends up accepting hedonistic economics, although only provisionally, as long as one is prepared to admit that its fundamental hypothesis of a continuous and always decreasing degree of utility is susceptible to empirical refutations.[68] If one accepts this hypothesis, mathematical economics, and only mathematical economics, is able to demonstrate[69] that the demand for a good is a decreasing function of the price, whereas when the price rises, the supply first increases and then decreases.[70]

At any rate, since, according to Pareto, the economic problem continues to lie in the assessment of how a provision affects people's welfare, its solution entails the need to measure that welfare. Finally, since it has not been demonstrated that this welfare 'is a quantity',[71] Pareto believes that the difficulty can be avoided[72] by making use of an index that 'clearly' distinguishes a greater welfare from a lesser one.[73]

While only admitting this idea as a postulate, Pareto has indeed no doubt that every human being, when put in front of two states of welfare (each deriving from a different combination of goods), is able to say whether he/she deems them equal, or one greater than the other.[74] Without worrying about the reasons behind the received answer,[75] this makes it possible to trace the lines of equal welfare (or of equal pleasure);[76] that is, the 'lines of indifference'[77] (that Pareto generally shows with a negative incline, but also illustrating the situation that will be later defined of lexicographical arrangement[78]). Pareto ascribes this concept to Edgeworth – although he stresses that the latter derives it from the hypothesis of the final degree of utility – whereas in Pareto's opinion it is a 'direct product of experience', which constitutes the new starting point of pure economy.[79]

According to Pareto, the analytical evolution that leads him from the final degree of utility (redefined 'ophelimity' in his *Cours d'économie politique*) to the index of ophelimity in the *Manuale di economia politica*, and finally to the index-function of the *Manuel d'économie politique* – which only indicates 'in which direction the individual will move' – constitutes a progress because it allows one to replace 'rather metaphysical concepts' with 'ever more exclusively experimental concepts'.[80]

General economic equilibrium

It is interesting to note that, though Pareto does not follow 'all the publications of mathematical journals',[81] at the beginning of the century he thinks that mathematics, 'with the reason, or the pretext, of rigour', is by now only searching for fine points. At any rate, for its applications, which include political economy, 'the ancient science' – as exemplified by the first three volumes of Jules Houël's *Cours de calcul infinitesimal*, published in Paris by Gauthiers-Villars in 1878–1881, and by the seven volumes of Hermann Laurent's *Traité d'analyse*, published in Paris by Gauthiers-Villars in 1885–1891 – is still 'always exclusively' sufficient.[82]

On the other hand, in an economist's training, the study of mathematics is of secondary importance; what is necessary is 'to study social sciences as one studies natural sciences', and in order to do so, one must rid oneself 'of metaphysics, of sentiment' and follow experience as the only guide.[83] Furthermore, mathematical economics, based on the aforementioned mathematical foundations, deals with matters that are quite different from the laws of supply and demand.[84]

Generally speaking, mathematical analysis is of little use in political economy if it is applied to specific, numerical problems, such as the calculation of single prices or the study of the final degree of utility.[85] It is, instead, of great use if it is applied to general, qualitative problems, such as, mainly, the identification of the conditions determining general economic equilibrium (GEE), which allows the expression of the 'interdependence' of the economic phenomena[86] through the concept of equilibrium (initially considered by Pareto as 'a fact',[87] and later simply as an analytically useful abstraction[88]). In fact, the use of mathematics in political economy is only justified for the purpose of solving the problem of GEE,[89] from which it is wrong to think of drawing practical applications,[90] which implies that there will probably never be the need 'to solve any economic equation numerically'.[91]

It is by following the experimental methodology outlined above, and in particular its suggestion that there is no single cause to social and economic phenomena, but they are interdependent,[92] that Pareto arrives at choosing GEE. Auspitz and Lieben's analyses of partial equilibrium, like those by Launhardt and Cournot, do not take into account either the reductions or the suppressions of consumption induced by customs duties. On the contrary, Walras' GEE succeeds in accounting for these complications of international trade,[93] though without matching the clarity and accuracy of exposition of Cairnes' theory of international commerce,[94] which Pareto somehow wishes to update with his article 'Teoria matematica del commercio internazionale' (*Giornale degli Economisti*, April 1895), which indeed shows a theory of international trade reformulated 'with Walras' formulae'.[95]

By putting together exchange and production, GEE gives an overall, albeit inevitably approximate, representation of the economic phenomenon and will be defined by Pareto as the problem of identifying 'what the actions of the people will be', 'given the tastes that people have and the obstacles they encounter in order to satisfy them'.[96] Moreover, the question of GEE consists in studying the way in which economic goods are distributed in a community of individuals who are 'entirely similar' – not only from a physiological point of view, but also in terms of their income and the quantities they own. GEE is based on the solution of the problem of the choices made by one single individual, which is a problem that in the end can be reformulated without making use 'either of ophelimity, or even of prices'[97] because they 'are a result of the position of equilibrium and do not determine it'.[98]

In this way, the theory of free competition – that is, the case of constant prices – is only a part of the theory of GEE, and it allows one also to consider variable manufacture coefficients and prices.[99] That which gives 'the conditions for mechanical equilibrium and for economic equilibrium (which is similar to the former), as it does in general for all kinds of equilibria',[100] is the equation of virtual velocities. And the representation of GEE given in the *Manuale di Economia Politica* is such that it brings 'the theory [closer] to the facts', since it is more general than previous representations.[101]

In 1907, while somehow taking stock of his investigations on GEE, Pareto deems the study of static GEE as still being in its infancy. This is despite the fact that it is 'much less difficult' than dynamic GEE,[102] the study of which one will be able to start only after finding out 'what relation exists, in economics, between force and acceleration'.[103] The progress of static GEE depends, instead, on the ability to solve its system of equations, or at least to study the properties of the solution for particular forms of the ophelimity function; for instance, $\varphi(x) = A/x\alpha$ or $\varphi(x) = A_0 + a_1 x + A_2 x^2 + \dots$, where the conditions $\varphi_x > 0$, $\varphi_{xx} < 0$, $\varphi_{xxx} < 0$ are satisfied.[104]

An important development of Pareto's GEE is the economy of welfare. It is interesting to note that, at first, the principle of the incomparability of the final degrees of utility, on which Pantaleoni insists so much, does not make an impression on Pareto. Indeed, like all other sciences, the science of economics is a science of averages. It is therefore crucial, for hedonistic economics, to find an average final degree of utility. This can be calculated if the demand is known,[105] since the demand for a good is a function of the final degrees of utility of its consumers – possibly starting from the family budgets of Le Play's school.[106] However, this research programme is soon abandoned in favour of the one that will lead to the well-known, innovative definition by Pareto of economic optimum.

Pareto has never been in any doubt that the total ophelimities of the individuals 1, 2, 3 ... Φ_1, Φ_2, Φ_3 ... are heterogeneous and therefore cannot be added up. If one varies the quantities of goods consumed by the individuals, it will be possible to group the ensuing variations $d\Phi_1$, $d\Phi_2$, $d\Phi_3$ ... in two cases. In the first case, some of them are positive and some are negative (which is, in other words, the situation from which it is not possible to move while at the same time benefiting all the members of the community[107]). In the second case, they are all positive or all negative. It is 'only in order to give a name to the first case' that Pareto called it 'maximum of ophelimity', and the continuation of his analysis consisted only in finding the quantities of goods corresponding to that maximum. He solved the problem by dividing every variation of individual total ophelimity by the individual marginal ophelimity of a single good (good x, for instance) ϕ_{1x}, ϕ_{2x}, ϕ_{3x} ... In this way he obtained the individually consumed quantities of x, $d\Phi_1/\phi_{1x}$, $d\Phi_2/\phi_{2x}$, $d\Phi_3/\phi_{3x}$ ..., which are homogeneous quantities and can therefore be added up.[108]

Pareto's criticism of other economists

The rigorous consideration of the economic phenomenon in terms of GEE is also the characteristic that, according to Pareto, distinguishes 'the new theories from the ancient ones'.[109] Goods and labour prices, the interest rate, and the rents of the various capitals are indeed unknown facts that are simultaneously determined by a system of equations in which some parameters also appear: one can therefore say that the facts are determined by all such parameters.[110] Non-mathematical economists, instead, were and still are looking for the parameter that determines the single unknown fact, which does not make sense[111]: the demonstration of the cognitive error of literary economics is, according to Pareto, one of the most important results of the application of mathematical economics.[112] The main difference between Pareto's economics and Austrian economics lies precisely in the fact that the latter still admits a cause for value. Pareto does not agree with this for the very reason that the exchange value one observes on the market depends 'on all the economic circumstances of barter, production, and capitalisation'.[113]

On the other hand, the distinction between economic schools must not be based on the use of mathematics (the knowledge of which is necessary but not sufficient in order to write about mathematical economics[114]), but on the 'more or less extensive [use] of the experimental method'.[115] As a consequence, Pareto feels as distant from Walras as he does from Edgeworth and Marshall (of whom he notes the inability to 'get an idea of economic equilibrium',[116] while always giving incomplete solutions to the economic problem[117]). Although making use of mathematics, the latter two consider economics as 'an art mixed with metaphysics, that leads towards the ideal they have set themselves'.[118]

According to Pareto, however, the scientific evolution of economics is characterized precisely by the disappearance of practical and ethical considerations.[119]

Initially, Pareto had credited the three above-mentioned economists, together with Gustave de Molinari (though disagreeing with the latter's dislike for pure economy),[120] with being his teachers.[121] The reconstruction of Pareto's relationship with Walras, as shown by his correspondence, is quite interesting. We do not know when, but Pareto's first reading of the *Elements d'économie politique pure*[122] had been interrupted because of the disgust caused to him by its 'metaphysical part, which is so large in it'. Pareto's subsequent reading of Pantaleoni's *Principi* had instead indicated to him that in Walras' work 'there was something other than metaphysics', thus prompting him to read the *Elements* again and to find in them 'a very important theory, namely the theory of economic equilibrium'.[123]

Once he has learnt about Walras' pure economy, judging that for the moment there is little to add to it, Pareto decides to do some applications of it, both to convince the public of the utility of the mathematical method in economics and to pave the way for further developments of pure economy itself.[124] One of the applications is the clarification that Walras' proposition, according to which it is necessary to take into account the utility of all the goods, implies that the final degree of utility of money cannot be considered as constant, since it varies when the price of any one good varies and when the available goods vary.[125] Pareto also believes that Walras gives little importance to the question of the *raretés moyennes*, even though in his own monetary theory there is a *rareté moyenne* of gold.[126] Finally, the 'perfect competition', as discussed by Walras, seems to Pareto to be just an extreme case that does not prevent one from taking into consideration, as suggested by Edgeworth, 'the obstacles to competition', thus giving rise to the study of the 'imperfection of competition'.[127]

On the other hand, Pareto immediately finds a point on which he disagrees with Walras: as a staunch supporter of the experimental method, contrary to his interlocutor, Pareto will never hesitate to modify or abandon a theory if it does not agree with experience.[128]

And, with their personal proximity in Lausanne, it quite quickly emerges that Pareto and Walras are scientifically poles apart,[129] since Pareto limits himself to study 'that which is', refusing to study, as his predecessor, 'that which should be'.[130] More precisely, Pareto believes that, even in discussing social and moral sciences, one must clearly distinguish the postulates from their consequences and from the facts of experience.

Walras, instead, does not linger on his postulates, which many would not accept, or even leaves them unexpressed, while dwelling at length on demonstrations that are 'extremely easy as soon as the postulates are accepted'[131] – in particular, the postulate of the positive effects, in social terms, of a wider role for the State.[132] By refusing to follow Walras 'in his metaphysical ramblings', Pareto ended up by making an enemy of him.[133]

The only point they have in common remains therefore 'a rather secondary question for social sciences',[134] such as the representation of GEE through mathematical formulae[135] for the case of free competition alone.[136] Pareto could have represented GEE in a different form from Walras', but he gave it up in order to fully acknowledge Walras' merit in clarifying to him the concept of GEE,[137] to which he just added the 'idea of successive approximations' in order to eliminate 'the too abstract aspect of Walras' doctrines'.[138]

Relation between political economy and sociology

As mentioned above, Pareto feels that, all things considered, political economy is showing little progress. He thinks that this is mostly due to the circumstance that, even though the GEE theory is a special case of the theory of social equilibrium,[139] political economy does not take into account the connections between the economic and the social phenomenon.[140]

Once one has differentiated between logical actions (i.e. those that directly depend on logic[141]) and non-logical actions (i.e. those that depend on sentiments[142] and are, for most people, much more numerous than the former),[143] social science or sociology should move on and classify the heterogeneous forces that affect people's will into categories (sentiments of sensual pleasure, moral sentiments, sentiments of justice, religious sentiments, without speculating what these sentiments are, or, as Spencer does, from where they come), and find out the resultant of each of those categories. Such a work of synthesis of facts is very difficult, but Pareto wants to try to accomplish it, since he rejects the easy alternative of adopting a metaphysical system.[144]

Social science will consist of two parts.[145] The first part will be a rational ethics that can be built only from postulates, from which precepts must be drawn for human actions: it is a discipline Pareto is not interested in, not because he despises it, but because no fundamental postulates exist for it, and he is not able to determine them.[146] The second part, which is the part Pareto studies, will consist in the description of the

manifestations of the social activity of the people and in the identification of the social variations corresponding to the psychological
variations – that is, the variations of the moral and religious states – of
the individuals.

Since the times of his liberalist campaign, which will be discussed
below, Pareto had guessed that concrete economic phenomena could
only be understood by combining their study with the study of the other
social phenomena.[147] He would have started such a combined study of
economics and sociology much earlier if he had earlier understood, also
in practical terms, that experimental study must only be founded on
principles that are 'given by experience'. This approach was precluded
to him by his 'blind' acceptance of 'some ethical principles' that were
present in the society in which he lived.[148]

Pareto's conception of economic policy: Positive and militant aspects

It seems to us that Pareto's entire theoretical-economic thought is largely
directed to the clarification of the political phenomenon in general, and
of the political-economic phenomenon in particular, not only with positive goals but also, at least for a certain period, with militant motivations.
I thought therefore that it would be of some interest to gather all the
materials on his political-economic thought that have been extracted
from his correspondence, under the topics of Pareto's liberalist militancy and his conceptions of liberalism, socialism and the problems of
practical economic policy.

The course of Pareto's liberalist militancy

At least until his *Cours*, Pareto's theoretical thought is certainly directed
towards supporting his liberalist militancy, which is founded on his early,
profound, and vivid adhesion to the general principles of liberalism.

Indeed, already in the first documents that record his thought,
Pareto – who will later attribute this attitude to sentiments innate to
him[149] – supports all individual liberties, including freedom of conscience. However, he stresses that they are often misinterpreted, in the
sense that they are defended by individuals who only invoke them for
themselves, ignoring the fact that partial freedom is indistinguishable
from oppression.[150] This observation leads him to apodictically affirm
that to be liberal means to be on the side of the oppressed against the
oppressor, whoever either of them may be.[151]

In an early exemplification of this concept of freedom, Pareto states that he has no doubt about 'the justice and utility of freedom of trade',[152] pointing out that in the relation between 'capital and labour' there are only two ways of organizing things. If the State wishes to regulate the price of work, then it gives the workers the right to demand that it also regulate the price of the goods they buy, which leads to socialism. On the contrary, one has the system of freedom if the State leaves the citizens free to deal with each other: this situation includes the freedom of trade union association, without which the workers would have their wages imposed on them.[153]

The first liberalist economist called upon by Pareto is Francesco Ferrara, author of the important article 'Il germanesimo economico in Italia' (*Nuova Antologia*, August 1874), which Pareto deems well written, although he is not impressed by the harsh tones Ferrara uses against his opponents. Such tones are even less justifiable, given the role that, as Minister of Finance, in 1868 Ferrara had in introducing the tax on milling, which was illiberal, since it was not proportional.[154]

Similarly, and in the same period, the conservative character of the arguments in favour of economic freedom put forward by the Florentine jurist Odoardo Luchini gives rise in Pareto to the temptation, which he says was swiftly and forever conquered, to cross to the side of the socialists of the German Historical School.[155]

And, after having frequented the fundamental Florentine group of the historic right for ten years, Pareto ends up by realizing that his coherently intransigent conception of liberalism[156] is by now followed only by a small and combative opposition party – the radical party – with which he sympathizes from the mid-1880s.[157] He only sees it as a lesser evil,[158] though, within a strategy of 'compromising on the means' in order only and always to pursue the aim 'of having minimal government action, of getting away from the clutches of the people who bleed the country dry'.[159]

Thus, he fights the customs duties imposed by Crispi in 1888 from the very time they are proposed.[160] He does this in a fashion that he acknowledges as being 'passionate' but fair, since such a new customs policy consists in the appropriation, by the agrarians and the government, of other people's property, in particular the property of poor citizens.[161] Pareto intends to quantify[162] the extent of this appropriation on the basis of the conviction that the custom duties are wholly transferred onto the national price, allowing the national producers to collect a sort of private levy equal to the customs duties multiplied by the national production.[163] Consequently, in the summer of 1891, he goes to Geneva and Lausanne not only, and not so much, to meet Walras in person,[164] but also in order to study the Swiss tax system, in an unfinished attempt to carry out an international comparison of the weight of taxes and customs protectionism.[165]

Pareto shares the thesis of the leader of French liberalism, Gustave de Molinari, that the best the liberals can do is to give all social classes the political and economic education they lack, which is the source of 'nearly all the evils of society'.[166] However, Pareto criticizes the liberal economists (whom in this period he regards as the economists *tout court*) because he considers them 'too bland to the powers that be, too lavish of excuses for the monopolies, too uncaring of the people's good',[167] whereas he wishes to invoke the theorems of classic political economy precisely 'against the oppression by the upper classes'.[168] In Pareto's intentions, the course of political economy that he conducts in Lausanne from the summer semester 1893 – which includes one semester of pure economics and three semesters of applied economics[169] – is therefore initially meant to be the exposition (without recourse to mathematics[170]) of the 'scientific principles of economic freedom', in the hope that some student may wish to teach them in turn.[171]

At any rate, Pareto acknowledges that the liberalists find themselves in the awkward position of attacking the interests of the small, but aggressive protectionist minority, while defending the interests of a majority who, through ignorance, is unappreciative to them of such battles,[172] which will lead to the victory of economic freedom only in a still distant future.[173]

And at the end of the century, together with the bitter realization of the unstoppable decadence of the liberals' – and particularly of the liberalists'[174] – influence, Pareto acquires the conviction that his liberalist campaign has been perfectly useless,[175] considering that he has finally realized the primordial fact that 'man is an evil beast' for his vices, ignorance, and prejudices, and that he will continue to be so for centuries to come.[176] Such a disenchanted attitude towards freedom emerges in Pareto in the wake of the Dreyfus affair, which gives him the opportunity to observe how the *dreyfusards*, having won their battle, use the same evil methods against their opponents that the French reactionaries had used against Dreyfus.[177] Pareto conceptualises the incident in the sense that only a minority, of which he has so far partaken, follow the principles of liberty, while the majority simply follow their own interests, which is a situation that the liberal governments have contributed to create naïvely.[178]

From all these considerations Pareto draws the conclusion that since it is impossible to change 'the nature and the custom of men', it is preferable to let them 'do, and serenely watch where they are going to end up';[179] thus, it is better for him to abandon all participation to active political life, in order to devote himself 'exclusively to science'.[180] In his following reflections on his, by now, past liberal militancy, Pareto deals with its lack of effectiveness, which he attributes to his not having understood that, in practical activities, knowing is often antithetical to acting. This is a subject that is synthesized in *Trattato di Sociologia* through the thesis of the 'distinction between the experimental truth of a doctrine and its social utility'.[181]

Theoretical foundations of free trade

Pareto's correspondence gives ample indications about his efforts to clarify the theoretical foundations of the liberalism he militantly pursued, with the intuitive argument in favour of free trade that is given by the opportunity it affords to procure every product where it costs least.[182]

Pareto's first in-depth reflection refers to a particular characterization of customs protectionism. National and international trade can be formally expressed through the ratios a_1/b_1, a_2/b_2, $a_3/b_3 \ldots a_n/b_n$, where a_n is the quantity of products that producer A_n gives producer B_n in order to obtain the quantity b_n of the latter's products. The case of equal protection for all economic agents (including those who are not involved in international trade) consists in making all the as and bs grow in the same proportion, with the consequence that the aforesaid ratios do not change. It is debatable whether such a kind of protection (different from the protection known so far, which makes only some of the ratios grow) is actually possible.[183] From this line of reasoning Pareto draws the political suggestion, which he very soon drops, that the most effective way to tackle protectionism is to protect all social classes, starting with the workers.[184]

In the early 1890s, the main proposition of political economy appears to Pareto to be that not only do protective customs duties destroy part of the income of the protected country, but they also effect a redistribution of the remaining income. And it is precisely the latter effect that explains the persistence of protection. This is because those who are damaged by it, being many, only suffer a small individual damage, which they therefore tend to ignore, while the beneficiaries, being few, receive great individual advantages, by which they are motivated to be very active in trying to achieve them.[185] In the case of Pareto's contemporary

Italy, it was precisely in order to obtain such advantages that the protectionists (industrialists and landowners) made their members of parliament approve the military expenses proposed by the government to meet the terms of the Triple Alliance.[186] Thus, the truth of the thesis, according to which it is necessary to fight at the same time against 'war and customs protection' – put forward by the more profound exponents of the Liberal School, such as Spencer and de Molinari – is proved.[187]

But, in general, Pareto only considers *laissez faire* as 'the lesser possible evil' for today's civilized peoples. The only demonstration that free traders must give[188] is therefore that the alternative policies so far applied are worse than *laissez faire*. Such a system is not required to be the best for the peoples of all time and all places.[189] It also needs to be considered that if *laissez faire* could be demonstrated, it would not at all entail the willingness by the people to adopt it.[190] Nevertheless, Pareto devotes himself to the search for this demonstration. At first he simply states that the hedonistic maximum is obtained from free competition between capital and labour in the production of private goods and services, and from free competition between State and private entities in the production of public goods.[191] The subsequent study of the variations of welfare for the society when production coefficients vary, which materialized in the article 'Il massimo di utilità dalla libera concorrenza' (*Giornale degli Economisti*, July 1894), is conducted by Pareto because, even though it is proved by very many facts,[192] it is by no means evident – as the socialists' claim that such a welfare can be increased by changing the competition coefficients demonstrates – that the coefficients that maximize welfare are actually those obtained 'by the competitive play of the entrepreneurs'.[193] With this article, in agreement with Walras' opinion, Pareto hopes to establish the theory of free trade 'on rational bases',[194] and to demonstrate that the propositions of pure economics apply to any arrangement, with or without private property.[195]

After having specified that he is for economic freedom 'as a means to achieve maximum utility for the people, and not to favour the wealthy',[196] Pareto does not hesitate anyway to acknowledge that 'free competition does not exist' yet,[197] whereas there exist 'monopolies of all kinds' (established by the State[198]) that must be destroyed, in order then to see what will happen to society.[199]

Pareto and socialism

Throughout his life, Pareto follows the progressive establishment of the socialist movement. His evaluation of it is influenced by the early and empirical idea according to which the State's economic ineptitude

is demonstrated by its inability to 'run well the industrial companies it has':[200] an inability that is caused precisely by the absence of
those incentives to efficiency and innovation that are provided by free
competition.[201]

Furthermore, after specifying, in strong terms, that liberal economists
are as interested in social problems as the socialists, and that they differ
from the latter only because, contrary to the socialist approach, they
require their solutions to be founded 'on experience and logic',[202] Pareto
thinks, at first, that socialism is 'an absurdity' if seen as the doctrine
pleading that each be given according to his/her needs; whereas if it is
regarded as the doctrine arguing that each be given according to his/her
merits, it represents the goal that true liberals should pursue.[203] In fact,
popular socialists (if they convince themselves that the revolution is
possible only from a situation that is not of extreme poverty) and true liberals could join forces to overturn the current bourgeois socialism – that
is, the use that the bourgeoisie makes of the State for its own interests.[204]
Once they have succeeded and have therefore temporarily increased the
people's welfare, the alliance will dissolve, because the popular socialists
will want to use the State to their advantage.[205]

Thus, Pareto opposes socialism because he deems it wrong in the economic part,[206] since, following his study of the facts,[207] he does not
see how the State's responsibilities can be expanded (as indeed required
by popular socialists) without 'considerably' reducing the production of
goods, and therefore without condemning to death by starvation a great
number of human beings.[208]

However, such a tragic phenomenon would be a decisive factor in
bringing about economic freedom, provided that the bourgeoisie finally
decides to respect everyone's property.[209] In general, the owners of fixed
and movable capitals have indeed always used them in two ways: the
first way consists in using them for the production of wealth, and this
has always been useful 'to all men without distinction'; the second way
involves using them instead to take possession of other people's riches,
and this has always been 'harmful to society'.[210] If the two uses cannot be
disentangled, it is likely that it is the socialists who are right in demand-
ing the abolition of ownership of capital. But if it is possible to prevent
the latter use (i.e. if it is possible 'to prevent the rich taking goods from
the poor'[211]), the main reason for the disastrous socialist experiment
ceases to exist.[212] Consequently, it is also necessary to take into account
that, by showing that distribution inequality does not vary with time and
place, Pareto's law of income distribution refutes the socialists' claim that
the capitalist system increases inequality, and therefore removes another

argument in support of their proposal to change the system.[213] However, from the aforesaid law, Pareto takes, above all, the proposition (which is of a liberal-radical nature and probably synthesizes his concept of ideal political economy) that a necessary and sufficient condition to increase the minimum income and/or reduce the inequality of personal incomes is increasing the national income more than the population.[214]

Thoughts on practical economic policy

Finally, from a reading of Pareto's correspondence one can extract a *corpus* of general positive reflections on the difficulties of practical economic policy.

Even though Pareto does not doubt, in the light of Darwin's studies, that the fight for existence is an 'indispensable condition for the betterment of the living races',[215] at first he believes that the goal of 'every man who is good at heart' is to obtain the good of 'most men, and of the most deserving ones among them',[216] in the sense of minimizing the sufferings caused by such a fight (including Malthusian repressive brakes).[217] Intuitively, the welfare of the people increases when the 'wealth' produced increases and when the proportion of wealth wasted by the State (mainly in armaments) and by the 'wealthy' (luxury expenses) decreases.[218] Once such wastes have been minimized, only poverty will remain. This is caused by reasons such as 'a too rapid increase of the population, and the vices, weaknesses, physical and moral faults of men', and these can be remedied only by educating the people – a task that can be accomplished only by private citizens.[219]

More precisely, however, in order to bring about social good, one has to assess the effects of each measure and, therefore, study them, irrespective of ideological considerations[220] and always taking into account that the complexity of social phenomena, of which only the direct effects are known to us,[221] makes it 'very difficult' to say whether a single measure will do more harm than good.[222]

In this general picture, which is marked by a profound scepticism about the possibility for economic policy to be truly scientific, one can still find interesting considerations on various aspects of practical economic policies. These seem to Pareto to be characterized by two features. First is the frequent contrast made between the solution to the problem of obtaining popular consensus and the solution to the problem of obtaining the 'greatest economic advantage' – a contrast that the government tries to hide from the public by resorting to arguments that are experimentally false (derivations), but make the two solutions look

as if they were coinciding.[223] Second is the fact that government effectiveness consists in 'knowing how to make use of existing sentiments
and interests'.[224]

With regard to monetary policy, Pareto – who is a committed supporter
of gold monometallism[225] (since bimetallism is a way 'to steal from many
for the benefit of few'[226]) – shares with Walras the idea that the function
of monetary means can be carried out by gold and silver, provided that
gold is the metal with the main role. Pareto and Walras part company
when Walras proposes that the relationship between gold and silver be
fixed by the State, because in Pareto's opinion the ways the State has
actually used this power have been catastrophic (i.e. inflationary).[227]
Similarly, Pareto believes that in order to ensure a 'healthy' monetary
circulation, it is necessary and sufficient that the State does not violate
the private citizens' freedom to accept or to reject the notes, irrespective
of whether they are issued by one or more banks.[228]

With regard to taxation, Pareto thinks that what matters is not its
legal form, but the quantity of the revenue[229] that the governments,
held back only by the resistance from the taxpayers, try to maximize[230]
so as to spend it entirely 'to pay their friends and to grease the politi-
cians' palm'.[231] Therefore, no fair tax system exists.[232] The best system
is that of reducing taxes because, since the incentive to work increases
when disposable income increases,[233] in many countries it is precisely
the excessive tax levying that prevents 'the betterment of the conditions
of the people'.[234] In general, while political economy and the science of
public finances both remain 'very unscientific', Pareto deems the delay
to be greater for the latter because it is only the art of 'putting to sleep'
the taxpayers so that they may better be used as 'food for a country's
rulers'.[235]

At any rate, from Pareto's correspondence some analytical elements
emerge of what he means as a scientific science of public finances. For
instance, in order to compare the effects of an extraordinary tax with
the effects of an alternative public loan, one must know the present
and future effects that such measures have on the social and economic
general equilibrium. The science of public finances 'knows little' of the
latter and ignores the former,[236] with the consequence that it replaces
'real' effects with imaginary effects. The two aforesaid measures would
produce different effects if the sums received by the State for the two different reasons did not give rise to alterations 'of the use of the economic
goods'.[237]

In reality, given that governments never repay the principal and pay
the agreed interests only for a short time (in real terms), the loan is only

one of the many subtle ways of 'fleecing part of the population for the benefit of another part'. This will be useful or harmful to the country according to whether or not it takes the country closer to the proportion of social classes, rentiers, and speculators, 'which gives the maximum utility' of the society.[238]

Conclusions

In order to reconstruct, even only partially, the thought of such a multi-faceted, prolific, and unsystematic author like Pareto, good philological practice suggests there is a need to take into account all of his writings, both public and private. The case study I have conducted seems to support this methodological indication.

Indeed, a reading of Pareto's correspondence gives us various interesting indications on his epistemology, which is one of the many topics of his intellectual biography that have not as yet been treated in an altogether satisfactory manner. In Pareto's correspondence we find the fundamental hubs of his conception of scientific knowledge, such as the purely relative and phenomenal character of it, the nature of interdependence of phenomenal relationships, the repetitiveness of scientific work, and therefore the predictability of its developments, as well as its irreversible incompatibility with metaphysics. According to Pareto, scientific research consists in making use of language as a simple but univocal way of labelling the phenomena; of mathematics as a means to follow lines of reasoning that would be too complex to expound verbally; and, above all, of the experimental method, which consists in directly observing the phenomena. Such research arrives at identifying uniformities – that is, simple concurrences of phenomena that make it possible, tautologically, to explain the phenomena in the very terms of their accompanying each other. The uniformities are expressed through hypothetical and descriptive propositions, and their truth is always provisional and can be refuted by reasoning and experimental proof.

It is within such a methodological grid that Pareto's investigations on economic theory must be studied. His correspondence indeed allows one to see his interesting and detailed application of his own methodological options to the concept of final degrees of utility, which he ends up accepting only provisionally, since its properties of being continuous and decreasing are the object of rather significant experimental refutations. As the impossibility for utility to be measured gives pure economy a metaphysical foundation, in line with his own methodology, Pareto ends up abandoning that concept for the concept of line of indifference, which, according to him, is experimental and finally makes it possible to found a scientific economic theory.

The role of mathematics in such a theory is justified only by its being indispensable in the treatment of the GEE problem, which Pareto chose as the representation of the economic phenomenon, because it is the only one that can account for the main characteristic of the latter, namely the interdependence of its components. However, the further development of political economy requires that the study of economic phenomena be carried out by also taking into account social phenomena, according to a scientific approach that Pareto is, in his own opinion, among the first to cultivate.

By being more a result of the experimental than of the mathematical method, GEE is also the discriminating criterion, not only between literary and mathematical theories, but also, within these, between English mathematical economics (which in Pareto's opinion is heuristically sterile) and Lausanne mathematical economics. On the other hand, GEE is the only point Pareto has in common with Walras, from whom he is epistemologically poles apart, since his predecessor only deals with that which should be, whereas Pareto only studies that which is.

Pareto's reflection on economic theory appears to be mainly aimed at guiding his study of the political phenomenon, in a broad sense, and of the political-economic phenomenon, in a strict sense.

Pareto's correspondence makes it possible to follow down to the most minute detail the 25-year-long liberal and liberalist campaign that he conducted, and to note that the reason for its conclusion is the verification that it is interests and sentiments, and not scientific knowledge, that prompt people to action. In that period, Pareto also deeply involves himself in an important attempt to renew the theoretical foundations of liberalism, which, anyway, he only sees as the least negative economic system for contemporary civilization and, all things considered, as yet to be built.

The related objections that Pareto raises against socialism are founded not on economic theory, but on the empirical argument that the statism foreseen by the socialists would lead to such an inefficient administration of the economic system that it would cause the death by starvation of vast numbers of human beings. Pareto is favourably inclined towards the possibility of a temporary alliance between liberalism and socialism, and against current bourgeois socialism – that is, against the use the bourgeoisie make of the State in favour of their own interests and to the detriment of the interests of the rest of the society.

The altogether limited knowledge one has of the social and economic phenomenon prevents the realization of scientific economic policies – that is, of economic policies which show consistency between their goals and means. The considerations one can make on practical economic policies, particularly on taxation and monetary economic policies, can therefore only highlight the aforementioned serious damages that the government more or less knowingly causes to the social classes that do not support it.

Acknowledgements

This research represents a part of the preparation of a detailed biography of Pareto. I am responsible for any errors and omissions. I thank Robert Leeson for kind encouragement.

Notes

1. Cf. Mincio D. – Mornati F. (1997), Melani L. (1983).
2. Cf. the bibliography. A number of Pareto's letter-books also exist, preserved in a small Italian bank, which owns them. Unfortunately, only a very small fraction of them has been published and so far they are not easily accessible, cf. http://www.popso.it/fondopareto/
3. Letters to Emilia Peruzzi, 13 and 24 April 1874, *O.C. 27.1*, pp. 342, 348.
4. Letter to Alceste (not Antonio, as was long believed) Antonucci, 7 December 1907, *O.C. 19.1*, p. 613.
5. Letters to Emilia Peruzzi, 8 April, 17, 18 June 1875, *O.C. 27.1*, pp. 501, 515–516.
6. Letter to Benedetto Croce, 12 July 1902, *O.C. 19.1*, p. 461.
7. Letter to Antonio Graziadei, 29 March 1901, *O.C. 19.1*, p. 422.
8. Letter to Maffeo Pantaleoni, 28 May 1897, *O.C. 28.2*, p. 77.
9. Letters to Giovanni Vailati, 23 October 1902, *O.C. 19.1*, p. 463; and to Guido Sensini, 18, 23 February, 16 May 1907, *O.C. 19.1*, pp.590–591, 598.
10. Letters to Benedetto Croce, 24 December 1896, *O.C. 19.1*, p. 317; and to Francesco Papafava, 1 November 1907, *O.C. 30*, pp. 461–462.
11. Letter to Maffeo Pantaleoni, 27 July 1892, *O.C. 28.1*, pp. 256–257.
12. Letter to Francesco Papafava, 1 November 1907, *O.C. 30*, p. 462.
13. Letter to Benedetto Croce, 27 May 1897, *O.C. 19.1*, p. 341.
14. Letters to Adrien Naville, 23 May 1905, and to Benedetto Croce, 21 March 1906, *O.C. 19.1*, pp. 545–546, 563.
15. Letters to Arturo Linaker, 21 May, 6 July 1921, *O.C. 19.2*, pp. 1065, 1067; and to Maffeo Pantaleoni, 22 May 1921, *O.C. 28.3*, p. 283.
16. Letter to Maffeo Pantaleoni, 6 July 1892, *O.C. 28.1*, p. 240.
17. Letters to Maffeo Pantaleoni, 25 January, 2, 7, 9 February 1898, *O.C. 28.2*, pp. 156, 159, 164, 167; and to Benedetto Croce, 7 July 1899, *O.C. 19.1*, p. 391.
18. Letter to Alfonso de Pietri Tonelli, 8 August 1917, *O.C. 19.2*, p. 978.

19. Letters to Emilia Peruzzi, 26 September 1872, *O.C. 27.1*, pp. 43–45; to Benedetto Croce, 27 May 1897; to Antonio Graziadei, 29 March 1901, *O.C. 19.1*; and to Giovanni Vailati, 23 October 1902, *O.C. 19.1*, pp. 340, 422, 463.
20. Letters to Léon Walras, 28 April 1896, *O.C. 19.1*, pp. 288–289, 291, 293; and to Adrien Naville, 9 May 1917, *O.C. 19.2*, p. 693.
21. Letters to Arturo Linaker, 7 October 1899, to Giuseppe Prezzolini, 3 March 1904, *O.C. 19.1*, pp. 394–395, 519; and to Maffeo Pantaleoni, 7 March 1907, *O.C. 28.3*, p. 17.
22. Letters to Benedetto Croce, 21 March 1906, *O.C. 19.1*, p. 563; and to Felice Vinci, 19 August 1912, *O.C. 19.2*, p. 783.
23. Letters to Maffeo Pantaleoni, 22 May, 3 July 1892, 22 July 1893, *O.C. 28.1*, pp. 222, 237, 386, 14 September 1907, *O.C. 28.3*, p. 55; and to Benedetto Croce, 14 November 1912, *O.C. 19.2*, p. 792.
24. Letter to Arturo Linaker, 7 October 1899, *O.C. 19.1*, p. 395.
25. Letter to Adrien Naville, 7 May 1897, *O.C. 19.1*, pp. 337–338.
26. Letter to Maffeo Pantaleoni, 2 April 1907, *O.C. 28.3*, p. 27.
27. Letter to Emilia Peruzzi, 26 September 1872, *O.C. 27.1*, pp. 43–45.
28. Letters to Adrien Naville, 11 May 1897; to Benedetto Croce, 27 May 1897; to Adrien Naville, 13 December 1899; and to Antonio Graziadei, 29 March 1901, *O.C. 19.1*, pp. 337, 342, 396, 423.
29. Letter to Adrien Naville, 9 May 1917, *O.C. 19.2*, p. 693.
30. Letter to Antonio Graziadei, 29 March 1901, *O.C. 19.1*, p. 425.
31. Letters to Giovanni Vailati, 12 September 1896; and to Benedetto Croce, 27 May, *O.C. 19.1*, pp. 301, 343.
32. Letters to Léon Walras, 28 April 1896; and to Benedetto Croce, 25 December 1898, *O.C. 19.1*, pp. 291, 380.
33. Letters to Giovanni Vailati, 10 February 1897; and to Adrien Naville, 7 May 1897, *O.C. 19.1*, pp. 333, 336.
34. Letter to Antonio Graziadei, 29 March 1901, *O.C. 19.1*, p. 425.
35. Letters to Carlo Placci, 30 December 1895; to Léon Walras, 28 April 1896; and to Benedetto Croce, 25 December, *O.C. 19.1*, pp. 281, 291, 380.
36. Letters to Maffeo Pantaleoni, 31 May 1893, *O.C. 28.1*, p. 382; to Léon Walras, 2 August 1893, *O.C. 19.1*, p. 226; and to Maffeo Pantaleoni, 28 July 1919, *O.C. 28.3*, p. 253.
37. Letter to Adrien Naville, 13 December 1899, *O.C. 19.1*, p. 396.
38. Letter to Emilia Peruzzi, 23 June 1875, *O.C. 27.1*, p. 517.
39. Letter to Adrien Naville, 13 December 1899, *O.C. 19.1*, p. 396.
40. Letter to Arturo Linaker, 6 July 1921, *O.C. 19.2*, p. 1069.
41. Letter to Léon Walras, 28 April 1896, *O.C. 19.1*, p. 291.
42. Letters to Emilia Peruzzi, 30 October 1872, 5 February 1873, 27 January 1874, *O.C. 27.1*, pp. 58–59, 153, 313.
43. Letters to Adrien Naville, 16 January, 11 May 1897; to Benedetto Croce, 27 May 1897, 7 July 1899; and to Arturo Linaker, 7 October 1899, *O.C. 19.1*, pp. 327–328, 337, 342, 389, 394.
44. Letters to Adrien Naville, 13 December 1899; and to Antonio Graziadei, 29 March 1901, *O.C. 19.1*, pp. 396, 422.
45. Letters to Emilia Peruzzi, 12 March 1874, *O.C. 27.1*, p. 326; to Napoleone Colajanni, 31 December 1891; to Léon Walras, 5 March 1893; and to Alceste Antonucci, 7 December 1907, *O.C. 19.1*, pp. 176, 213, 614.

46. Letter to Alceste Antonucci, 7 December 1907, *O.C. 19.1*, p. 614.
47. Letters to Emilia Peruzzi, 10 February 1873, *O.C. 27.1*, p. 165; and to Léon Walras, 2 August 1893, *O.C. 19.1*, p. 227.
48. Letter to Francesco Papafava, 13 December 1888, *O.C. 23*, p. 621.
49. Letter to Francesco Papafava, 27 November 1888, *O.C. 23*, p. 589.
50. Letter to Francesco Papafava, 2 December 1888, *O.C. 23*, p. 592.
51. Letters to Maffeo Pantaleoni, 7 October 1890, *O.C. 28.1*, pp. 7–8; to Felice Cavallotti, 21 October 1890, *O.C. 19.1*, p. 146; and to Luigi Bodio, 20 April, *O.C. 31*, p. 19.
52. Letter to Maffeo Pantaleoni, 17 October 1890, *O.C. 28.1*, p. 14.
53. Letters to Maffeo Pantaleoni, 2 May 1891, 22 July 1893, *O.C. 28.1*, pp. 33, 387.
54. Letters to Maffeo Pantaleoni, 2 May 1891, 25 January 1893, *O.C. 28.1*, pp. 33, 338–340.
55. Letters to Maffeo Pantaleoni, 1, 4 January 1892, *O.C. 28.1*, pp. 147–149.
56. Letters to Maffeo Pantaleoni, 21, 28 June 1891, *O.C. 28.1*, pp. 37–38; and to Francesco Papafava, 14 August 1892, *O.C. 30*, p. 167.
57. Letter to Maffeo Pantaleoni, 8 July 1891, *O.C. 28.1*, p. 49.
58. Letter to Maffeo Pantaleoni, 8 July 1891, *O.C. 28.1*, pp. 46–47.
59. Letter to Maffeo Pantaleoni, 8 July 1891, *O.C. 28.1*, pp. 46–49.
60. Letters to Maffeo Pantaleoni, 26 May 1893, 6 June 1896, *O.C. 28.1*, pp. 375, 453.
61. Letter to Maffeo Pantaleoni, 6 July 1891, *O.C. 28.1*, pp. 42,46.
62. Letters to Maffeo Pantaleoni, 20 September, 9 December 1891, *O.C. 28.1*, pp. 63, 109–110.
63. Letters to Lèon Walras, 21 September 1891, *O.C. 19.1*, p. 167; and to Maffeo Pantaleoni, 9 December 1891, *O.C. 28.1*, p. 109.
64. Letters to Maffeo Pantaleoni, 3 October, 9 December 1891, *O.C. 28.1*, pp. 66, 110.
65. Letter to Maffeo Pantaleoni, 20 September 1891, *O.C. 28.1*, p. 63.
66. Letter to Maffeo Pantaleoni, 3 October 1891, *O.C. 28.1*, p. 67.
67. Letter to Maffeo Pantaleoni, 3 October 1891, *O.C. 28.1*, pp. 65–66.
68. Letter to Maffeo Pantaleoni, 9 December 1891, *O.C. 28.1*, pp. 115–116.
69. Letter to Antonio Graziadei, 29 March 1901, *O.C. 19.1*, p. 423.
70. Letter to Antonio Graziadei, 10 January 1901, *O.C. 19.1*, pp. 419–421.
71. Letter to Giovanni Vailati, 4 December 1901, *O.C. 19.1*, p. 435.
72. Letters to Maffeo Pantaleoni, 14 December 1898, 28 December 1899, *O.C. 28.2*, pp. 253, 287, 292.
73. xvi Letters to Hermann Laurent, 11 January 1899, *O.C. 30*, p. 339; and to Maffeo Pantaleoni, 28 December 1899, *O.C. 28.2*, pp. 289–291.
74. Letters to Hermann Laurent, 14, 19 January 1899, *O.C. 30*, pp. 339, 348–349; and to Maffeo Pantaleoni, 23 July 1900, *O.C. 28.2*, pp. 323–324.
75. Letter to Maffeo Pantaleoni, 30 December 1900, *O.C. 28.2*, p. 348.
76. Letter to Hermann Laurent, 19 January 1899, *O.C. 30*, p. 349.
77. Letters to Hermann Laurent, 11 January 1899, *O.C. 30*, p. 339; to Maffeo Pantaleoni, 24 October 1902, *O.C. 28.2*, p. 409; and to Vladimiro Furlan, 28 September 1907, *O.C. 19.1*, p. 607.
78. Letter to Maffeo Pantaleoni, 28 December 1899, *O.C. 28.2*, p. 293.
79. Letter to Maffeo Pantaleoni, 28 December 1899, *O.C. 28.2*, p. 288.

80. Letter to Luigi Amoroso, 11 January 1909, *O.C. 19.1*, p. 649.
81. Letter to Luigi Amoroso, 7 January 1910, *O.C. 19.2*, p. 685.
82. Letters to Guido Sensini, 18 January 1905, *O.C. 19.1*, p. 533; and to Hermann Laurent, 7 January 1899, *O.C. 30*, p. 337.
83. Letter to Felice Vinci, 19 August 1912, *O.C. 19.2*, p. 782.
84. Letter to Antonio Graziadei, 10 January 1901, *O.C. 19.1*, pp. 419–421.
85. Letter to Maffeo Pantaleoni, 3 October 1891, *O.C. 28.1*, p. 67.
86. Letters to Maffeo Pantaleoni, 10 February 1897, *O.C. 28.2*, p. 30; to Wilhelm Franz Meyer, 16 December 1901; to Maffeo Pantaleoni, 15 September 1907, *O.C. 28.3*, p. 61; and to Luigi Amoroso, 21 April 1908, *O.C. 19.1*, pp. 436, 630 and 28 November 1911, *O.C. 19.2*, p. 745.
87. Letter to Maffeo Pantaleoni, 19 February 1897, *O.C. 28.2*, p. 35.
88. Letter to Alfonso de Pietri Tonelli, 8 August 1917, *O.C. 19.2*, p. 978.
89. Letters to Antonio Graziadei, 29 March 1901, *O.C. 19.1*, p. 424; and to Maffeo Pantaleoni, 15 September 1907, *O.C. 28.3*, p. 61.
90. Letter to Alfonso de Pietri Tonelli, 8 August 1917, *O.C. 19.2*, p. 978.
91. Letter to Luigi Amoroso, 28 November 1911, *O.C. 19.2*, p. 745.
92. Letter to Pierre Boven, 25 May 1912, *O.C. 19.2*, pp. 769–770.
93. Letter to Lèon Walras, 15 March 1892, *O.C. 19.1*, p. 183.
94. Letter to Maffeo Pantaleoni, 5 January 1892, *O.C. 28.1*, pp. 151–153.
95. Letter to Maffeo Pantaleoni, 26 January 1892, *O.C. 28.1*, p. 166.
96. Letter to Antonio Graziadei, 29 March 1901, *O.C. 19.1*, p. 424.
97. Letters to Maffeo Pantaleoni, 19 November, 28 December 1899, *O.C. 28.2*, pp. 278–279, 287.
98. Letter to Maffeo Pantaleoni, 23 July 1900, *O.C.* 28.2, p. 324.
99. Letter to Attilio Cabiati, 13 February 1908, *O.C. 19.1*, p. 624.
100. Letters to Irving Fisher, 11 January 1897; and to Luigi Amoroso, 11 January 1909, *O.C. 19.1*, pp. 320, 322, 650.
101. Letter to Maffeo Pantaleoni, 22 June 1905, *O.C. 28.2*, p. 444.
102. Letter to Luigi Amoroso, 14 May 1907, *O.C. 19.1*, p. 593.
103. Letter to Luigi Amoroso, 14 May 1907, *O.C. 19.1*, p. 594.
104. Letter to Luigi Amoroso, 24 April 1909, *O.C. 19.1*, pp. 661–660.
105. Letter to Maffeo Pantaleoni, 14 August 1892, *O.C. 28.1*, p. 275.
106. Letter to Maffeo Pantaleoni, 18 September 1892, *O.C. 28.1*, pp. 283–284.
107. Letter to Attilio Cabiati, 13 February 1908, *O.C. 19.1*, p. 626.
108. Letters to Giovanni Vailati, 6 February 1908; and to Attilio Cabiati, 13 February 1908, *O.C. 19.1*, pp. 622, 626.
109. Letters to Tullio Martello, 23 June 1894, 30 August 1906, *O.C. 19.1*, p. 249, 572; and to Maffeo Pantaleoni, 28 September 1907, *O.C. 28.3*, p. 64.
110. Letter to Wilhelm Franz Meyer, 16 December 1901, *O.C. 19.1*, p. 439.
111. Letter to Maffeo Pantaleoni, 17 June 1895, *O.C. 28.1*, p. 417.
112. Letter to Wilhelm Franz Meyer, 16 December 1901, *O.C. 19.1*, p. 440.
113. Letters to Antonio Graziadei, 16 June 1901, *O.C. 19.1*, p. 428; and to Domenico Berardi, 18, 29 August 1901, *O.C. 31*, pp. 136–137.
114. Letters to Maffeo Pantaleoni, 18 May 1902, 22 July 1904, *O.C. 28.2*, pp. 403–404, 432.
115. Letters to Maffeo Pantaleoni, 19 February 1897, *O.C. 28.2*, p. 36; and to Felice Vinci, 16 January 1912, *O.C. 19.2*, p. 757.

116. Letters to Maffeo Pantaleoni, 17 June, 9 July 1895, 6 June 1896, *O.C. 28.1*, pp. 417, 423–424, 453–454, 10 February 1897, *O.C. 28.2*, pp. 29–30 and 15, 28 September 1907, *O.C. 28.3*, pp. 61, 64.
117. Letter to Maffeo Pantaleoni, 10 February 1897, *O.C. 28.2*, p. 31.
118. Letters to Luigi Amoroso, 21 April 1908, *O.C. 19.1*, p. 630; and to Felice Vinci, 16 January 1912, *O.C. 19.2*, pp. 630, 757.
119. Letters to Maffeo Pantaleoni, 19 February 1897, *O.C. 28.2*, p. 37; and to Felice Vinci, 29 January 1912, *O.C. 19.2*, pp. 758–759.
120. Letters to Emilia Peruzzi, 30 April 1893, *O.C. 27.1*, p. 547; and to Guido Martinelli, 24 August 1894, *O.C. 30*, p. 257.
121. Letter to Léon Walras, 2 August 1893, *O.C. 19.1*, p. 226.
122. Letter to Léon Walras, 12 September 1891, *O.C. 19.1*, pp. 163–164.
123. Letters to Maffeo Pantaleoni, 27 July 1892, 17 June, 9 July 1895, *O.C. 28.1*, pp. 217, 417–418, 422–425, 10, 19 February 1897, *O.C. 28.2*, pp. 3, 35; and to Guido Sensini, 8 August 1911, *O.C. 19.2*, p. 735.
124. Letters to Lèon Walras, 15 March 1892, *O.C. 19.1*, pp. 183–184; and to Maffeo Pantaleoni, 13 January 1894, *O.C. 28.1*, p. 412.
125. Letters to Lèon Walras, 20 March 1892, *O.C. 19.1*, p. 184; and to Maffeo Pantaleoni, 20, 28 March, 18 September 1892, 22, 26 May 1893, *O.C. 28.1*, pp. 197, 200, 287, 373, 375–378.
126. Letter to Lèon Walras, 30 July 1893, *O.C. 19.1*, p. 225.
127. Letter to Lèon Walras, 12 August 1893, *O.C. 19.1*, p. 228.
128. Letter to Lèon Walras, 15 March 1892, *O.C. 19.1*, p. 183.
129. Letter to Guido Sensini, 8 August 1911, *O.C. 19.2*, p. 735.
130. Letter to Maffeo Pantaleoni, 19 December 1908, *O.C. 28.3*, p. 121.
131. Letter to Adrien Naville, 7 May 1897, *O.C. 19.1*, p. 338.
132. Letters to Maffeo Pantaleoni, 26, 28 May 1893, *O.C. 28.1*, pp. 379–380, 19 December 1908, *O.C. 28.3*, p. 121.
133. Letters to Maffeo Pantaleoni, 26, 31 May 1893, *O.C. 28.1*, pp. 378, 382, 17 May 1893, *O.C. 28.2*, pp. 73, 19, December 1908, *O.C. 28.3*, p. 121; and to Guido Sensini, 16 February 1911, *O.C. 19.2*, pp. 735–736.
134. Letter to Adrien Naville, 7 May 1897, *O.C. 19.1*, p. 336.
135. Letter to Adrien Naville, 7 May 1897, *O.C. 19.1*, p. 334.
136. Letters to Maffeo Pantaleoni, 19 December 1908, 27 September 1909, *O.C. 28.3*, pp. 121, 144.
137. Letter to Guido Sensini, 8 August 1911, *O.C. 19.2*, p. 735.
138. Letter to Maffeo Pantaleoni, 19 February 1897, *O.C. 28.2*, p. 36.
139. Letter to Alfonso de Pietri-Tonelli, 14 March 1914, *O.C. 19.2*, p. 863.
140. Letters to Maffeo Pantaleoni, 10 February 1897, *O.C. 28.2*, pp. 32–33, 13 October 1907, *O.C. 28.3*, p. 68; to Alfonso de Pietri-Tonelli, 14 March 1914; and to Luigi Amoroso, 17 April 1914, *O.C. 19.2*, pp. 863, 867–868.
141. Letter to Maffeo Pantaleoni, 15 March 1907, *O.C. 28.3*, p. 23.
142. Letter to Maffeo Pantaleoni, 15 March 1907, *O.C. 28.3*, pp. 22–24.
143. Letters to Maffeo Pantaleoni, 17 May, 11 November 1897, 5 February 1898, 24, 26 October 1902, *O.C. 28.2*, pp. 73, 121, 163, 407–408, 413–414, 2 May 1918, *O.C. 28.3*, p. 231.
144. Letter to Adrien Naville, 11 January 1897, *O.C. 19.1*, p. 325.
145. Letter to Adrien Naville, 11 May 1897, *O.C. 19.1*, p. 339.
146. Letter to Adrien Naville, 11 May 1897, *O.C. 19.1*, p. 339.

147. Letter to Emanuele Sella, 11 June 1913, *O.C. 19.2*, p. 832.
148. Letters to Maffeo Pantaleoni, 9 December 1906, *O.C. 28.2*, p. 465; to Emanuele Sella, 11 June 1913; and to James Harvey Rogers, 7 April 1916, *O.C. 19.2*, pp. 833, 922.
149. Letter to Alceste Antonucci, 7 December 1907, *O.C. 19.1*, p. 613.
150. Letters to Emilia Peruzzi, 20 August 1873, 27 January 1874, *O.C. 27.1*, pp. 254, 313, 8 March 1888, *O.C. 27.2*, p. 375; and to Guido Martinelli, 14 August 1892, *O.C. 30*, p. 164.
151. Letters to Emilia Peruzzi, 30 April 1886, *O.C.* 27.2, p. 323; and to Carlo Placci, 25 August 1898, *O.C. 27.1*, p. 370.
152. Letter to Emilia Peruzzi, 5 November 1872, *O.C. 27.1*, p. 73.
153. Letter to Emilia Peruzzi, 20 August 1873, *O.C. 27.1*, p. 255.
154. Letters to Emilia Peruzzi, 20, 24 August 1874, *O.C. 27.1*, pp. 398, 401.
155. Letter to Emilia Peruzzi, 27 October 1874, *O.C. 27.1*, pp. 444–445.
156. Letter to Maffeo Pantaleoni, 23 April 1893, *O.C. 28.1*, p. 369.
157. Letters to Emilia Peruzzi, 8 August 1885, *O.C. 27.2*, pp. 301, 304–305; and to Maffeo Pantaleoni, 1 August and 27 December 1897, 2, 3, 11, 17 February 1898, *O.C. 28.2*, pp.96, 137, 160–161, 171, 173–174.
158. Letter to Maffeo Pantaleoni, 17 February 1892, *O.C. 28.1*, p. 185.
159. Letters to Maffeo Pantaleoni, 23 February, 27 July 1892, *O.C. 28.1*, pp. 189, 255.
160. Letter to Luigi Ridolfi, 9 March 1887, *O.C. 23*, p. 571.
161. Letters to Emilia Peruzzi, 8 March, 11 May 1888, *O.C. 27.2*, pp. 375, 378–379.
162. Letter to Emilia Peruzzi, 17 November 1888, *O.C. 27.2*, p. 388.
163. Letter to Francesco Papafava, 6 January 1891, *O.C. 30*, p. 112.
164. Letters to Léon Walras, 23 July, 12 September 1891, *O.C. 19.1*, pp. 160, 163; and to Emilia Peruzzi, 26 August 1891, *O.C. 27.2*, pp.481–482.
165. Letters to Maffeo Pantaleoni, 18 August, 17 September 1891, *O.C. 28.1*, pp.57, 61; to Léon Walras, 18 August, 6 September 1891, *O.C. 19.1*, pp. 161–163; to Emilia Peruzzi, 26 August 1891, *O.C. 27.2*, pp. 481–482; to Philippe Monnier, 22 September 1891, *O.C. 19.1*, p. 168; and to Paul Speiser, 30 September 1891, *O.C. 30*, p. 140.
166. Letters to Francesco Papafava, 27 November 1888, *O.C. 23*, p. 590 and 17 January 1891, *O.C. 30*, p. 125.
167. Letter to Francesco Papafava, 2 December 1888, *O.C. 23*, p. 591.
168. Letter to Francesco Papafava, 2 December 1888, *O.C. 23*, p. 593.
169. Letter to Maffeo Pantaleoni, 11 November 1893, *O.C. 28.1*, p. 400.
170. Letter to Giovanni Vailati, 2 November 1896, *O.C. 19.1*, p. 305.
171. Letters to Teodoro Moneta, 2 May 1893, *O.C. 31*, p. 57; to Guido Martinelli, 24 May, 9 December 1893, 29 March 1895, *O.C. 30*, pp. 189, 211, 268; to Maffeo Pantaleoni, 25 November 1893, *O.C. 28.1*, p.404; and to Carlo Placci, 28 May 1894, *O.C. 19.1*, p. 246.
172. Letters to Emilia Peruzzi, 13 June 1891, *O.C. 27.2*, pp. 474–475; and to Maffeo Pantaleoni, 18 August 1891, *O.C. 28.1*, p. 56.
173. Letters to Maffeo Pantaleoni, 7 October 1891, *O.C. 28.1*, p. 76; and to Carlo Placci, 9 February 1894, *O.C. 19.1*, p. 239.
174. Letters to Maffeo Pantaleoni, 30 April, 11, 20 May, 22 December 1896, *O.C. 28.1*, pp. 442, 444, 449, 500, 11, 22 February, 16 May 1898, *O.C. 28.2*, pp. 171, 175–176, 196.

175. Letters to Benedetto Croce, 21 January 1898, *O.C. 19.1*, p. 358; to Maffeo Pantaleoni, 21 November, 7 December 1899, 18 July 1901, *O.C. 28.2*, pp. 281, 284, 432; to Arturo Linaker, 18 October 1900; and to Arcangelo Ghisleri, 18 September 1901, *O.C. 19.1*, pp. 412, 432.
176. Letters to Maffeo Pantaleoni, 17, 22 February 1898, *O.C. 28.2*, pp. 174, 177; to Filippo Turati, 16 September 1898 , 5 March 1899; and to Arturo Linaker, 24 September 1903, *O.C. 19.1*, pp. 377–378, 382, 496.
177. Letter to Alceste Antonucci, 7 December 1907, *O.C. 19.1*, p. 614.
178. Letters to Maffeo Pantaleoni, 22 February 1905, *O.C. 28.2*, p. 436, 7 March, 25 April 1907, *O.C. 28.3*, pp. 18, 38; and to Alceste Antonucci, 7 December 1907, *O.C. 19.1*, p. 615.
179. Letters to Arturo Linaker, 18 October 1900; and to Arcangelo Ghisleri, 18 September 1901, *O.C. 19.1*, pp. 412, 432.
180. Letters to Maffeo Pantaleoni, 3 July 1902, *O.C. 28.2*, pp. 405–406; to Giuseppe Prezzolini, 17 December 1903; and to Carlo Placci, 4 June 1904 *O.C. 19.1*, pp. 507, 513.
181. Letters to Teodoro Moneta, 27 March 1898, *O.C. 31*, p. 113; to Emanuele Sella, 11 June 1913, *O.C. 19.2*, p. 832; and to Maffeo Pantaleoni, 26 October 1907, 7 August, 10 December 1916, *O.C. 28.3*, pp. 70–71, 192, 198, 252.
182. Letter to Francesco Papafava, 23 February 1889, *O.C. 23*, p. 631.
183. Letters to Maffeo Pantaleoni, 20, 26 March 1891, *O.C. 28.1*, pp. 21–23, 25–27.
184. Letters to Maffeo Pantaleoni, 18 September, 21, 23 October 1892, *O.C. 28.1*, pp. 285, 302–303.
185. Letters to Francesco Papafava, 14 August 1892, *O.C. 30*, p. 165; and to Emilia Peruzzi, 22 February 1894, *O.C. 27.2*, pp. 564–569.
186. Letter to Francesco Papafava, 14 August 1892, *O.C. 30*, p. 165.
187. Letters to Maffeo Pantaleoni, 19 May, 12 August 1892, *O.C. 28.1*, pp. 218, 268–269; and to Guido Martinelli, 17 September 1893, *O.C. 30*, p. 202.
188. Letter to Léon Walras, 12 September 1891, *O.C. 19.1*, p. 164.
189. Letter to Maffeo Pantaleoni, 6 December 1891, *O.C. 28.1*, pp. 98–99.
190. Letter to Carlo Placci, 9 July 1900, *O.C. 19.1*, p. 402.
191. Letter to Luigi Bodio, 4 January 1893, *O.C. 31*, pp. 40, 49.
192. Letter to Carlo Placci, 30 December 1895, *O.C. 19.1*, p. 281.
193. Letter to Léon Walras, 20 July 1894, *O.C. 19.1*, p. 250.
194. Letter to Léon Walras, 23 July 1894, *O.C. 19.1*, p. 251.
195. Letter to Benedetto Croce, 30 June 1899, *O.C. 19.1*, pp. 387–388.
196. Letter to Carlo Placci, 28 May 1894, *O.C. 19.1*, pp. 246–247.
197. Letters to Emilia Peruzzi, 11 October 1892, *O.C. 27.2*, pp. 517–518; to Teodoro Moneta, 29 May 1894, *O.C. 31*, p. 80; and to Carlo Placci, 30 December 1895, *O.C. 19.1*, pp. 281–282.
198. Letter to Lèon Walras, 28 April 1896, *O.C. 19.1*, p. 290.
199. Letter to Carlo Placci, 30 December 1895, *O.C. 19.1*, pp. 281–282.
200. Pareto's deposition, 7 January 1880, to the parliamentary Commission of Inquiry on the operation, Italian Railways, *O.C. 23*, pp. 196–197.
201. Letter to Maffeo Pantaleoni, 16 March 1893, *O.C. 28.1*, p. 427.
202. Letter to Léon Walras, 28 April 1896, *O.C. 19.1*, p. 287.
203. Letter to Francesco Papafava, 3 December 1888, *O.C. 30*, p. 596.

204. Letters to Napoleone Colajanni, 31 December 1891, 2 January, 27 March 1893, *O.C. 19.1*, pp. 176, 207, 216; to Maffeo Pantaleoni, 7 March 1893, *O.C. 28.1*, pp. 352–353; and to Teodoro Moneta, 9 June 1896, *O.C. 31*, p. 94.
205. Letters to Francesco Papafava, 9 December 1888, *O.C. 30*, pp. 603–604; and to Maffeo Pantaleoni, 20, 22 July 1898, 19, 21 November, 7 December 1899, 30 June 1901, 1 April 1905, *O.C. 28.2*, pp. 223–224, 227–228, 278, 282, 284, 366–367, 442.
206. Letters to Francesco Papafava, 9 December 1888, *O.C. 30*, pp. 616–621; to Guido Martinelli, 30 January 1895, *O.C. 30*, p. 266; and to Maffeo Pantaleoni, 19 December 1896, *O.C. 28.1*, p. 498, 1 August 1897, *O.C. 28.2*, p. 96.
207. Letter to Léon Walras, 28 April 1896, *O.C. 19.1*, p. 292.
208. Letters to Napoleone Colajanni, 5 May 1892 and 14 January 1898, *O.C. 19.1*, pp. 187, 357; to Francesco Papafava, 9 January 1894, *O.C. 30*, p. 215; to Léon Walras, 28 April 1896; and to Adrien Naville, 1 July 1899, *O.C. 19.1*, pp. 289–292, 388–389.
209. Letters to Filippo Turati, 11 November 1893; and to Carlo Placci, 9 February 1894, *O.C. 19.1*, pp. 235, 238, 240.
210. Letter to Carlo Placci, 15 November 1895, *O.C. 19.1*, p. 269.
211. Letter to Carlo Placci, 30 December 1895, *O.C. 19.1*, p. 281.
212. Letter to Carlo Placci, 15 November 1895, *O.C. 19.1*, pp. 269–270.
213. Letter to Gustave de Molinari, 18 November 1896, *O.C. 19.1*, p. 307.
214. Letter to Maffeo Pantaleoni, 14 July 1896, *O.C. 28.1*, p. 461.
215. Letter to Francesco Papafava, 2 December 1888, *O.C. 23*, p. 593.
216. Letters to Francesco Papafava, 2 December 1888, *O.C. 23*, p. 591; and to Maffeo Pantaleoni, 22 December 1891, *O.C. 28.1*, p. 122.
217. Letters to Francesco Papafava, 2, 3 December 1888, *O.C. 23*, pp. 594–596.
218. Letter to Francesco Papafava, 4 December 1888, *O.C. 23*, pp. 599–600.
219. Letter to Francesco Papafava, 10 December 1888, *O.C. 23*, pp. 610–611.
220. Letters to Francesco Papafava, 2 December 1888, *O.C. 23*, p. 591; and to Lèon Walras, 28 April 1896, *O.C. 19.1*, pp. 292–293.
221. Letter to Alceste Antonucci, 7 December 1907, *O.C. 19.1*, p. 615.
222. Letter to Carlo Placci, 10 June 1897, *O.C. 19.1*, p. 344.
223. Letter to Maffeo Pantaleoni, 24 June 1920, *O.C. 28.3*, p. 267.
224. Letter to Maffeo Pantaleoni, 1 October 1921, *O.C. 28.3*, pp. 294–295.
225. Letter to Maffeo Pantaleoni, 9 August 1892, *O.C. 28.1*, pp. 264–265.
226. Letter to Maffeo Pantaleoni, 8 November 1897, *O.C. 28.2*, p. 115.
227. Letters to Lèon Walras, 2 August 1893; and to Carlo Placci, 30 December 1895, *O.C. 19.1*, pp. 226–227, 281.
228. Letter to Maffeo Pantaleoni, 20 December 1892, *O.C. 28.1*, p. 329.
229. Letters to Napoleone Colajanni, 12, 24 December 1893, *O.C. 19.1*, pp. 236–237.
230. Letter to Edwin Robert Anderson Seligman, 5 January 1896, *O.C. 19.1*, p. 282.
231. Letters to Edwin Robert Anderson Seligman, 5 January, 1 March 1896, *O.C. 19.1*, pp. 282, 284; and to Benvenuto Griziotti, 2 September 1917, *O.C. 19.2*, p. 984.

232. Letters to Maffeo Pantaleoni, 12 August 1892, *O.C. 28.1*, p. 267 and 21 December 1897, *O.C. 28.2*, pp. 133–134.
233. Letter to Maffeo Pantaleoni, 24 November 1898, *O.C. 28.2*, pp. 249–252.
234. Letter to Lèon Walras, 28 April 1896, *O.C. 19.1*, p. 290.
235. Letters to Guido Sensini and to Tullio Martello, 5 April 1917, *O.C. 19.2*, pp. 958–959.
236. Letter to Guido Sensini, 3 September 1917, *O.C. 19.2*, p. 985.
237. Letter to Benvenuto Griziotti, 2 September 1917, *O.C. 19.2*, p. 984.
238. Letter to Benvenuto Griziotti, 5 October 1917, *O.C. 19.2*, p. 989.

Bibliography

Melani L., *Alcuni manoscritti autografi di Vilfredo Pareto conservati nella Biblioteca nazionale di Firenze: catalogo*, Firenze, Giunta regionale toscana, La nuova Italia, 1983.

Mincio D.-Mornati F., *Inventaire du Fonds Vilfredo Pareto conservé au Département des manuscrits de la BCU*- Lausanne, Département des manuscrits et Centre d'études interdisciplinaires Walras-Pareto, 1997.

Œuvres Complètes de Vilfredo Pareto (from now on O.C.), 19, *Correspondance, 1890–1923*, edited by Giovanni Busino, Genève, Droz, 1975.

O.C. 23, Lettres 1860–1890, edited by Giovanni Busino, Genève, Droz, 1981.

O.C. 27.1; O.C. 27.2, Lettere ai Peruzzi, 1872–1900, edited by Tommaso Giacalone-Monaco, Genève, Droz, 1984.

O.C. 28.1; O.C. 28.2; O.C. 28.3, Lettere a Maffeo Pantaleoni, edited by Gabriele De Rosa, Genève, Droz, 1984.

O.C. 30, Lettres et correspondances, edited by Giovanni Busino, Genève, Droz, 1989.

O.C. 31, Nouvelles lettres (1870–1923), edited by Fiorenzo Mornati, Genève, Droz, 2001.

Author Index

Subject Index

American Economic Association, 2, 96
American Economic Review, 81
American Political Science
    Association, 15
Annals of Social and Economic
    Measurement, 149, 150
Austrian economics, 183

Bank of England, 97, 113–35
Bank of International Settlements, 129
Bretton Woods, 113–35

Cantonal University, 173
Capital, 56, 58, 65, 90
Carnegie Foundation, 47
Carnegie-Mellon University (formerly
    Carnegie Institute of Technology),
    76, 102, 139, 145, 146, 156, 159,
    163, 165
Chase Manhattan bank, 76
Chicago School, 1, 10–14, 21, 53, 57,
    62–3, 66, 100
Chicago Workshop in Money and
    Banking, 99–100
Circular flow diagram (wheel of
    wealth), 23, 28, 37–8
Coase conversion evening, 2, 4
Cobden Prize, 16
Columbia University, 14, 16, 18,
    82, 151
Communism, 17, 74
Conservative Party (UK), 3, 130
Consumer expenditure, 52
Cornell University, 165
Council of Economic Advisers, 75, 128
Cowles Commission, 162

Duke University, 18

Earhart Foundation, 75
Econometric Society, 140
Econometrica, 142, 144, 151, 154,
    164, 165

Economic Journal, 100
Economica, 107
European Economic Community, 3
Exchange rates, 3, 113–35

Federal Reserve System, 122, 128,
    155, 166
Ford Foundation, 75, 103
Formalism, 2, 83–4, 93
Free enterprise, 31, 37, 38
Free trade and protection, 187–90
F-twist, 78–9, 93
Full employment, 48, 63, 83, 97

General equilibrium, 14, 58, 81,
    180–5, 195
General Strike (1926), 3
George Washington University, 74
German Historical School, 187
Gold standard, 3, 113
Great Depression, 90

Harvard University, 77
Hoover Institution, 10

Inflation, 2, 52, 66, 105
Inflationary expectations, 1, 2, 96–109
Inflationary gap, 47–68
Institute of Public Administration, 47
Institutionalism, 17
Interest rates, 90, 127, 183
International Monetary Fund (IMF), 3,
    113, 115, 119, 122
Investment, 82, 83, 141, 142
IS-LM model, 48, 154

Journal of Economic Dynamics and
    Control, 159
Journal of Economic Issues (JEI), 7
Journal of Money, Credit and Banking
    (JMCB), 162, 163
Journal of Political Economy (JPE), 3,
    30, 149